I have great respect for Michel̵ _____ ling skills and her unwavering integrity ͮ _____ ͦ to work with the increasingly powerful en _____ ͭt is illuminated in her writing. Michel̵ _____ ____ ͧ ͨ gap between indigenous and present day medicine ways, in a most respectful, loving and impeccable manner.

Gini Gentry, Nagul Woman, teacher of the Toltec Eagle Knight lineage
Founder of the Garden of the Goddess in New Mexico

Comprehensive and Heartfelt; deeply insightful journey into a greater awareness of the pathway to the Fifth World. I also know Michele as a dedicated and powerful ceremonialist, who is able to transform a group working with the magical energies of Earth and Sky.

James Jereb, visionary artist, creator of 'Star Dreaming' Temple Complex

Many thanks to Michele for birthing 'Journey to the Fifth World', at a time when it is needed the most. There were so many gifts that this book and the work with her has afforded me. The gift that offered the most comfort for me was the knowing that the changes, which I am going through, physically and emotionally, are being experienced by many and that I am not alone. The information she has gathered and generously shared in her study with many indigenous people around the world, shed light on that which I sensed but had no language for. Her words helped to bring the teachings of many great souls into my home and heart and transformed the way I live in the world.

I have been fortunate to live in Santa Fe and share both one on one work, as well as a shamanic journey group that she leads, that goes through the 'journey of healing' laid out in the book, and have found the work to be life changing. There is no greater warrior to get to the heart of the matter and assist us with the work of clearing the past in order to better bring in a more positive future.

Kristal Wolf March, Southwestern College Counseling student

A clear guide for personal growth. If the reader does not have the opportunity to see Michele in a private, group or workshop session, this book is a transformational process that will create movement and change with every page that you turn. Each line is a living fabric that asks you to go deeper. In my personal transformation journey with Michele, I have experienced a sacred place where I have been held and seen for the spiritual being I truly am. She pulls back the veil for us to see the full circle of our lives and the greater world!

JoAnna Conte, Southwestern College Counseling student

Journey to the Fifth World

Coming Full Circle in
Healing and Transformation

Michele Ama Wehali

Llumina Press

ISBN: 978-1-59526-656-9

Printed in the United States of America by Llumina Press

Library of Congress Control Number: 2006911144

Journey to the Fifth World

Coming Full Circle in Healing and Transformation

Dedication

*T*his journey is dedicated to all of Mother Earth's inhabitants, as a blessing for 'coming full circle in healing and transformation,' so that we may truly experience Heaven on Earth.

To the 'Great Spirit' in all of us, that prevails even when we can barely see the Light or feel the Love.

To the forgiveness and transformation of all we have been and the fulfillment of all we truly are!

To my Mother Margarete Viktoria-Luise Heinecke Rozbitsky who passed through the death doorway on Mothers Day, 2006, near the completion of this book.

To the healing of the deep feminine and the evolution of the masculine in all lineages!

Giving Thanks!

I am thankful to Great Spirit, the Mother of all Creation, and to the Mother Earth and the Rainbow Goddess and all my helping guides and spirits, for inspiring me to look deeply into the 'Eyes of Creation,' searching for the way home. I would like to share my heartfelt gratitude for my parents, my sister Monica and especially my daughter Quinoa Maya, for being my close relations in this life, as I thank all my relations. Deepest thanks to my Aunt Irmi for leaving me an inheritance that allowed me the time to write. I am deeply grateful for all who have been part of my journey in friendship, as teachers, and in partnership. To the Earth and the Stars and all the incredible beauty of Mother Nature that has kept me connected to myself, in spite of being in computer world for so much of the last year and a half. In awe of the many animal guides and messages that have showed up to support me in my writing isolation and a wish that they get to live a happy and easy life on the Earth. In great respect for the many indigenous teachers I have had the great honor of learning from. In thanks for Gary who provided a space in which I could quietly write. In deep appreciation and love for the support of my true Soul sister Deborah, the first to read and give feedback on the book, who truly gets who I am. I would like to also heart-fully acknowledge my friends Marshal, Michael, and Chantal, who were able to give me valuable suggestions for changes that were helpful for a more flowing read of my book. I am also deeply appreciative of Cindee Pascoe who did the final edit. I wish them many blessings! I give thanks, I give thanks, I give thanks.

Symbology of Cover Art

*T*he cover of this book has extensive symbology that expresses the content of what is contained within the book. The symbols came from my Soul without conscious thought and I did not understand their meaning until it had birthed through on paper. You may understand more of what I share after you take a journey through the book. The pastel drawing was left somewhat kidlike and unfinished looking, to show we do not need to be perfect individuals, but on a path of becoming more aware, forever uncovering our spiritual wholeness.

The black staircase at the bottom of the picture represents the levels of the Underworlds we must pass through on our journey of evolution. Each step represents a challenge of the human psyche to be faced. The flower in the center represents the 'True Flowering Soul' of the human being that keeps contact with its spiritual Source and its impetus for evolvement, even in the darkest night. The Light below it is the 'Light without a Shadow' that is coming from the Fire in the belly of the Earth, birthing humanity into a non-dualistic reality.

The prayer feather fans located on the stairs come from the use of these sacred implements in the Native American Church's all night prayer meetings, where they are used after midnight to assist one in staying connected to Spirit while going within (among other uses). They represent another tool for humanity to utilize, to keep praying through the difficult times. These fans also bring our prayers out through the dreaming of the dancing stars, so that they can reach the Heavens.

The stars on the stairway represent our connection to the celestial Heavens while in the Underworlds. This connection keeps us excited and fired up about evolving, even when we get tired from the seemingly endless steps ahead of us, in our return home to Source. The rope or Aka Cord that joins the stars is well explained in the contents of the book, but briefly let us say that it is our dream cord that connects us to the 'bigger picture,' our Higher Self, and to all our various parts. You could call it our 'life line.'

The Rainbow Serpent is the guardian of the next Era of the Fifth World, who assists humanity to heal the wounds of the Heart, the emotional body, and the shadow realms, so we can enter into the Upperworlds. It transforms the energy of the Underworlds into the many colored wings of illumination and true spiritual freedom, thus becoming the Feathered Serpent. The Feathered Serpent is also known as Quetzalcoatl to the Aztec, Kulkulcan to the Maya, and to the esoteric Rosicrucians, as the Christ consciousness. The return of these spiritual beings or energies assists in the healing of the 'Heart of Humanity.' The rainbow wings are protecting humanity's 'journey of healing' to the Upperworlds, where the higher consciousness is to be accessed with the guidance of our Higher Self.

The Yellow Sun or 'True Cross' in the center (similar to the Peruvian Incan Cross), is representative of the balancing of consciousness and a non-linear, holistic manner of access to the Thirteen Heavens. The gold color is connected to the energy of the Sun as well as to the element of gold that is an alchemical doorway to higher consciousness. The Yin/Yang symbology in the very core of the picture is the resolution of duality. The Fourth World or Era humanity has been living in for over five thousand years according to the Maya, has been a time of experiencing and learning through a dualistic reality of good and evil, day and night, masculine and feminine, etc.

The Hummingbird, at the top of the Heart, is the bird that leads the way into the Fifth World, as shared by the Q'ero of Peru, descendants of the Inca. This sacred bird assists us in being able to handle more Joy, Light, and Love; as we drink from the nectar of the Heavens, we become the 'Flowering Souls', thus enriching the 'Soul of Mother Earth.' The crowning of our consciousness occurs as we do so.

Contents

Introduction

S omething is stirring deep inside; feeling the flood of movement all around, I search for understanding with the sight of knowing I have grown to depend on, sensing the immensity of what can no longer stay hidden in the depths of my being.

Wishing to shine the light of knowing into the hidden caverns of this darkness, rising up through the tenuous grounding patterns of my daily life, I gather my spiritual energies so that I may not lose myself.

Seeing the greater web that connects me to all beings, as it vibrates with the rejoining of that which has been held separate within and without, I shudder with the immensity of what is occurring for humanity and the Planet.

Feeling the great sorrow of the hearts, minds, and bodies of the many who are caught in the throes of the purification of Water, Earth, Fire, and Air, I go deeper into my own Soul search.

Sensing strongly that I must open to the most powerful spiritual consciousness my meager being can reach for, while the collective fear of surviving the storm, at times encroaches on my ability to know a greater truth.

But as the Holy Waters cleanse my Soul, I surrender to the Will of Great Spirit and that which has birthed me into the playing fields of the Earth, and begin to trust in the guidance of my Higher Self to place me wherever I need to be, for my journey to the Fifth World.

I invite you to accompany me on the journey!

We have recently experienced the devastation of Hurricane Katrina in the Gulf Coast, the Tsunami in Indonesia in December 2004, the bombings in England, and the destruction and ensuing fear and government control caused by 9/11, not too many years ago; not to mention the war in Iraq and the continuing violence in much of the Middle East. Are you feeling the deep stirring inside of unrest and ill-ease? Are you feeling a deep urge to take action and make change, but feel frozen and unable to move except in the habitual patterns of your life? I have also felt this way at times. But a deeper aspect of my Soul has not allowed me to forget these and so many other tragic experiences that can be used as a powerful motivation for awakening! Humanity must not waste these strong messages and ignore the great shifts we are being asked to make. Many more Earth changes and natural and man-made disasters will be occurring, for the time of awakening is upon us. The great need to evolve as a species is becoming painfully apparent as we witness increasing levels of suffering in the World and truly face the fact that humanity's ability to continue to live on Mother Earth is not a given .

We live in a time where there has been an increase in natural catastrophes, acts of terrorism and genocide, destruction of the environment, population growth over the limit of sanity, as well as corporate greed and takeover, loss of governmental integrity, and an increase in suicides, depression, and violence. In the very same breath, a large part of humanity is opening its heart in compassion and altruistic acts, to the suffering of our brothers and sisters, offering assistance to those in great need. We see that the effects of global warming and the strong movements of Earth's elements do not care what country we are from or the color of our skin. All people are subject to suffering and struggle on this third Planet from the Sun. All life and all people are connected as the five fingered ones. as planetary citizens.

In the midst of so much suffering, many are also on a fast learning curve towards higher states of consciousness, evolving to heightened states of awareness and love. We are experiencing the times of purification and the resolution of duality spoken of by the Hopi and many other indigenous cultures. We are experiencing a great amplification of the polarities of the dark and of the light, the negative and the positive, and of the great energies of destruction and creation. We are up against the consequences of creating a society greatly out of balance with Mother Nature and our spiritual essence. Our alienation from the Earth, each other, and our own totality, is at a critical point and we are being asked to take an evolutionary leap. As we individually take more responsibility for what we create, then maybe religions, governments, and the larger forces that profoundly affect our reality, will also be more able to take self-responsibility for their thoughts and actions; great change may then occur.

Many are experiencing being pushed to the edge of their own sanity to deal with the great demands of the evolutionary vortex we are in. This vortex or vibration of change is requiring humanity to take a leap in consciousness unlike any other time previously experienced on the Planet.

All that is occurring is not just in the awareness of those who are spiritually and psychically sensitive. It is also being experienced in the overall psyches of humanity, our society, our religions, and in the natural environment we call home. The spiritual impetus to evolve is affecting all aspects of life.

The Mother Earth is taking the lead in speaking very loudly for all to hear, that she must be respected and honored and is not here solely for our pleasure and misuse. She has her own divine consciousness and it is time for her to evolve. We have been given a time to go through our adolescent stages of growth and it is now time to advance into adulthood and take better care of our inner and outer environments. The Earth is balancing and cleansing herself, moving to the higher dimensions for the evolution of her elements as well as the evolution of humanity. It has been stated in many prophecies that the 'Great Change Times' would be coming and that we have a choice as to how the changes will be carried out. These prophecies indicate that the time of purification will be experienced more severely if the elements of Mother Nature are polluted and disrespected, if the governments and society become ruled by greed and misuse of power, and if individually we have not done our inner work on realigning with the powerful spiritual forces entering onto the Planet. It is time to heal and love the places of separation and un-love in our own beings and in the World. The consciousness of humanity is being pushed to the wall to move to the next stages of growth. It is as if we have been sleeping for a long time in forgetfulness and separation, and are having great difficulty waking up.

The Tsunamis of the Waters are stirring up and bringing to the Light the waves of the unconsciousness of humanity. The Waters of the unconscious are being revealed and are entering conscious life. The spiritual barriers that have kept the negative energies in the Underworlds are being broken open as the Mother Earth twists and turns in responding to her own evolution, releasing all forms of negativity out of her elements and her cellular structure. Humanity is being pushed to respond to the breaking open of these long held negative patterns and emotions as well, for we are made from the Waters and sacred elements of the Earth. We are being forced into awakening, not only through difficult, personal experiences, but through being affected by the increase in suffering of thousands of people throughout the World experiencing catastrophe after catastrophe. We are being asked to go deeply into the individual and collective psyche to understand what is occurring. It is a time of great purification and change.

Water, the element that has been speaking so loudly, not only creates destructive change but also restores the wasteland, bringing in the renewal of life force energies, breaking up the inertia and rigidity of the Underworld. The toxicity of negative thought and emotions as well as pollution and social inequity can no longer be pushed aside. Our fears are being brought to the surface and are being asked to be transformed. We are being stretched to our limits to release our cataclysmic fears and believe in our ability to create another more positive outcome. We have lost contact with our instinctual natures through the imbalanced use of technology and misuse of power gone wild, and it is most important that we reconnect deeply with the natural forces of Mother Nature. In spite of all the instability and confusion, the doorways to the houses of Great Spirit are also wide open, inviting us to truly awaken.

The powerful passage we are moving through has been spoken of by many ancient traditions throughout the eons of time and is not a surprise to the Wisdom Keepers of the indigenous people of the World. We will go on a journey through this sacred information so that greater understanding is given as to what is being asked of humanity, for it goes well beyond the need for changes in government, human greed, overpopulation, and pollution. Ready or not, we are being asked to evolve at core levels. These are exciting and challenging times.

Much is being revealed of the secrets of ancient traditions and the higher levels of esoteric knowledge, as well as the dark secrets and power plays at political and corporate levels. It is the time when what has been hidden in our psyches that has created imbalanced and unhealthy realities for humanity and the Planet will come to the surface. We are being given that which we need in order to transform, if only we take the time to inquire on a very deep level. It is important to take pause and to move beyond the demands of time and space, to look into the spiritual depths within, and to discover answers from a much more enlightened part of our psyches, hearts, and Souls. Our reality, which is in a vortex of great change, is moving very rapidly and by the time the information contained in this written journey gets out in the World, much more will have been revealed, I am sure.

I began writing this book, this 'Journey to the Fifth World,' as a way to understand a journey of healing I was putting together to be experienced in individual, group, and workshop format. It was meant to be a short booklet, but has ended up being an entire book. I have felt pushed forward, as if the message had a life of its own, to continue writing month after month until the journey was done. This information is an accumulation of years of teachings, ceremony, and healing work with others and within myself. The writing of this book began in late winter of 2005, but has been gestating in me throughout many lifetimes. It has become a journey unto itself, expanding into the pages that lay before you, that has taken me on a ride of a continuous change of consciousness every bit of the way. It has been both an extremely difficult and at times highly inspired and ecstatic experience.

My hope is that as you go through the passages of this book, you will also be engaging in a spiritual initiation that will change your life. During these 'Great Change Times,' we get to choose what experience or reality we want to focus on; either the suffering of the full death throes of the Old World or the opening to the New Heaven being birthed here on Earth. These are simultaneous realities that we may flip in and out of, as we complete and 'come full circle in healing and transformation,' shifting from beings of separateness to beings of inter-connectedness. These passages might be an impetus to go further into your own spiritual journey, or simply expand your conscious mind to ask more questions about what you perceive as reality. I hope that this journey offers you some kind of map so that you may have guidance in navigating through the turbulent waters of the psyche during these change times. My wish for you is that you take this journey of healing with as much ease and grace as possible, taking the path of the Beauty Way, where all is known as a gift from the Creator in spite of the experiencing of many challenges at times.

I am neither a scholar nor a trained writer. Much of the book is written from the perspective of embodying higher aspects of conscious awareness so that it may be experienced as a powerful spiritual journey that is beyond the mind, especially from the perspective of the Divine Feminine. It is my hope in the embodying of the higher level energies of the healed feminine that an ascension rhythm of healing and transformation is invoked and that you are actually taken on a healing journey. At times I switch, from one chapter to another, from writing from the right brain intuitive, feeling sense, to the more left brained state of details and information. I do this so that there may also be more of a balance between the left and right brain invoked in the reading, as it is important that this balance is cultivated in our psyches at this time.

You will notice that there are many words that are capitalized beyond the norms of the English language. This extra capitalization is to give respect and power to certain words. Many chapters are headed by spirit animals as guides who would appear to me, wanting to assist by offering the healing energy of what they carry. The section on the 'Door of Heaven' especially has such guides to assist in grounding the otherworldly energies of the heavenly realms. Some words or phrases are also put in quotations to emphasis their importance. There are many shamanic and New Age terms, which should be understandable because of the context in which they are used. Some important phrases like Light and Love are used again and again, so as to give a mantra like effect to the words in the reading thereof. When I refer to God, Creator, Great Spirit, I am referring to the Mother-Father God-Goddess, all that is, that is the central spiritual force of all life that is beyond definition.

You could say that this journey is where indigenous knowledge, New Age, shamanism, and psychology meet. Many of my teachings and spiritual experiences have been connected to indigenous teachers, ceremonies, and sacred sites. Much of what I share comes from my personal interactions. I mean no disrespect to any tradition, nor do I pretend to be an expert on native prophecies or spiritual traditions, but this is how the wisdom was often to come my way, as well as through my own sacred journeys, healing practice, and inner guidance. An Iroquois Elder, Mad Bear Anderson, once said: *"Eastern spirituality looks inward, western religion outward, and the Red People are the middle road where all roads come together."* I believe we have all gone down many roads through many lifetimes and it is a good day to come together. There is no other way. We all have something good to teach each other.

The information I have included that is taken directly from others, I have given credit to and once again mean no disrespect. I have brought together the knowledge of various Wisdom Keepers as well as the many realizations I have come to, for this is how we will remember our inter-connectedness. None of us can understand the immensity of what is occurring on the Planet without listening to the teachings of many. Each person shares their unique view.

This path is one of many, and I encourage you to take what you need and leave the rest. I am one Soul who wishes to assist others through these transformational times, as I have been guided to do. I wish to save others from some of the pain and suffering of being in the dark night of the Soul that can occur if we have disconnected from our true selves and do not understand the bigger picture of what is occurring. I wish to be a midwife to those who have been on the path of spiritual growth and are ready to take further steps. But most of all I surrender to the Will of the Creator of all life, in union with the destiny path of the Mother Earth. I am in service with Love and Light, holding out for the highest fulfillment of humanity's evolvement, dreaming the World awake!

You can read a mini version of my story to understand better who I am, or you can move on to the Vision Chapter. I share a small piece of my personal story so that you may see some of yourself in me and be comforted by the reminder that you are not alone. We all have our stories to share, as well as the joys and the pain, and the multitudes of experiences that we have had here on Planet Earth. We can use all of these stories for the 'grist for the mill' of our evolving selves; not to stay attached to and over-identified with, but to carry us forth, 'full circle in healing and transformation.'

The healing journey is a breathing living entity of its own that will continue to move and expand as the 'World Turns,' going through its stages of metamorphosis like the butterfly, trusting in becoming even more of itself.

My Story

*W*ho am I? Why listen to a word that I say? I am a traveler here on
Earth. Like you, I have been on a journey of forgetting and
remembering, opening and closing, dreaming while awake, dreaming
while asleep. But I can no longer stay asleep and be afraid of the
grandness of who I am in the eyes of the Creator. I can no longer be
unable to stand up and be counted as one who tried her best. Can you?

I birth these words from my Heart in simplicity. I have gathered such a
large quantity of information throughout my life, especially over the last
few years, that I have often felt very overwhelmed in the task of bringing it
all together while continuing on my own path of transformation. I know it
inside very deeply. I have taken the journey myself in all the healing work
and spiritual experiences I have gone through. I taste it like good medicine
that is so powerful that I must bring it out of myself or I will just burst. So
I share just a small part of my journey that you may know me better.

In my childhood, I began my strong connection to Mother Earth by
spending much time outside in her beauty. I felt more connected to her
than to my birth family most of the time. I experienced a special
connection to her and to the Christ energy that would come like a burst in
my Heart while I was praying before bedtime as a child.

I also had an early meeting with the death doorway while experiencing
a 100-foot fall off a cliff as a teenager, resulting, amazingly enough, in
only minor injuries. Being at the tail end of the sixties, I went on a
consciousness raising journey, attempting to break out of the confines of
the box into which my parents and society had put my peers and me. These
were mind expanding times and were powerful groundwork for all that I
have experienced since. I moved out West in the mid-seventies to
California from the East Coast, and caught the end of the wave of
consciousness change.

My first degree was in Horticulture, which assisted me to stay
connected to Mother Nature, even in my work. In my twenties, I worked
closely with her, being involved with community gardens, seed gathering,
and the studying of herbology. During that time the planting ceremonies

that are part of acknowledging the cycles of Mother Nature, began my ceremonial life. In a move to New Mexico in 1984, I ended up living at San Juan Pueblo north of Santa Fe for three years, as part of an agricultural revival of native seeds project. This began my journey with Native American culture and ceremony, and the wake up call of the Four Corners region. This was and still is, not the place to stay asleep.

I experienced ill health for many years after the difficult birthing of my daughter. After living in New Mexico for a year or so, various medicine people and alternative forms of healing became available to me as a vehicle of self-inquiry and healing. I was able to work with shamans and healers from a variety of backgrounds and modalities. I also did intensive work on the healing of a multitude of past lives that were still affecting me in my present life. I doubted the intensity and information I would receive in trance, but would get affirmation soon after that would validate what I had remembered. One memory that was particularly intense was confirmed by a book I picked up a week after my journey.

The major themes and lessons I have gone through life after life gave me a greater understanding of who I am, in a much greater connection to the big picture of my Soul's evolution. Again and again my life experiences would be connected to parts of me that had unfinished business from past lives. I was able to see that the consistent thread of my Soul, lifetime after lifetime, has been involved with bringing consciousness to the World as priestess, healer, herbalist, and mystic. I have been driven to travel much of my life, which in retrospect has felt like a clearing and regaining of many aspects of my former self. Certain sacred sites around the Planet would send me into another World of total recall and memory of more spiritual times. Since that time of deep transformational work, I see how so much of this lifetime is about finishing the lessons of the past, both recent and ancient, so that I can be more ready to make a shift into a whole new way of being, into the Fifth World. I have never stopped that deep self-transformation, by making changes with the help of others, or by working with my own ability to self reflect and transform. It has been an amazing journey.

After my time living on the Pueblo, I went back to school for a Masters Degree in Transformational Counseling. After I received my degree I was hired by Eight Northern Indian Pueblos Council to establish and run a Domestic Violence program, practically by myself, for eight Pueblo, mostly Tewa speaking communities. After one year I saw the absurdity of being a one woman show, wrote a grant, and for five more years developed and participated in a program I named Peace Keepers. It was quite a learning experience as I strived to better understand the wounding and oppression of this particular native culture, as well as much about their ability to survive with great dignity, humor, and spirit.

Throughout the process I was pushed to learn how to stay in my power, while bringing up very deep cultural wounding in a respectful manner.

For years I attended many Native American connected workshops, as well as ceremonies and teachings from a variety of indigenous cultures. I mention Ohkie Simine Forest (of Mohawk lineage, connected strongly to Mayan and Mongolian shamanic teachings), in the main body of the book, because she is the teacher I have learned from the most consistently and her ways have spoken strongly to me as a female on the shamanic path. I truly respect her knowledge and how she brings it to the World. I have tried to give her acknowledgement and respect when the information has come from her, but I ask forgiveness for any places I did not give credit to the source, as the teachings of many Wisdom Keepers has come through my life and has integrated with my own healing work. These teachings and ceremonies, as well as my own spiritual growth and journeys in sacred places, had led me to want to provide assistance to others, more as a spiritual guide than as a psychotherapist.

I began to study and become educated on the path of the shaman and found myself a natural at it. It was interwoven with all the spiritual experiences I was having ceremonially, both in Nature and in healing sessions. I was fortunate enough to have a number of shamans and medicine people as teachers, which has kept me grounded in Earth Wisdom, along with so called New Age teachers who helped open further doorways to the cosmos.

I am very thankful for the many awakenings and spiritual magic I have experienced in my life, too endless to list them all, but I will mention a few. I list them in a continual movement of experiences, even though each experience would warrant a full story of its own:

The 100-foot fall off a cliff at age fifteen, beginning my journey of facing death *The appearance of many plant devas in my many years of living in the garden* *The amazing spirit messages in the Mayan Fire Ceremonies I learned to work with in profound ways* *The opening of my Soul to the Heart of myself and others in deep connection to the Earth, the Water, the Fire, and the Air, during ceremonies of the Native American Church for many years; the transformation into the 'Spirit of Water' during one of these ceremonies that brought great bliss and healing; Water falling on me from a dry sky when I began singing a prayer song inside the teepee* *The many miracles of the shamanic healing journeys I went on for others and the positive changes they experienced in their lives* *Being witness to the trance-like beauty of hundreds of Katsinas (please note that this is the proper spelling of Kachinas in this reference), dancing in and out of the Hopi Kivas* *Seeing lightning strike the Tree of Life at the end of a Santee Sioux Sun Dance* *Taking part in Tibetan Buddhist Ceremonies, working with the underground Water Serpent Spirits of New Mexico, called Avaynu, to heal the Fire energy gotten way out of balance, connected to the teachings of the Tewa people* *Being guided by Spirit to go to a particular temple in Peru where the image of my personal animal totem was imbedded in the ancient stone of the Incan trail (no other like it anywhere else on the trail), which opened me to my lifetime as a Nust'a, an Incan Priestess; completing the ceremony of the marrying of the Sun that was left incomplete from this powerful lifetime in Peru, which stopped my Moon Cycle from ever returning again* *Rainbows appearing again and again while praying to the Native Hawaiian guardians of the volcanoes* *Being chosen to be a Goddess caretaker of the Temple of the Rainbow Serpent by my now dear friend James Jereb at 'Star Dreaming' Temples and Labyrinths in Santa Fe, who did not know that Feathered Serpent is my day sign in Mayan Astrology* *Gathering ashes from the Ceremonial Fires at the Temple of Magic, where thirteen indigenous grandmothers gathered to do their closing ceremonies (a huge standing stone waiting for each one), during the time I was writing that part of the book* *Being guided by unseen forces to perform a multitude of ceremonies both solo and community connected, especially the most recent Venus Passage of June 8th, 2004, along the sacred pathway south of Santa Fe between Sleeping Buffalo and Quetzalcoatl Mountain, where the sacred number of thirty-three attendees was most auspicious* *The most amazing experiences at sacred sites all over the Planet, where the spiritual Worlds were revealed*; and so much more.

The list of spiritual experiences is long and continues as I experience my earthly reality in search of the sacred in all life. I know this is also true for many of you. Spirit is already alive and well here on Earth and has enlivened and inspired our journeys even through the dark times.

I have taken the journey of healing in a deep and profound manner and I know that the journey is not over yet. Every step of the way and with every chapter I would write, I would have to go through the process myself. Every step of the way my World would synchronize to fit exactly what I was writing about. Even though I have spent twenty-two years on a very strong healing journey, I was asked to 'up the ante' and go even deeper into my personal healing. What an adventure I have been on, being so thankful one minute, and then cursing the next. But I know it is important to have gone through everything that I have, to bring me to where I am today. It has been truly about the deepening of my own initiatory process.

I have been aware of myself on a symbolic, spiritual, and mythical journey for much of my life, searching out and seeing the deeper meaning in whatever I was experiencing. It is who I am. I know no other way. We have destiny paths to carry out in this lifetime and I know that my gift is in the transformation of consciousness. Some of you are meant to step forth and be healthier leaders, some are to be agents of social change, others protectors of the environment, while some are to stand up for the children and the animals. The jobs are as numerous as are the gifts that are given to each and every one.

In the writing of this book I have been in an altered state of consciousness the majority of the time, in between the distractions and demands of day to day life, as I continue my initiation rite to greater, expanded consciousness. The journey has taken me to places and experiences that were not what I expected. Every step of the process, I was put through my own tests, as well as having synchronistic experiences and information come my way. The animal guides who had messages for me would come to me almost daily, for the natural World is very present, as are the lakes and waters near the White Mountains of New Hampshire, where I wrote the majority of this book. Mother Nature still rules here in a very obvious way. Wild Turkey, Eagle, Hawk, Osprey, Loon, Moose, Fox, Woodpecker, Blue Heron, and Coyote, are just a few of the animals that have spoken loudly. Then there are the many dreams and visions that would instruct me. I had also been living with a Ball Python Snake that goes by the name of 'Beauty,' which is incredibly symbolic, as you will see. The symbolic connection became endless as the synchronicities increased. I found myself connected to Moon Cycles, Equinoxes, Solstices, and Eclipses, as well as Holy Days of various spiritual traditions, writing the appropriate information related to each, specific energy during these most auspicious times. I believe the power of this will come through the contents of this book.

The final rewrite and integration of all that it has taken to complete this book, is occurring back in Santa Fe, New Mexico, the Sipapu of my own rebirth into spiritual consciousness. I also ended up writing in Portland, Maine, a very Piscean City of much gentleness and in Costa Rica, a place where the vitality of Mother Nature is quite present.

Who would have known I would be brought to these so very different locations on Mother Earth in order to bring in what was needed for my own transformation to birth forth the energy of this book, as a breathing, living healing journey. Then again it makes total sense I would be guided to do so in the completion of the transformation of the 'Four Direction Pillars' that shape the World and the 'Four Basic Elements' of each direction, in preparing me for rebirth. It was necessary to work with the powerful Earth energies of each location. You will understand this better after you take the journey through this book. Santa Fe is the place of Fire, Ossipee the place of Earth, Costa Rica the place of Air (many trees), and Portland the place of Water; even though each place carries a portion of each. This journey in its telling has truly had a mind and will of its own, taking me from place to place, spiritually, physically, mentally, and emotionally. I have been purified in the Fire, cleansed in the Water, clarified in the Air, and brought to my knees as I have fallen to Earth, to embody all I have learned and to bring it forth.

These and many more are the experiences that have opened me to see beyond what the normal vision sees, to hear so much more than we normally hear, and to feel the pull to be so much more than I thought I could be. I have put every ounce of what I have transformed into the energy of this journey so it may gather momentum for your own spiritual movement, bringing you closer to the Light and Love of your own being. May my breaking out of the restraints of what has held me back from my true self, be of major assistance at this time of 'Great Change.' Changing Woman has worked through me, changing everything she touches.

Each and every one of us is needed at this time, to discover who we truly are and to meet ourselves again in a new way, understanding the 'Good Medicine' that we carry in the particular beings and characters we have manifested during this turn around the 'Great Wheel of Life.' We each have a Soul signature that is our very own, not in an egotistical way, but in a way of positive ownership for the gifts we carry.

I know myself in many ways: as a human being who struggles with her demons, as well as rejoices in the experience of embodiment; as a Star Child from Sirius coming through the Beauty Way of Venus; as Feathered Serpent, Priestess of the Rainbow Serpent Temple; as a Pisces woman ruled by the Waters; a daughter of Isis lifetime after lifetime; Ama Wehali (Water Eagle spirit essence); a shaman and ceremonialist of many ways; a daughter of the Earth, a mother and daughter, a lover and beloved, but most of all a child of the Love and the Light of the Creator of all things, ready to birth what I have come here to do as I come through into the Fifth World. Will you join me there?

I

The Vision

1

The Cycle of Transformation

The dream I have carried within me of a World where Spirit and the sacredness of all things will be honored and felt on the Planet with every breath, with every step, with everyone, is being awakened! The spirit of Water Eagle (Ama Wehali) opens in me to share the vision. The gift of this power animal has integrated within me, opening its sacred being to share what it sees and feels. The Water Eagle assists in expanding clear vision in the watery worlds of what previously has been hidden in the recesses of our unconscious and is now being revealed. May it open in you so that you may also see, feel, and hear the vision and the calling to awaken out of humanity's deep slumber.

Humanity is in the midst of great evolutionary times. According to many indigenous prophecies, we are shifting from one Age to another as we draw nearer to the year 2012, having already passed through three Worlds. We are finding it necessary to look deep within, as we reach out far to the Heavens, to find answers and solutions from a much more enlightened part of our consciousness. Both Light and Love are pouring into the Planet from the 'Heart of the Earth' and the 'Heart of the Heavens,' activating us to deal with our places of separation. In the Fourth and present World, we have been learning from the lessons created from a dualistic and out of balance reality. It is of vital importance that we complete and learn from the lessons of the past in order to enter fully into the Fifth World, a much more spiritually aligned and infused reality.

It may appear that the darkest energies of human nature are taking over the Planet, but take a deeper look and you will also see the opposite in acts of great generosity and kindness. We are in the middle of the resolution of dualities. This is the nature of the shift. The 'Great Center Core' of our Mother Earth, in her connection to the Light and Love of the Godhead, is emanating to her children a great calling to wake up! To wake up to what we have forgotten and to face what needs to be healed and transformed. The Fire in Earth's belly can no longer be held back from her evolution as a being. Have you not experienced her voice speaking loudly as she balances that which is not in sync with her sacred energies?

We can no longer do the dance of humanity without remembering and respecting our true home and coming into alignment with her cycles and wisdom, as well as uniting our own separated parts in reconnection to our divinity in every part of our being. Mother Earth is not separate from the Creator of all life. She speaks with her undulations and movements, that which come from the Center of the Wheel, the Center of Creation. The message to awaken and to come into harmony and balance is no longer just a whisper on the wind. We are being pushed to the wall individually and collectively by the unconsciousness and pain of humanity and the imbalances thus created on Mother Earth.

Do you feel the stirrings inside? Are you experiencing great unrest and angst in your life, not being in a place that feels quite right;, the very uncomfortable sense of how much loss of life and instability has been created by natural and man-made disasters, while awaiting the next crisis; the great confusion over the destructive mismanagement of our society by our government and the corporate powers, and the ensuing fears of survival and the possible breakdown of our economy and society, as well as the great suffering and seeming lack of control the general public has over war? Do you feel the sadness of living a life without community, a loss of old goals and friends, grieving over many close relations passing away, increase in physical ill-health, the anxiety and stress of all it takes to live in the World and to keep up with your life, the hopelessness that no matter how much healing you do, you are still seemingly on an endless loop of more to heal? Are you aware of how much anger you are holding towards the powers in the World that are out to destroy Mother Earth and many of her children, the frustration that you are being held back by some unseen force that is not allowing you to make not only the changes that are needed in your own life, but to stand up and take action to make it a better World for your children's children and beyond? Do you feel the overwhelming nature of all of the above and more, and lastly the often unnamed fear that you will not survive through these challenging times and neither will the rest of humanity? These deep feelings, as well as many others, may be difficult to be with, as we try to cover them up and go on with our daily lives. Take a deep breath and let go, while trusting in your abilities as a spiritual being. It is important to find the place deep inside where you can see and feel all this, and at the same time remember who you are beyond the turmoil; not by ignoring what you are experiencing, but through a journey of spiritual transformation. These feelings are a doorway to transformation as we ride the waters of awakening!

At the same time many are being overwhelmed by these intense feelings, many are experiencing profound moments of transformation, going through immense shifts of spiritual growth and awakening; opening to realities out of the norm, seeking a higher plane of existence. This can be inspirational as well as disorienting, as we will explore in later chapters. But it is important to know how to navigate through all the many experiences and feelings, for these are powerful times.

I ask of you at this time to take an even more intimate look into yourself and see if you are experiencing the stirrings deep inside that are asking for a change in your being and in your life at a very core level. Do the old ways of being fit anymore? Have you taken the inner journey to grow as a person? Are you willing to bare your Soul in honesty and truth when it is time to look at yourself in the mirror of self-reflection? Can you love yourself back to wholeness? Have you given the attention you need to your thoughts, your feelings, your actions, your relations, and your treatment of the Earth? Is your spiritual self leading the way? If you are reading these words, I believe you have begun the journey. It is time to travel even further.

I understand deeply how difficult it is to undertake the journey within and face all parts of one's being. Stay in love and compassion for yourself and the World as much as you can. This is very important, step by step, moment by moment. Most of us have not been taught that there is a rich inner world in which to journey and reflect, as well as many other dimensions of which to be aware. Most of us have not been taught that there are many unseen helpers available to us who are gifts from the Creator to help us on our way. Most of us have not been shown the necessary tools to use on a daily basis to evolve our beings, from the simplest and most basic relationship skills, to the most elevated teachings of the enlightened ones. Most of us have not been honored in the major passages of life which would have assisted us to truly mature. But during this time of great shifting on the Planet, there are many who are standing up as guides to assist us to be on a more conscious journey, to become 'Flowering Souls' of awakening. Invite the petals of your Soul to open and let in the Light and be blessed by the Holy Waters of the healed Heart, through whatever way is most aligned with your Soul. You will know. Trust yourself.

The catalyst to take the time to focus on your personal awakening may be any of the uncomfortable feelings mentioned above, or may be because you are tired of your life not working, being unmanageable, or unfulfilling. The impetus to make powerful changes may be the state of the World around you. Whatever the reason, whatever the way, make a choice; it is time for self-responsibility in the fullest sense of the word, because no one is going to save us. According to the Hopi Elders, "We are the ones we have been waiting for," and the twenty-five years of purification that are strongly upon us, are inviting us to transmute all negativity. There is help, there are gates opening to assist, there is grace; but not without the movement of the seed growing towards the Light, becoming its realized self. It is being asked of the many, not of the few, to make a leap in consciousness and evolution at this time, a paradigm shift unlike any we have ever been able to make in any of the previous Worlds. Evolution, as I see it, has to do with returning to and being able to embody more Light and Love, to transmute the darkness, and all of humanity is being asked to take part in this awakening. As we take responsibility to shift our consciousness, we affect the whole of humanity as well as life here on the Mother Earth. It is not a self-centered thing to do. It is for the good of all life. As we heal, we heal the World.

We are at a time where the need for evolving as a species is becoming more apparent to much of humanity, in spite of the resistance to change. This awareness is not only being experienced by spiritual seekers, but through personal feelings and experiences of the masses. The presence of weapons that can destroy the entire Planet, the increase of acts of misuse of power by governments and corporations, destruction and pollution of the Earth and volatile Earth changes, are being made apparent to us, wherever we may live. We can no longer afford to stay asleep in the illusionary safety of our daily lives. It is time to wake up from the deep slumber of the trance of forgetting who we truly are. We have evolved, but mostly in an individualistic, separatist manner; seeing anything or anyone that is different as 'wrong' or 'less than.' It is time to take a leap into an entirely new way of evolvement, where we are capable of loving all our parts and all of humanity, in a return to the knowing of the 'Oneness' of all life.

It is time to gather and heal the energies and lessons learned from the unconscious parts of our psyches, as well as from the collective unconscious of our Ancestors, our religions, and our countries, and then to bring all back into harmony and wholeness, so we can move forward in a new way. We are birthing into a World that is a new creation for humans to experience, and we must have faith and trust the journey. It is time to evolve. For that is what we are here to do. We must transform our emotions, our beliefs, our psyches, and Egos, bringing all into conscious awareness. We have created a reality out of our Shadow Unconscious that must be loved through the door of Light that is opening for us, shining the Light on the path back to wholeness. It is most important that humanity become more conscious as co-creators of our reality.

In the passage and birthing of our beings into the denser energies of this third dimension or Earth plane, there was a fragmentation of the unified sense of self. The body was experienced as separate from the personality, which in turn was experienced as separate from the Soul. Access to the higher frequencies was no longer so easily available. We shut down our higher feeling states in fear of being overwhelmed and confused. Our basic self kicked in, requiring us to move into states of physical survival without being fully connected to the gifts of higher knowing. New energies were developed, such as the Ego and its Shadow that birthed out of the places of separation. This way of existing is due for an evolution change, not only because it is in sync with the prophecies of many cultures, but the places of separation have been away from the Light for too long and need to return home. These energies, these Shadow beings that are part of us but also bigger than us, have evolved through time into 'Shadow Complexes' that can at times negatively rule an individual, a family lineage, a tribe, a country, a World. The ancient unhealed wounds amplify at times, where they get so out of control that they personify for example, in the great unrest in the Middle East. The ancient wounds of looking at the other as the enemy, have been collecting more and more fuel to feed the collective ancestral and cultural Shadow, to a place of explosive combustion. Even the place or location of trauma can hold the unhealed energy until resolved.

These individual and collective Shadows have been away from the Light and the Love of Spirit for too long and need assistance to find their way back home to wholeness. These Shadows of separation cannot exist in the unified field that is pouring onto and emanating throughout the Planet. These places of separation, distrust and at times feelings of great anger, hurt, and revenge, must heal back into wholeness or we will destroy ourselves. Many who appear as if they are adults in adult bodies, are acting out like teenagers with big destructive toys, resisting moving into adulthood and a higher state of being, attempting consciously and unconsciously to slow down the collective movement of change while they hold onto false illusions of power. These Shadow or Unconscious parts exist in and are the responsibility of each and every one of us. Our capability to face this openly, may depend on how split we have become during this time of separation. As difficult as it may be to look at ourselves in unwavering honesty, there is help available for all who travel through this passageway. Ask with a sincere Heart and assistance will come your way.

Many people look at the Epoch humanity has been in, as a 'Fall from Grace' that has created a long cycle of suffering because of the choices of humanity, especially around free will (Adam and Eve story). I look at this time and the entirety of humanity's earthly journey, in the Light of the perfection of Creation and all things, as part of our Souls' need for deeper experience. The Epoch we have passed through may have been an experience necessary for us to gain the maturity needed to come back to God out of our own free will, even in the midst of much suffering and non-respect for the sacredness of all things. Maybe it is time to finally move out of the adolescent stage (which is acting out in refusal to grow up), into a more adult stage of our development as a species.

As mentioned previously, according to many indigenous teachings and prophecies, we are in the midst of great evolutionary times as we shift from one Era to another, as we head towards the year 2012. I will be referring to the terms Era, Epoch, and Age, interchangeably as 'Cycles of Time,' as a way to chart the characteristics of the stages of human evolution. It is important to have at least a minimal understanding of these Cycles, in order to have some perspective on the immensity of the changes that are upon humanity. We tend to focus on the needs of our daily lives and it is a must that we expand our view into greater horizons. Humanity is being called to dig deeper, to find answers and solutions from a more enlightened part of our consciousness, as the questions and challenges get bigger. In the present Age of the Fourth World that we have been journeying through (approximately 5,200 years according to the Mayan delineation of time), we have been learning from the lessons and painful patterns and emotions created from separation and disharmony, including the experiencing of suffering and death. The Fifth Sun or World is the next Era, in which Spirit will once again readily be seen and felt in Matter, making us aware of the inter-connectedness of all things, within and without. The Fifth Element Ether, Spirit in Matter, will be more present here on the New Earth. This Light of awakening will assist us to come back into a unified field of loving consciousness.

The concept of Ages and Cycles has been charted since time immemorial by many ancient cultures that have held great knowledge. More and more the modern World is looking to the ancients for the wisdom that had been hidden or left behind. The Western World is now beginning to respect many indigenous teachings that were practically eradicated, as was prophesied in the healing of the Sacred Hoop. The Sacred Hoop was broken when the gifts of the various races and Nations were disrespected. Many Indigenous Elders are now sharing their teachings with the World as they were instructed to do when the time was right, in honoring of their traditions and to assist with the great shifting of the consciousness of humanity. There are many versions of these Cycles according to cultural context and I will name but a few.

According to Hindu lore we are nearing the end of the Great Cycle of the Kali Yuga, during which humanity has been primarily learning through the experiencing of pain and suffering. We change what we do, or change our perspective about what we've experienced, because we want to stop being in pain and to feel better. This Cycle is the last of four major Epochs that humanity has gone through, each representing an element or building block of Nature; of Earth, Water, Fire, and Air. Different cultures have varying concepts of which element rules each Cycle. The Kali Yuga is the Epoch where humanity has lost or forgotten most of its connection to its sacred God Source and divine beginnings and for the most part has wallowed in its lower appetites, with an increase in materialism and greed. This last Cycle has been a time where for the most part, selfishness has ruled; that when someone has something, they wish to keep it for themselves. This last Cycle has been a time when the collective norm has been to look outside of oneself for the answers and for a connection to Divine Source and the majority of the population has often been controlled by a hierarchy that does not have the best interest of the people in mind. The cumulative result of this is a system that is collapsing because its foundations have been irresponsible to the whole.

In the many years it takes to gain entrance into the next Era, the old paradigm is held onto more tightly as humanity fears the change into the great unknown, while the energies of the next Era are creating a new reality right alongside the old. The influence of the next Era is already shining its Light of awakening onto the many imbalances created in the last Great Cycle. This has been a Cycle where the many are controlled by the few, and those few control much of the World's resources while many still live in poverty. The next Epoch is called the Satya Yuga, which is believed to be the return 'full circle' to a Golden Age, as the 'Fifth Element' Ether (Spirit manifest in Matter) changes us at our core. This will be a time for the best of humanity to shine and to discover the divine within which has never truly lost its connection to spiritual Source.

According to the Mayan Calendar, time will stop as we know it on Winter Solstice of December of 2012. We are being given a chance to evolve out of the time and space limitations of the third dimension. The way it was explained to me by a Mayan Elder, is that this is not the end of the World, but the end of life as we know it; that this next Era is a way of being that we have never experienced before. The past Great Cycle has been called the Nine Bolomtikus (approximate length of 5,200 Mayan years), of the Thirteen Baktuns, of the Fourth Ajaw, a time of learning through the Nine Underworlds. These nine levels have to do with facing energies such as greed, self-importance, selfishness, and judgment, to name a few; the World of our Shadow side. No one is exempt from this experience. Even advanced medicine people and shamans have to keep facing the lower energies of their Basic Self and negative Egos when embodied in this dimension, and more so, as the temptation to misuse power is amplified. Even the 'Holy Ones' who come back to assist humanity and inhabit an Earth body, must be able to face the aspects of their lower natures before they can embody the higher truths.

In the next Great Cycle, the Fifth Ajaw, we get to experience the Thirteen Upperworlds, a much more divinely connected dimension. This is where we may get the chance to experience a true 'Garden of Eden' where we become much more conscious co-creators of our reality, remembering that the Creator is everywhere, within and without. We get to heal the distortions of what has been created. The year 2012 is the arrival of the Fifth Balam, where the union of all races, the fusion of the polarities, and the presence of a unified field of energy created by the presence of the 'Fifth Element' Ether (Spirit in Matter), will occur. Polarity is the force or magnetic dance of energies that have sustained the physical reality of matter in the Third Dimension, where humanity has been living in duality. The Fifth Balam will herald the time of a chance for a more evolved humanity to be birthed. This date begins the possibility of a Great Cycle of wisdom, harmony, peace, love, of consciousness and the return of natural order. This doesn't occur overnight but has cycles of preparatory initiations to assist us to resolve the old way of being.

We are presently in the transitional period where it is becoming difficult to accept the ways of this last Cycle, as well as confusing to know how to relate to the energies into which we are moving. The rules are changing and we are not quite sure what the new guidelines are. It is the time of purification where our beliefs and concepts about what constitutes reality will be turned upside down. It is the time where we will be pushed to the edge of emotional, physical, and psychological pain to resolve the places of un-love and judgment in our selves and in our lives. We are being asked to operate from a much more divinely aware part of our beings and to trust and connect to our divine selves.

The twenty-five year period of purification began in August of 1987, during what is known as the Harmonic Convergence. At this time, the new consciousness needed to start gradually awakening humanity to bring in the 'Fifth Sun,' began showering down on us from the core of the galaxy through the inner Sun or Fire within the Earth. Since then, there has been a high level of disturbance in the Earth's core as she adjusts to the higher vibration (earthquakes, changes in weather, etc.). It is ever increasing as we get closer to the time when the doorway is wide open, December 21st, 2012. There will be vortexes of great intensity that our Planet will be spiraling in and out of, giving us a chance to work with the Fifth Dimensional frequencies. Our Sun is increasingly exhibiting solar flares in response to the intensity of the heavenly Light that will be joining with the Light from deep within the Earth. There has also been a greater feeling of unrest and unease in humanity in response to these energies as we are pushed to our limits in order to complete the lessons and change the ensuing patterns of the Cycle we are leaving. At this time all Worlds are coming together to give us a chance to be bathed and reborn in spiritual Love and Light.

In the Book of Revelation it is stated that we have already gone through three Worlds that were destroyed because of humanity's inability to follow the tenets given for spiritual living, and that God made a promise to the people that this Fourth World would not be destroyed by God. Is humanity's own unconsciousness going to be the cause of the World's destruction this time? Or is there going to be transformation without total destruction, a possibility of two Worlds, two choices; one choice, the holding on to the old ways, and the other, of expanding consciousness and opening to the New World? It is stated in some prophecies that when two Suns appear, this will be a sign that another dimension or World will be forming alongside the one we have known. According to some traditions, as this dimension opens, we will experience three days of darkness, which will be a time when it will be decided if our consciousness has evolved sufficiently to grant our entrance into the New World. Is it possible that during this time of passage, we will go through the bardo state without dying, akin to the death doorway, where decisions are made by the Holy Ones as to whether or not one is ready to birth into the Fifth World? There is a sense of urgency felt by many to gather together as many of our brothers and sisters as we can to make it through the passageway, as a large majority of humanity is needed to hold open this doorway to create a New World. The choice is ours. Do we surrender to the conscious transformation of our beings or continue in a World of separation and Ego rule that cannot truly support human life? Can we gather together enough of our brothers and sisters to make it through?

The prime symbol of the Kabala, the Tree of Life, is the energetic representation of that which holds up the World and our individual energy fields. These are the Four Sacred Trees, or Four Worlds. Each one represents an element in its highest form; Air being the archetypal World of pure divinity, Water representing the creative World of the Archangel, Fire representing the formative World, and the Angelic realm, and Earth representing the material 'World Tree.' As we evolve into the Fifth World and incorporate the Fifth Element, it is possible we will activate the code of a new sacred, symbolic, and energetic Tree of Life, forming a more spiritually infused reality, transforming the Tree of Knowledge.

To the Q'ero, the descendants of the Inca of Peru, we are moving towards the Great Cycle of the Taripay Pacha, the 'Age of Meeting Ourselves Again,' a Golden Age during which we can step more fully into our energetic, spiritual bodies. Connecting to these most important unseen energies that make up a human, is a way in which Ether, Spirit in Matter, will be consciously embodied. Many techniques and processes which can facilitate our work with the spiritually unseen forces are appearing and being shared within the human experience. Some examples of techniques that are useful in assisting us to connect with the not-so-easily-seen-with-the-naked- eye world of spiritual energy and guides are: Shamanic Practices, Reiki, Chi Gong, Chakra clearing, Light Body and DNA Activation, and Breath Work, to name but a few. It is becoming more natural for people to acknowledge and work with these energies. We are being asked to learn how to bring more awareness and connection to Spirit and to the subtle energies of life.

According to the Q'ero we are living in the midst of a nineteen year period during which humanity has the potential to establish its own spiritual evolution. According to their prophecies we have gone through a pachakuti, an overturning of space time, beginning somewhere around 1990 to 1993, in which a cosmic reordering with human consciousness and the creative force of the cosmos occurred. This has provided humanity a chance to evolve rapidly and affect positively the outcome of the future. The Q'ero call this the 'Fifth Level' of human consciousness, manifest on Earth. The understanding is that many Paqos, spiritual seekers of any ethnic heritage or cultural or religious background, are needed to raise the vibrational energy of humanity to the level required to complete transformation. This process of emergence and transformation is available to all people. Many prophecies of Earth changes have stated there would be much worse devastation than has already occurred, around the turn of the century. It is possible that because of the 'consciousness awakening' that is growing around the globe, we may have alleviated some of the severity of the destruction that we would have experienced without it. However, it is obvious with the catastrophes still occurring, our work is far from over.

One of my teachers, Ohky Simine Forest, who is a Mohawk shaman (also connected to Mayan and Mongolian traditions), has been instructed by Mongolian Elders about the four major Eras of 5,400 years each, similar to the Mayan length of 5,200 years. They tell first of the Era of Earth, predominately led by huge communal and matriarchal societies, inclined to worship the Goddess. Next is the Era of Sky, when great enlightened and spiritual civilizations flourished (the heyday of great civilizations such as the Egyptians and the Maya). Third is the Era of Man (the Cycle we are now coming out of), the time of the patriarchal societies and their dominance in all forms. The fourth Era is the Era of Women, with a prevalence of the universal feminine forces. Some believe that this Era is a quickened Cycle in which to balance all other Cycles with the energies of the higher feminine which honors all in 'full circle.' We have gone through the sacred elements of Earth, Air, Fire, and now Water, and will then join all these together in the experiencing of Ether.

There are many references made to the 'Flowering of the Soul' throughout. Many years ago, the very first shaman I went to for my own healing, informed me that I would be just fine when I lived in the Land of the Flowers. Since then I have heard of a place in Peru called 'the Land of the Flowers,' where a community is supposedly already living within the vibration of the Fifth World. I also have been told that many Mayan Elders refer to the next stage as 'the Land of the Flowers'. Flowers have represented the Tree of Life for many cultures, especially the Lotus, Lilies, and Orchids. Flowers bring forth a state of beauty and grace and greatly assist the re-balancing of the feminine energies. Seeing the beauty in a flower, the most evolved form of plant life, a physical representation of Spirit in Matter, is a reminder of our true spiritual essence self.

The Mayan prophecies state that the change being initiated which will come to fullness in 2012, is a time where the polarities of the reality that we have known will begin to be unified, and opposite energies will learn to join together in harmony more often. Each of the Eras that humanity has already experienced, was a time when the majority of humanity saw the various energies, races, tribes, and sexes as something separate and different and did not understand the inter-connectedness of all things. This experience was rooted in separation, with a forgetting of much of the original spiritual instructions on how to live. As the Ego developed a stronger and stronger presence, one of the ensuing outcomes was the creation of an enemy to be attacked, conquered, and taken from. Much of humanity was overtaken by greed and materialism, misusing the Earth and the powers and gifts given to each race. Only a few faithful people who followed the original tenets survived with consciousness each time that humanity went through destruction. The great majority of the population went into the World of unconsciousness, not remembering what had been experienced before. This time around the 'Great Wheel of Life' as we are nearing a passageway of great rebirth, we are being given a chance to gather the wisdom from what we have learned from these previous Cycles and move ahead with consciousness. That is why so much is being gathered from the ancient history of humanity's time here on Earth.

The Hopi, Native Americans who are located in Northern Arizona, have prophecies that have been handed down from generation to generation. Their prophecies are known throughout the World. They have tried many times to be heard at the United Nations and are considered the 'Record Keepers' of the Native Americans. One time a special group of Hopi Elders was heard by a small gathering of members of the United Nations. They spoke of many things. The Elders shared how the teachings were passed down to them from ancient times. They spoke of how the First World Creator made in perfect balance, where humans all spoke one language, but humans turned away from the spiritual principals given to them. They misused their God given powers for selfish purpose. They did not follow Nature's rules. Eventually the World was destroyed by the sinking and separation of land by what you would call major earthquakes. Many died and only a small handful survived. Then this handful of peaceful people came into the Second World. They repeated their mistakes and the World was destroyed by freezing, which was the great Ice Age.

Only a few survivors entered the Third World. That World lasted a long time. The people invented many machines and conveniences of high technology, some of which have not yet been seen in this Age. They even had spiritual powers that many used for the good. But eventually they too turned away from the natural laws and most began to pursue power and material gain, turning away once again from the God-given laws and principles. Only a few tried to stop this course and the World was destroyed by a great flood that many nations still recall in their religions and historical records. The Elders said that once again only a small group survived and came to this Fourth World where we now live.

The Hopis call this the Fourth Age of Man and say that we are soon to enter the Fifth Age, which they call 'The World of Illumination.' They believe that the Four Corners area of the Southwest is the Sipapu or entrance point of the Fourth World we have been living in, and is the place where the higher energies coming to the Planet are to be brought in and grounded here on Earth. This birthing place is to be kept protected and spiritually elevated with sacred ceremonies and dances. What happens in this 'Cosmic Birthing' place is a microcosm of what will occur in the World. The connection and correlation to the number four, in the Four Directions, the Four Races, the Four Elements, the Four Corners, and Fourth World, is hard to ignore.

There is a rock that I have been gifted to see, that is called Prophecy Rock located in the land of the Hopi in Arizona. This ancient petroglyph shows a juncture of two paths to take as part of the foretold future, where there will be a choice to make by the people. The choice to make, as interpreted by the Hopi Elders, is to go either the road of the two-hearted people (those who think with their head rather than Heart, who misuse technology and power by thinking with the mind only), or to go the road of the Heart, where connection to Mother Earth and all her relations, and the return to the natural ways are followed. It is said that the split between those two paths is ever widening, as exhibited in the great suffering and heartlessness occurring in part of humanity.

I was able to personally experience being in a solar energy house of a leader of one of the clans in Hopi, where I was told that advanced technology, in balance with the Earth, is acceptable to the old traditional ways. Use of anything out of balance with the Earth, is not. The original instructions and responsibilities given to each race on how to live in a spiritual manner in connection to the Earth are to be remembered and adhered to by all people. Part of the Hopi message that has been communicated in the last five years, is that the time is now; we are the ones we have been waiting for. Are we waiting to be saved or are we going to become the shining ones?

One of the most glaring changes that many people are aware of during this paradigm shift, is that they do not experience time in the same way as before. Some people have shared with me that they have felt like time has sped up and that they cannot accomplish the same amount of projects in a day that they used to, that they cannot keep up with themselves, and that it is difficult to focus for any length of time. Others speak of it time going both slower and faster with no rhyme or reason. We are also being brought into the dream world of great fluidity and into the next dimension and Era and are in the 'Time of no Time' according to the Maya (the Time Keepers). Time and space are but a boundary for the 3D reality of Matter and the same limits will not be necessary in the next World. It appears as if we are being sped up (with the great influx of Cosmic Light), but the key is to slow down, to handle the shift. Then we can be prepared to let more Light and Love into ourselves and onto the Mother Earth. In times of major shifting it is important to ground and slow down so one does not spin out of balance or topple over.

The Fifth Dimension that is opening up is much less linear and much more spatial with spirals of movement within incorporeal space. It is taking some getting used to while still performing the tasks of the 3D World. But within this field we can have greater access to the spiritual energy in all things and can learn to be better co-creators of this reality, as what we believe and think comes to pass much more quickly than previously experienced. We are in the Fourth Dimension transitional phase, where we get to practice before the Fifth dimension is fully upon us. The dream time is also infiltrating our waking time as the veils between the Worlds get thinner and we open up to dimensions where we get to work with the wholeness of our beings, bringing that which is out of alignment back in sync. This is quite the expansive experience and may be disorienting at times.

A number of years ago I asked a Peruvian shaman friend of mine why was humanity so interested in the cultures of the past at this time? He shared with me that in order to rise up to the next Age, the next World, we needed to come 'full circle' with what we have learned from the past. This invoked an image for me wherein as one circle completes its Sacred Hoop, a new one spirals above. The indigenous cultures of the past carry much wisdom that can assist us to understand and heal from this time of separation, being more based in an Earth connected, spiritual manner that adds much to the Western World's perspective.

In learning about the shifting into the New World, therefore a new dimensional reality, I became aware that the unlearned lessons of the Era we are completing cannot follow us into the future. Those Souls or energies who have not worked on the clearing and integrating of the aspects of their being that have developed out of separation, will not be permitted entrance into the New World; they will have to stay on the karmic loop (learning through actions taken in separation from our God-self).

Here we have again the choice of two Worlds. This time there is a safety loop in the evolutionary journey that assures those energies of separation cannot even exist in the Fifth World or Dimension. Each time one World has ended and another begun, we have taken with us the unlearned lessons from the past, with the majority of humanity not carrying the knowledge of what has occurred in the previous existence. This level of unconscious material can no longer keep biting us from behind as we strive to evolve. It is necessary this time to bring all into conscious awareness, so we can birth ahead with wisdom, not in forgetfulness.

There is more information given on the prophecies in the next chapter, but I want to give an overview of the concept of Ages and Eras, which gives the backdrop for the more detailed story of this time of change. I also hope this may help you to hold some kind of vision of the bigger story behind the impetus for humanity to transform. I would like to share that there is at times, a discrepancy between the concepts of what number World or level or dimension we are moving into, even though there are more commonalities than differences. This ultimately does not matter, but the messages that are given do.

It is also important to mention that according to the perspective of Astrology we are entering a very unique Cycle which aligns with what is spoken of in many indigenous prophecies. We are nearing the end of a 2,160 year Piscean Age and are entering the energies of a very different Cycle of the Aquarian Age. West of Pisces and below the neck of Pegasus, lie the stars which make up Aquarius, the Water Bearer, one of the oldest recognized constellations. It is generally believed that the Aquarian Age started in the year 2,000. Regardless of the actual so called start date, this star grid has been influencing the shifting of consciousness for many years and will continue to do so, as the stars above have always done when they shift in their connection and influence on earthly reality. This influence and focus will be on self-transformation, self-realization and self-actualization. Through the focus on evolving the self, we are being asked to transform the Ego's illusions of control that perpetuate separation, power over others and selfishness that have developed in this time of duality. When our Ego is brought back into integration with the spiritual and whole self, the more altruistic parts of our beings can come into play. These are the aspects of humanity that know how to cooperate with others, that combine individuality with group integration, that do not believe in hierarchical control, and care about the well-being and equality of all people. The Aquarian Age will inspire new awareness and ways of thinking and believing that will open us to the Universe in new and mysterious ways.

According to many prophecies, in alignment with the Aquarian energies, this is the time where all races and cultures are meant to come together to work in harmony with their individual gifts, as well as the birthing of the Rainbow Warriors spoken of in many traditions as the Thirteenth Tribe. A Native American Elder, Standing Bear, speaks of the Rainbow Prophecies: *"During the changing of the polarities of the Earth, mass unconsciousness will arise. A new neo-indigenous people will rise up from the Earth's ashes like the thunderbird, symbolizing rebirth. They will bring balance and harmony back to Mother Earth and humanity. They will carry the traditions of the native people in a new way. They will gather the four sacred directions, all distinctly separate but forever connected in the 'Circle of Life.' They will bring together the four races of man to live in peace and will carry the ways of many people. They will be called the Rainbow Warriors. During this awakening, the Rainbow Woman will emerge once more to give rebirth to this new tribe and to awaken as much of humanity as possible. The tasks of these 'Warriors of the Rainbow' are many and great. There will be terrifying mountains of ignorance to conquer and they shall find prejudice and hatred. They must be dedicated, unwavering in their strength and strong of Heart. They will find willing Hearts and minds that will follow them on this road of returning 'Mother Earth' to beauty and plenty once more."*

The Cherokee, the Hopi, the Cree, and the Sioux, are among many indigenous tribes who have a similar prophecy about the Rainbow Warriors. We are out of balance and it is important for all cultures to step forward and bring their wisdom to the whole. The colors of the rainbow symbolize new hope to many, as well as the totality of the gifts available from Great Spirit. It is the bridge to consciousness and to the Heavens. The rainbow is the beautiful way that pure Light comes into our earthly dimension so that it can be accessed by the human energy field, bridging the physical with that of higher Light.

According to the Inca shaman, Don Eduardo Calderon, the shamans of the coming Age will arise from people who come from the race of the American Indian oppressors, as they become the needed teachers, guides, healers, and caretakers of the Earth. It is interesting how karma works. In my own small way, I have integrated a variety of teachings through the whirling dance of my own transformation, seeing the truth and the connection that there is in each path. The shaman has always been a bit of a Heyoka, a Coyote Spirit; and in my personal shamanic journey I have respectfully used a variety of sacred ways in the creative process of transformation for myself and others. We are only limited by our beliefs and judgments. Of course, there is always a need for discernment and respect of all teachings, learning them to the fullest. But there are universal truths that connect us in all paths. I do not take any path lightly and respect those who follow one path deeply; but Great Spirit and Mother Earth are the ones who speak the clearest to me and it is time to clear away the restrictions that do not allow growth and open the gates to another way.

Each Era or World has a guardian spiritual energy that personifies the energy of the time. The Tlish Diyan Elders from Mexico have been guardians of a Sacred Snake Clan Bundle that carries the energy of Clan Guardian Katoiya, who has been protector and guide of humanity for the outgoing Fourth World of separation. They have performed initiation rites to recognize and be in tune with the next guardian's essence. This spiritual being is called Nakia, the Rainbow Snake Guardian, and is here to assist in the purification and awakening. The door has been opened. Will you enter?

My intention with what I have shared is to reach you in your 'Heart of Hearts,' to become Spiritual Warriors of the Earth and humanity's evolution as a species. As difficult and overwhelming as it may seem, it is a glorious time to be present for the awakening. We are being given the chance to make a paradigm shift, unlike any other major shift, without the majority of humanity being destroyed.

The energies of grace that are available at this time, can assist us in working with the parts of us that have developed in separation, much more rapidly than before and will positively affect our lives once we make the passage. This does not mean that the road will not be difficult at times as the resistance to change comes up, but loving grace can come in to ease the way. This is the time where we truly can become more conscious co-creators of our reality with the use of our greater imagination and higher minds, without the baggage of the past's limitations. I believe that everyone who is alive during these great times has a great responsibility to awaken. Everyone! With this awakened consciousness we can also take action in the World that will bring in the New Cycle, in a walk of peace, unity and non-judgment, while encouraging the blossoming of the new 'Rainbow Flower,' whose fragrance and splendor will invite all to participate in a walk of beauty.

I have been aware of myself on a spiritual, mythic journey most of my life, and have been focused on personal transformation as well as providing guidance to many others on their road to healing. Because of the experiences I have had and what I have learned, I have gathered together a process, a ceremonial healing journey, a Beauty Way path, to assist in the awakening of those who want to blossom. This is what I offer as one of the many who have a deep feeling of responsibility to provide assistance during these powerful times. I encourage you to open to the mystery and magic that may occur for you in what emanates from the pages of this journey, even if we never meet.

The information in this book is meant to provide a background, a basic understanding of the deeper meaning of what I am putting forth; a way to prepare for the healing journey; but at the very least or the very most, it is meant to spark a journey of awakening, whatever the path you choose. What I have been shown is that as we do our healing work and uncover the beautiful flowering beings that we truly are, we can move ahead into the future with more ease and grace. If we do not align with the energy pouring onto the Earth from the Cosmic Center, our lives will become individually and collectively more painful, as all that is out of balance will have to come back to center. If we resist the changes needed in our beings and in humanity, the World around us will become the negative fulfillment of our greatest fears instead of our greatest hopes. It is time to dream a new dream into this reality.

When we have reunified our places of separation, we will be more able to handle the higher energies coming in and not have to suffer as much. It is not always necessary to experience internal and external earthquakes to shake up the stuck old paradigm that no longer serves humanity. We can learn to take responsibility for our innermost thoughts and feelings, so as not to project them out on others, thereby making the most needed change in the microcosm of our own psyches as well as in the collective unconsciousness. This is not impossible. Many are stepping forth and have made the choice to do whatever it takes to awaken from the deep slumber of this trance, a way of being that no longer serves to instruct us in the experiencing of the 'Underworlds.' There are passageways between the changing of the Worlds. We are entering one now. How will you go through? Will the door stay open long enough for you to pass through? Do not wait!

I feel like a cheerleader urging you on, for I feel the emergence, the pressure of the new flower breaking through the hard crust; just like the crow in the morning that wakes you up from a deep slumber, at first irritating, but eventually noted as a blessed messenger that stirs you to enter the mystery.

This process, this 'Journey to the Fifth World,' is meant to be a powerful, graceful movement into remembering who you really are in beauty and purity, in rhythm with the Light and Love pouring from the Center of the Universe, for the blessing of humanity and your children's children, for the Ancestors, for the animals, for the helping spirits and guides, for the Holy Ones, for the Earth and for the Creator of all life.

In humbleness I ask forgiveness for any misinformation I have given, especially in the sharing of indigenous teachings. I am human. I try my best. From the core of the Earth, through the depths of the spiritual beings we have always truly been, up to the stars, in gratitude for all that has been and all that will be. Namaste! Blessings on all!

2

Indigenous Prophecy and Wisdom for Our Times

T he future is calling me, pulling me ahead to some unknown destination. I want to listen more carefully to what the whisperings on the wind are saying, for I feel a strong presence reaching out to touch me, to teach me, to help me see beyond the ordinary steps I am used to taking on the path of my life. This time is different; there is a profound nature to what I sense that asks for greater understanding! Where will I find this wisdom?

There have always been individuals throughout history who have been able to receive divinely inspired messages and prophecies of the future, to apprise us of what will occur if we continue on certain paths of behaviors and related actions. I believe this divine guidance has been brought forth at times of major paradigm shifts throughout humanity's history, to inspire us to make more conscious choices, not to hold us to futures written in stone. At this time of 'Great Change,' it is of utmost importance that we obtain the information we need in order to take the big leap and advance into maturity as co-creators of our reality. Sometimes the messages can be experienced as very 'strong medicine' and may be hard to swallow. But ultimately they are precious gifts from the Creator. We are fortunate at this time to have profound knowledge and wisdom made available to us from higher sources, to help us better understand the bigger picture of where we are in the Great Cycle of evolution. Part of becoming more conscious humans is to be able to lift our heads out of the trance of daily living and to look around at what surrounds us; to feel, to experience, to grow, to think outside of the box and the ordinary boundaries of our lives.

I am not an expert on prophecy and indigenous wisdom, however I have gathered information throughout the years that I believe is pertinent in order to truly understand the nature of 'healing and transformation' that is being called for at this time. This is not about doom and gloom but rather about hope and the gift of grace and self-responsibility. Much of what I have gathered comes from cultures that I have had deep contact with, such as the Mayan, Native American, and Peruvian traditions. There are numerous prophecies that come from all nations and I am focusing on what I consider the most vital information concerning the call for the evolvement of humanity. I have been fortunate to have a personal connection with native shamans and medicine people from a variety of backgrounds from both North and South America, who have given me first hand information on knowledge that comes from their personal traditions.

In the previous chapter I highlighted prophecies that spoke of the Great Cycles that we are leaving and the Cycle that we are entering, as an overview of the energies we are working with. In this chapter I will focus on information pertaining to why I see the healing journey the way that I do. Much of what has inspired me to choose a particular way, a ceremonial path for working with individuals and groups in a deeper, more profound manner, comes from the power of what has been shared with me. For years I have been listening to great wisdom that has assisted me in making sense of the transformation I have experienced in myself and in others, in alignment to that which has been prophesied throughout the Ages. I hope to weave together the threads of what I have experienced; a synthesis of what is to be birthed.

The Maya speak of these times as being when hidden knowledge will be re-awakened in the human DNA as we move from the 'Age of Belief' (dogma and control outside of ourselves) to the 'Age of Knowledge.' Important information is being shared and revealed to those open to receive directly from the spiritual library of the Soul and the higher dimensions.

Many prophecies focus on the destruction of humanity and the Earth. What I have gathered has to do with might be useful to help us evolve and to make the needed changes in ourselves and our lives, so that we can make it through these challenging times and if possible, still live here on our beautiful Mother Earth. As we inform and align ourselves with what is occurring, we can co-create a very different reality from a place of greater consciousness. It is important not to be in denial about what may be difficult to hear, but it is as important not to go into a state of overwhelm. We need to expand our awareness and increase our spiritual connections and vital life force in order to take positive action towards what we want to create. It is important to breathe deeply and be with the information one moment at a time, while we keep an awareness of the bigger picture.

I previously spoke about how the Q'ero from Peru believe a doorway opened in 1987 that provided an opening where humanity could have a greater positive effect on the future. This was the time of the Harmonic Convergence where, since then, there has been a great increase in humanity's ability to look more deeply within and learn how to consciously delve into negative patterns and energies. The self-help consciousness of the seventies has advanced into more spiritual modes of healing and transformation.

Prophecies are sacred information meant to be helpful in assisting humanity to pay attention, and are subject during various paradigm shifts to the free will effects of the Creation to shift the foreseen outcomes. This is one of those major Cycles. Just as we have evolved rapidly with technology, which has affected our daily lives greatly, we can also rapidly evolve our consciousness. If our fate were written in stone, what would be the impetus for personal growth and spiritual evolvement? The process of 'becoming' is more important than the prophecies themselves. It is the journey to the awakening of our true beings that matters. I believe we are not meant to forever suffer as a way of life while on the Earth, nor sacrifice the Earth in waiting for the 'Great Rapture' that will take us to the Heavens.

I will not always be making reference to every source that my information has come from, to keep the flow of the messages. Some of the information will be given in a more detailed manner within the journey being offered in the workshops and individual teachings. I do give credit to one of my teachers, Ohky Simine Forest, who I refer to in the previous section, because she is the one who has shared with me the most concise synthesis of a variety of traditions that contain many useful messages, and I respect her greatly.

Take this information in and open yourself to that which evokes response. Pay attention to that which you already know. My words are shared in a simple way. I mean to engage you with all of your being, not just with the mind. Listen with your Heart and Soul.

At Sunrise on December 21st, 2012, for the first time in 26,000 years, the Sun will rise to conjunct the intersection of the Milky Way and the plane of the ecliptic, opening a channel for cosmic energy to fully activate on the Planet, cleansing it and all that dwell upon it, raising all to a higher vibration. This intersection will realign the cosmic Tree of Life that has differentiated the Worlds with the True Cross of the Four Directions. This will bring back into balance the energetic and archetypal Cross, so that we once again have equal access to the Upperworlds or Heavens, instead of the World being focused mostly on the Underworlds, as the Christian Cross has symbolized for this last Era. Access to the more spiritually infused Worlds will enable us to reunify and enlighten the Shadow realms. This is what has been shared by the Mayan Elders.

The Cosmic Cross that is created from the intersection of great forces in the Milky Way, is a balanced Cross (like the representation of the Four Directions in the Medicine Wheel) that is considered to be the sacred Tree of Life, which is where the blueprint, the Sacred Geometry of this Creation was birthed, according to many traditions. This Cross balances out the fields of reality, giving equal acknowledgement to Heaven and Earth. This conjunction is a reforming of the cosmic grid that has gone out of balance in the journey through the Underworlds. This Cosmic Grid is also a part of what keeps our World existing with the spiritual forces that emanate from this Celestial Center. Could it be time to realign the blueprint of our beings, to come back into more wholeness and well-being and a time of great rebirth?

All planetary bodies are electromagnetic and this Great Cycle of cosmic and stellar proportions is already changing the electromagnetic field of the Earth. Our solar system makes one revolution around the galaxy of the Milky Way approximately every 228 million Earth years, a Galactic Cycle. The completion of a pass of the precession through all twelve signs of the Zodiac (we are coming out of the Age of Pisces for example), represents one Grand Cycle of 26,000 years. We are journeying towards a precession where the poles and therefore the core of the Earth, will align with the Galactic Center of our Universe. We will get to experience an influx of spiritual energy similar to that which was present when the first wave of individuation began, when our Souls differentiated from the Godhead. It may feel like we are returning home to Source. This will give us a chance to experience the 'Oneness' that has been hidden deep inside in a new way, while we review what our Souls have learned in this last Great Cycle. Then we can spiral onward, infused with divine consciousness. We will be able to reconnect with our Higher Self and the core of our Soul, in order to assist in the great reunion with the part of ourselves that has never truly left the Spiritual Center of Creation.

The Light that is transforming humanity that has been coming through the Center of the Earth since the Harmonic Convergence, is a very different Light in that it does not have a Shadow, therefore activating us to heal our Shadows and unhealed places. This vibration is asking for us to resolve the forces of duality in which we have been living and creating. This Light without a Shadow that is coming through the core of the Mother Earth in varying degrees of intensity also brings in a high level Love that does not judge. This Love heals the Heart of the Child within, the Basic Self that has been wounded during this cycle of separation. This Light does not carry a Shadow because it carries the Love of the Divine Mother of Creation. It is as children that we may enter the Gates of Heaven. As we transform our core wounds we can more fully embody the ecstasy of the Divine Child. It is this Divine Child reborn that will greatly assist us in making it through the gateway into the Fifth World. This requires great trust and surrender. Until 2012, the main entranceway for this special Light will be through the core of the Earth; this supports the concept of our bodies and the Earth's body evolving together, as our bodies and psyches are striving to keep up with this Light of great evolvement. This Love and Light is breaking open the wounds and the beliefs that bind us to the old, painful way of existence. It will fully join with the Light coming from the heavenly portals in 2012, creating a unified field between Heaven and Earth, Spirit and Matter, Divine Masculine and Divine Feminine. Let go of trying to understand this Great Mystery solely from your head and listen with your Heart.

The scientific world has perceived invisible rays since the sixties, coming from the photon belt, the Medicine Field of the Pleiades, reaching our solar system in ever increasing frequency. When these photons or split electrons reach the Earth, all molecules become excited and all atoms of Matter and life forms undergo a transformation of great magnitude. These rays appear to be a form superior to normal Light, without heat or a Shadow, appearing like an invisible mist (Ether?). The null zone of this gateway or in-between Worlds passageway is such that the magnetic fields are so tightly strung together that it is impossible for any type of third dimension to pass through without being altered. The Light without a Shadow will illuminate all things from the inside out, casting out all Shadows, bringing in a higher degree of spiritual refinement and wellbeing.

According to the Maya there is a 'Fifth Element' that is becoming available as we enter into the next World, which is Ether; a celestial energy lacking in material substance but no less real than wood, stone, or flesh. It is able to permeate all space and transmit waves of energy in a wide range of frequencies. The dictionary defines Ether as 'a rarefied element that fills the upper regions of space,' or should we say, the Heavens. When higher energies filter into the hearts and minds of humanity, the impetus to spiritually evolve is stimulated and long held secrets become revealed! Further strands of DNA are activated, opening us up to much greater knowledge and consciousness. This spiritual substance permeates our cellular structure, down to the core of this Creation. Our positive intentions and feeling states and the calling in of the Light and Love, creates further activation. The forces that wish to keep a hierarchical system in place cannot hide from this celestial energy which needs to be revealed. It is the time of no secrets, from ourselves, about ourselves, and from those who wish to deceive and hide the truth. All is to be revealed. The Light will prevail and the amplification of the polar extremes will be experienced, and there will be nowhere to hide. The masses will have to wake-up from the deep slumber of false comfort and material indulgence, because the loss of freedom and the wrongs inflicted will be so obvious and jarring.

With the presence of Ether, Spirit in Matter, there can be a greater fusion and harmony between the polarities for those who have brought the Light into the darkest recesses of their beings. We are moving towards a time when the two most basic energies that make up the polarities, the feminine and masculine forces, are going to have an opportunity to work together in greater support and harmony. There will no longer be a hierarchy of one over the other in the larger arena of archetypal energies. I believe that before this graceful union can occur, it is necessary to be more in touch with the higher archetypes of these energies.

A few years ago I was speaking to a friend of mine from Mali, Africa, about the union of the polarities, and his response was, "Why?" He liked the polarity pull of the force of opposites between men and women! I shared my thoughts with him that it would be a long journey before we no longer felt the pull between the energies of masculine and feminine, and that we still had plenty of time to look forward to the joy of being together with more evolved versions of both. He also shared that in his native culture in Mali, it was said that traditionally the women were to teach the men how to evolve into true wisdom; however the men had stopped listening, which has created more imbalance. We will go into the dynamics of these most important polarities of Creation a bit later.

Because of the importance of bringing together the separated energies, there is also a request by the respected Mayan Elders, for the forces of Light to come into unity so that a unified field of energy can be created in which to birth the Fifth World. At this time it is important to not focus on ideological differences but for the spiritual paths to come together as well as people of good Heart and intent. There are many unifying events being broadcast on the internet at this time in which to take part that can also be organized locally. There is no reason to stay isolated and alone.

A Mayan Priest shared with me that as we evolve our consciousness we also make it possible for more advanced beings, the Holy Ones, to enter this realm to assist with humanity's evolution. In order for their presence to embody in this dimension, it is important to raise the vibration. It is possible that in the infinite wisdom of the Creator, it is time for us to truly take our next steps in embodying more Light and Love. It is very important that we keep being in self-accepting kindness and Love towards our transforming beings because we are being asked to grow quickly. At times I have felt the presence of the higher spiritual energies of grace come in like a cool watery substance that permeates my entire being, and I am most thankful for these moments.

According to Mayan researcher, Carl Johan Calleman, since 1999 we have entered a new paradigm of consciousness, as part of a Galactic Greater Cycle, which transmits a very high frequency of change. This energy is activating the more typically feminine right brain or hemisphere, which carries characteristics of intuition and spatial awareness, in-the-moment energies. It is now very important to balance the overuse of the masculine left brain, which activates our more linear and logical thinking energies and that we have been mainly functioning from for a very long 'Cycle in Time.' We are being asked to make the transformation into using the more feminine part of our brain in a short amount of time, as we speed up to come to the balance point needed for the shift into the Fifth World by the year 2012. Many will find that as their minds are overloaded with trying to function in a left brained World, as well as handling the intense energy of the shift, that they may be experiencing states of either intense emotional breakdown or heightened states of awareness (or a mix of the two). The right brain activation is a step towards greater connection and trust in the more spiritually connected realms. Putting major focus on enlightenment and evolvement, as well as meditation, ceremony, yoga, and breath work, to name a few, and not spending as much effort in the doing and more in the being state, can help make the transition easier, as well as being a necessary balance needed in our daily lives.

This 'Time of no Time' as spoken of by the Mayan Elders, is also giving us a chance to return to a more natural and Earth connected rhythm instead of the false technological one. Returning to and grounding in this, gives humanity a chance not to collapse with the immense change of energy and spiritual force that is coming onto our Planet. Waking up the 'rainbow brain' that is the union of the hemispheres, may be one way to deal with the evolutionary crisis of humanity's artificial timing mechanism, which is at odds with both the Earth and the universal time frequency. This unification will give us many more creative solutions to planetary concerns, and a much more joyous and fulfilling connection between the masculine and feminine. Connecting to the thirteen Moon Cycles of twenty-eight days is part of the return to the real rhythm of life, and can assist in creating balance in the midst of much disconnection and chaos.

With the coming together of the polarities, in the effect that the element Ether is having, it is also important for the 'Four Root Races' as well as the 'Four Elements' that make up the Creation forces, to come together in a new way. The Hopi believe that the Four Corners region of the Southwest is where the Sipapu or birthing place of the Fourth and present World is located, and that what happens there is a microcosm of what will occur in the rest of the World. They believe that the Creator sent the Four Races out to the Four Corners of the World from this place of emergence with responsibilities and spiritual guardianship. Each race was given the responsibility to care for and learn the medicine of what they were given.

To the Red People, Creator gave the spiritual guardianship of the element of the Earth, with instructions to learn from the Earth, the plants that grow, the herbs that heal, and the animals that are to be honored. They were to be the steadfast keepers of the secrets of the Earth, as well as the keepers of the ceremonies to ensure her continued fertility and to connect with her unseen helpers. To the Yellow Race was given the guardianship of the Wind. They were to learn from the sky and the breath how to keep in balance with this element for vitality and spiritual advancement, as well as inner discipline. This race became well versed with the flow of energy in the body. To the Black Race the Creator gave the guardianship of the Water, which is the most humble and powerful of the elements, linked to the emotional body and its movement. The gifts of resourcefulness and flexibility are to be learned through this precious element. To the White Race was given the guardianship of the Fire, Fire being the creative force that truly brings in the power of the Sun and sparks quick action in carrying out Great Spirit's instructions, when in balance with the other elements. Fire is at the core of most technology. All of these elements are the building blocks of humanity, as is the wisdom that is carried within the people.

Each race was also given teachings called the 'Original Teachings,' which were ways of living and ceremonies to be carried out. These 'Sacred Teachings' were given as a way to keep connected to the Creator's great wisdom, as a way not to fall into forgetfulness and disconnect while in the third dimension. Each of the Four Root Races that all colors, tribes, and traditions are birthed from, was given two stone tablets which contained the sacred instructions for the spiritual way to live through this time of the rule of the Underworlds. The people who were given the sacred tablets were: The Hopi, representing the Red Race; the Tibetans, the Yellow Race; the Kukuyu tribe of Africa, the Black; and the ancient tribes from Switzerland, the White. The Four Races were to come back together to share what they had learned near the end of this last Great Cycle, and to join together in bringing peace on Earth, birthing a great and more unified civilization. But many of the original daily practices, ceremonies, and teachings have been lost. Much of the importance of each element as a vibrant, life giving energy was forgotten. A few of the original Hopi Clans have continued doing the originally instructed ceremonies and holding to traditions as they were shown; to hold the cosmic doorways open until the 'Great Change Times.' Many indigenous tribes are also remembering the ancient ways that are needed to move forward into the New World at this time. Their commitment to their spiritual traditions, in spite of great oppression and encroachment of modern ways, has kept open a possibility for humanity's evolvement and a chance to choose the high road.

It is very interesting that the White Race in its guardianship of Fire, created the atomic bomb at Los Alamos Labs in the Four Corners region of the Southwest, affecting much more than the local environment. The powerful element of Fire was developed without the balance of the wisdom of the other races and elements. During my years in the Southwest, I witnessed a fire called the Dome Fire. This fire was a very strong showing of the Fire element gone wild, burning through much of the surrounding forest and parts of the town of Los Alamos. A Mayan

Priest has shared with me that it is important to heal the energies of the Earth that have been misused. In the past the local indigenous tribes had a sacred altar in the area of Los Alamos that was fed to balance the elements. That area is now part of Los Alamos Labs. I was told it is also important to heal the energy of the spine of the Earth that goes from the Four Corners region down to South America. The making of the Panama Canal split the energy of the Earth's meridian, allowing for the head (located in the Four Corners) of the Serpent Earth energy, to become imbalanced from the overuse of the gifts of the mind and the power of Fire. The head was missing the Heart of South America. What happens to the Earth energies also affects the human body and psyche.

It is now time for the children of the Four Directions to come together, as well as the four basic elements which are the base of the Four Directions, keeping balance with all life. It is time to remember how to be in sacred space, with daily rituals and prayers, to keep us in tune with the sacredness of all things. It is time for the blessings of the rainbow, where the sacred teachings of all colors and races are to be brought together as a whole, offering that which is needed to bring in the power of Unity and Love. As the 'Wisdom Carriers' of each tribe reunite with the sacred ancient teachings, they will bring forth the healing of their individual lineages, becoming re-empowered, willing to join and unify with other healed individuals and tribes. At the same time that ancient chasms, differences, and emotional charges between individuals, races, tribes, and nations, are coming to a place of extreme polaritization, the Wisdom Keepers, as well as individuals dedicated to healing, are paving the way for transformation to take place for all beings.

I was able to partially witness one of the 'Gatherings of the Elders' in New Mexico, where Indigenous Elders had gathered from North, Central, and South America to share their knowledge and wisdom. Their intention was to continue meeting each year in different locations. This gathering occurred because of 'The Legend of the Eagle and the Condor,' which comes from ancient times, from both the Andes and other parts of the Americas. This Legend speaks of a time when the Eagle of the North will fly with the Condor of the South. This prophecy is also connected to the Maya. In Mayapan, a sacred Ceremonial Center, there is a great figure that has a Condor in one hand and an Eagle in the other, with three double circles meeting with the navel at the center (the place of the Dream Center as we will see later). This time of coming together will activate the healing of the wounding and separation of the Wisdom Keepers of North and South America over the last five hundred years of oppression and takeover. The Red Nations will bring them together, issuing in a new spirit of unification, which will then reach out to erase oppression, exploitation, and injustice. This healing would open up the Wisdom Keepers in their

Hearts, so that they would be willing to share their teachings with the other colors of the rainbow.

The White Buffalo Calf Woman Legend of the native people of the Northern Plains speaks of a Sacred Maiden who brought the Holy Pipe and Seven Sacred Ceremonies, because the people were forgetting the sacred ways, especially in the honoring of the women and the feminine. The Sacred Pipe is the symbol of balanced shields, masculine and feminine, the Red Road and Blue Road, and of the reminder to give thanks for all things. When this deity departed, she said she would return when the people were in trouble and turmoil. As she turned to leave she turned into a black, then red, then yellow and finally white buffalo. In August of 1994, a white female buffalo calf was born in Wisconsin, who changed into four colors as her coat matured; from white to yellow, to red, to black, as well as other details that were in alignment with the prophecies. Since then a number of white buffalos have been born. This sign is to represent the coming together of the four races, as well as a return to peace and a time of honoring of Native American wisdom, as well as the return to the respect of the feminine in all things. It also is to mark the return of many Red Ancestors who would not necessarily come back to the 'Good Red Road' in red bodies, who will learn to walk the Earth Mother in balance again, as well as reform the ideas of the white chiefs. This would also be a great teaching, encouraging all to look deep into their Hearts and to move out of the battle of their Egos, being thankful for the return of true wisdom in as many beings as possible.

As was stated before, the Rainbow Serpent will be the sacred guardian of this new time. The serpent represents many things and has been greatly revered or feared throughout history. The snake has been seen as connected to the energies of the Underworlds, and it is time to evolve the Shadow energies contained there to the Upperworlds of the Heavens. This sacred energy may then assist us in freeing and transforming the emotional toxins of un-love and judgment, as well as unifying the polarities and the split between the different Worlds or realms. This will convert the energy held in the Underworld so that we can use it to transform, and also to bring forth the knowledge and wisdom gained from this journey in the Fourth World, into the next Era. It is time for the healing of the past, bringing all back into the light of healing and transformation.

The Hopi have a story describing the origin of the Snake Clan. I will share a shortened version. *The Hopi God of Death, the Earth, and the Underworld, Masau'u explains to the snake mother why her children can no longer have a house in which to live. The wife of the cultural hero Tiyo gave birth to a brood of venomous snakes that have bitten and killed many Hopi and will never again have a house, but should live under the rocks and holes in the ground. The same myth or legend concludes with the healing of these most primal of energies, with an offering to the snake beings and the establishment of the Snake Clan. The snakes were all collected, the first snake having its head washed, naming it Chua (one of the Earth), decorating it with beads and ear rings. The Hero Tiyo opened a bag and gave the people cotton and beads and said as the snakes brought rain, the people should on every celebration of the snake festival honor them with good blessings and gifts.* The Snake Society is a powerful clan well connected to the elemental forces. The snake energies are known to be able to communicate directly with the Creator. All beings are to be given a chance to heal. I will speak on the healing of the serpent energies, later in our journey. All beings in this dualistic World carry both Light and Dark, and are being given a chance to come back to wholeness.

We have been on a long journey through the Underworlds in this Great Cycle we are coming out of. The Light of the Creator that exists in each and every one of us has assisted humanity in keeping a sense of consciousness through the dark times of being half asleep in the Unconscious. According to the Maya, this time of learning through the Cycle of the Nine Underworlds (more later), has created a Shadow component of humanity that needs to be dealt with and transformed so that we can evolve to the Thirteen Upperworlds, which is the next paradigm we are moving into, and it is important to let in and embody much more Light. As we remember who we truly are, bringing all back into Love and acceptance, without judgment or fear, grace can manifest much more easily in our lives. The entire journey of healing is truly about reclaiming our sacred beings, so that our Shadows and places that have split off from the whole, can evolve and come back home.

In the creation of the Nine Underworlds, the law of karma came into existence. A respected teacher of mine speaks of the twenty-five year purification passageway spoken of by the Hopi, as being a chance to release our individual and collective karma from many lifetimes. This special passageway will assist humanity to realign our personal Tree of Life matrix back into a unified field.

What is karma? Webster's Dictionary states, *"in Hinduism and Buddhism, the whole ethical consequences of one's acts, considered as fixing one's lot in future existence."* Some believe that karma comes from the separation from spiritual source and the resulting energies and actions that come from creating and living out of sync with the 'Sacred Laws of Life' given to humanity at the beginning (spoken of by the Hopi). The laws of karma were developed possibly because our Higher Self was no longer the main director of our actions. As the Ego took over and the spiritual connection to our higher guidance was given over to other voices, humanity needed a system of checks and balances in order to keep some sense of connection to the original instructions and spiritual 'Laws of

Creation.' It seems we were being giving a chance to mature as co-creators of our reality and see more quickly the results of our creations. This Law may no longer be necessary when we are once again unified with our Higher Self, and the Shadow realms healed. How else could we truly understand that we were responsible for our thoughts and behaviors unless we experienced the consequences of our actions. The Buddhist religion explains this in detail.

I do not begin to imagine that humanity has a full understanding of what karma truly means. But, in my personal experience and that of many others with whom I speak, it appears that the negative patterns and lessons we have been dealing with most of our lives are increasing in their appearance and intensity as they are being presented to be looked at and transformed. This seems to be occurring not only in our actions but in our thoughts. If we find an avenue, a way to move forward with our personal work, then with the aid of the spiritual energies now present it may be possible to release the unresolved karmic energies of the past. I have felt this release myself while in a heightened state of awareness in the sacred circle of healing and ceremony. If we learn to live in a more non-judging and less reactionary way of living, working towards more neutrality and non-dualistic ways of being, maybe we can also stop creating more karma. When we heal the painful emotions, such as shame and guilt we carry from past negative behaviors, and truly forgive ourselves and others, the higher level energies will have room to enter. It is important to take responsibility for the resolution of our Egos' control that feeds the existence of the Shadow side of humanity, which blocks the voice of the Higher Self.

Is it possible that when we come fully into present time without the karmic, emotional residue of the Era we are coming out of, that we can be free to begin each day as 'a brand new day, never been used?' Yes! It is possible to be free to live in a way that brings more joy and peace and less suffering for all! The saying, 'A brand new day never been used' are the words of a Dine' (Navaho) medicine man at sunrise, after praying all night in a Native American Church Ceremony. I believe this was meant to let me know I could begin again, with the rising of the Sun, feeling all cleaned up, ready to start anew with the innocence of a child.

The Prophecy Rock in Hopi shows two roads, or two choices humanity and individuals have to make. One road is the way of the one-hearted people who follow their Hearts and Spirit; the second road is the way of separation and the misuse of Creator's elements and gifts, and the road of destructive power and technology. I believe these two roads show both the way of karma and the way of the absence of karma.

As we get closer to this great paradigm shift and grow further into our conscious responsibilities at being co-creators of our reality, we get to experience our thoughts and visions manifesting more rapidly, both individually and collectively. It is of utmost importance that we pay close attention to how we express our thoughts and emotions in the World. The results will show up right in front of us at this time, instead of being hidden in our unconscious. We can make a daily practice of consciously reframing and retraining ourselves to pay more attention more than ever. We can see this power constructively exhibited when groups of people across the Planet come together in prayer, ceremony, and positive intent, for the good of all. This is a great agent of change, and being together in consciousness raising circles can assist us to come back into balance in ourselves and each other, for the creation of a New World.

The healing of our sacred Waters, our emotional bodies, and the movement out of a fear based reality, can assist us in working together. Every moment, we are being asked to face our fears and other so called negative emotions as we move out of reacting to our past traumatic experiences. We can move ahead towards using discernment in each situation as we decide how we wish to respond, supporting personal and collective true empowerment instead of creating more fear based karma collecting dramas. Fear has had its purpose in keeping us safe and warning us of danger; this is akin to a child learning that the fire is hot and will burn. But now this emotion has become extreme and is keeping us separate from ourselves and each other and is food for the energies of separation, which do not remember that they truly live on Light and not fear. The Shadow beings created from and fed by the fear, have been away from the Central Sun of Love and Light of the Creator so long that they may go out of their way to obstruct the healing energy of grace. It is difficult for these energies to remember their ancient original connection to the Spiritual Center of all life.

As part of awakening to our self-responsibility, it is very important to live in deep respect of the Earth, our Mother, in all ways possible. This has been stressed as the most important part of the prophecies spoken of by all indigenous people, so I will not focus on specific prophecies. They all basically say the same thing. It is not something new or a complex prophecy to be understood, but I must mention it here again as I do throughout the journey, for it is of vital importance. The Earth is moving and shaking in ways and in places that may not be easy to understand. There is destruction and suffering created by her rebalancing that which is out of balance and which needs to evolve. There is release of the pain inflicted on her by the misuse and dishonoring of her great bounty and natural resources. There is the strong reaction to attempts to control her forces by scientific, disconnected systems of disrespect that treat her as if she were a lifeless entity! There is the awakening of her body to the Light and to the great shifting of energies that is occurring at an accelerated rate as we near the year 2012. We can only truly evolve as a larger collective of humanity as she evolves, for we are not separate from the Earth. This time of great transformation is not for the chosen few. All Souls present on Earth at this time are being given a great opportunity to participate.

When Mother Earth is spoken to and respected as a living being, she will take you into her changes as a participant and not as a victim. The technological Age we are in has created lifestyles that separate us from that which gives us life in physical form. This time of transformation can be experienced less painfully as we get a chance to move into a higher version of these bodies of touch and taste, which can occur when we go through the great journey of 'transformation and healing.' Whatever path you choose, come back home to connecting to the Earth's unseen helping forces, breathing her in, singing to her, dancing on her, giving thanks to her, and taking a stand for her.

I have been given the honor of participating in a Dine (Navajo) Ceremony where I was able to witness the ability of humans to work in harmony with the great forces of Mother Nature. A Dine Medicine Elder had a vision many years ago about a ceremony at Turquoise Mountain, their holy mountain, where the Rainbow People of the many colors and nations were to gather and pray together. The ceremony was fulfilled on May 8th, 2004, and was connected to Mother Earth rituals throughout the West at specific mountains and lakes. The main ceremony at Yellowstone had to do with the vision of a Shoshone Elder, for the quieting of the volcanic activity waking up under Yellowstone Park. 'The Reunion of Mother Earth with Her Children Blessing Ceremony,' as it was called, was also connected to ancient Earth wisdom knowledge about realigning the magnetic poles. It was a powerful ceremony where many joined in beauty and harmony, and the rains soon came back to the drought ridden Southwest. It is important to regain the knowledge of how to work with her sacred energies.

I believe true healing cannot take place in humanity's evolution without engaging in working with Mother Earth's energies. It is crucial. Those who do not care for her will not be able to gain entrance into the Fifth World or Sun (the Hopi use the word Sun). Her new energy body will no longer tolerate abuse. It is not about if she will survive; it is about our ability to evolve with her.

A Mayan Elder had revealed to me that it was very important that enough of Mother Earth be left unpolluted and undamaged so that we could take our bodies with us to the next World. I believe this meant that we are so inter-connected with her elements that we need enough of the original pure energies present in which to shift from and to. If we are to bring in the element Ether, it must have a place of beauty and purity from which to create more conscious realities.

Many are being motivated to move to different locations during this time of great shifting, possibly to rebalance consciousness and energies in themselves in different geographic locations. Or it might be that an individual or group brings certain vibrations that are needed in an area. This is also because we are being asked to break our patterning and habits from staying in one place, and to get less attached to material safety and trust more in the Divine. Many are journeying to sacred sites to wake up that which is connected to and in harmony with the higher consciousness coming through individually and globally. These are powerful times.

With the stirring to relocate, I have felt the urge to live in another culture, another country. But over and over again I hear the message from the Indigenous Elders that there is a reason we were born in this land, at this time. According to the prophecies of many Native American traditions, this country (the U.S.A.) is where the greatest tool for the misuse of power was created (atomic bomb), and where the responsibility of the right use of the Fire was given to the White Race. It is very important to bring the use of this element back into balance, as well as honoring the place where all races are to come together. I feel the need to not abandon this responsibility at this time.

There are teachings from the indigenous 'People of the Dawn' from the northeast coast, that speak of how the female deities that held the place of helping the people remember to care for the Earth and all of the community, departed when the Europeans came. Both women and children, who had always held a place of honor, were abused and mistreated, as well as was the Earth greatly dishonored. The patriarchal energies moved like a wave of destruction throughout the country. Interestingly enough, the Northeast is also the place where many women that came from Europe, who were in any way connected to the wise woman tradition, suffered annihilation during the witch hunts. It is also said that California, the golden land, is rumored to have been the last dwelling place of the Great Mother and Star Woman, the deity who fell from the stars. Maybe she has been in safe keeping until this time of awakening, in places like the Hawaiian Islands as well as many other volcanic places (Bali) of birthing and renewal, where the Fire in Earth's belly has been alive in the creating of new life for thousands of years. The Divine Feminine is now in a time of powerful rebirth.

With this return to the care of the Earth, how could it not be time for the reawakening and rebalancing of the feminine? This has been foretold in indigenous prophecies throughout the globe. (Remember, according to the Mongolian shamans we are moving into the Era of Women.) Most indigenous people (which all races once were), have always kept an awareness of the need to honor Mother Earth and the women of their tribes, as well as keeping alive the knowledge of ways to stay in balance with all of life. It is time to be able to respond to the pain of Mother Earth and humanity. Even though much was lost in the takeover of and destruction of the native cultures, the roots of the respect and sacred ways were not totally forgotten. Their wisdom is most needed at this time for the great awakening! The wise women grandmothers of the tribes are being asked to come forward and take their rightful place as Wisdom Keepers and Elders, for they understand the most sacred of teachings as they remember to care for our 'children's children' as well as 'all our relations.'

This reawakening and empowerment of the feminine is not about women ruling the World or about the control and subjugation of men. It is about the higher feminine aspects of this energy coming alive in the Hearts and Souls of all beings and on the Earth. We have learned much through these times of focus on the characteristics of the masculine and the dominance of the patriarchal energies of duality and separateness. In spite of the suffering experienced from learning through pain, there have been gifts in the experience. We have moved out of pure survival mode and have used the focused intellect to create many great things. But humanity has moved way out of balance, and it is most important to come out of the Fourth World paradigm where one individual or group keeps the abundance and power to themselves, and into a World where each being is respected and honored.

Because we contain both the energies of the masculine and the feminine, we all have our work to do, both men and women. The masculine part of us must go through an Ego transformation in order to be able to encourage the rise and balancing of the feminine, without fear, without control. The feminine aspect has to move out of its oppression and all emotions that have been suppressed. One is not to overpower the other. This is not about the return of the matriarchal times, but about evolvement into a higher state of the feminine. There was an imbalance of power in the matriarchal times, which we are to evolve out of and not re-create. This is about the unifying of the masculine and feminine, as the imbalances of the last four Eras come into harmony and union before the leap into the Fifth World. There have been more sightings of Mother Mary (who personifies the Divine Feminine for many) during the last millennium than in all of documented history as she announces the return of the Divine Feminine with grace.

We have recently gone through a Venus Transit (on June 8th, 2004), when the path of Venus directly crossed the disc of the Sun in an eclipse lasting seven hours. The energies of Venus and the Sun blended together, weaving Love and Unity for the empowerment of all beings. This transit occurs every 130 years, and every time this transit has taken place in human history, it has represented a new level of harmonization on the Planet. Interestingly enough, Venus transits always comes in pairs and the next one takes place on June 6th, 2012. The planet Venus is rich in archetypal symbology. It is often known as the Morningstar, the Bringer of Light; it is related to Love, true abundance, human unity, beauty, and 'Oneness.' Venus is very special in that it not only brings in the healing of the feminine energies, both human and divine, but also unifies the polarities, exemplified in how it transforms itself from morning to evening star. What better sacred Goddess than Venus, who is able to bring Divine Love to the earthly plane, to usher us through this doorway of transition and transformation.

In ancient Mexico the planet Venus is also associated with Quetzalcoatl (Aztec) or Kukulcan (Mayan). Quetzalcoatl, the Plumed Serpent, a deity of Light and duality, was known as the Creator of civilization. This deity was believed to be embodied in a number of incarnations and was also known to have been present as a most important priest who sought to halt the practice of human sacrifice. When Quetzalcoatl ascended, he went to the planet Venus and vowed to return someday. Some believe he was another incarnation of the Christ energy and that his return really has to do with the waking up of the energies of Love and forgiveness and the enlightenment of humanity. This most auspicious transit, which occurs in pairs, may not only be ushering in the healing of the feminine and the embodiment of the Divine Feminine, but also may thus assist in bringing forth the healing of the masculine and the embodiment of the Divine Masculine, as we move towards the second transit and the year 2012.

In this time of transition from one Age to another, from the accumulation of all I have gathered, I believe that it is the healing and return of the Divine Feminine and the empowerment of this force in all people and on Earth that will initiate healing in the World with Love, compassion, cooperation and harmony, bringing in the next World with grace and beauty.

I am not going to name the many indigenous prophecies that mention the return of this sacred energy. I am going to tell the next chapter, like a beautiful story of the blossoming of a flower, first germinating as a seed that has stayed dormant for many years and is now reaching for the Sun, awakening with the return of the sacred 'Waters of Grace;' for this is what the Queen of the Heavens asks of me.

3

The Return of the Divine Feminine Through the Gateway of Venus

I know myself by many names; I know myself because I have always been; I know myself by the deep feelings I have in the center of my being; I know myself by the colors of the rainbow that swirl through me; I know myself as the Queen of the Heavens because it has always been so. I have no beginning and I have no end. My womb is fertile with the stars of Creation, eternally birthed through the 'Waters of Grace' in the waterfall of my gateways.

Long ago in the very ancient time of humanity's presence on Earth, I was honored as the Creatress of Earth and was able to offer my gifts and teachings to the Hearts and Souls of humanity. But there came a time when my children were to learn what it was like to not feel held in the arms of my loving embrace; the Heart of the Heavens and the Heart of the Earth were no longer fully connected to the Heart of humanity. The Great Shadow fell over humanity as the World turned away from me. Like an earthly mother who awaits the return of her loved ones who have had to leave home to mature, I have awaited the return of my children.

Some have kept their vigil, kept their singing, their dance, their prayers, their rituals, in spite of the great pain and suffering of separation that has threatened to close the Hearts of even the strongest of my beloveds. Many have looked to the Blue Star for guidance, as in the days of Egypt during my reign in the form of the blessed Isis. The Blue Star of Sirius had been the gateway to me at that time because consciousness could travel quite far. It knew no limits. Some of you may have kept contact through the healing blue lights that come into your vision and create a doorway into my celestial home. I have been honored by many in their connections with the Moon and the many names of the Goddess that have spoken through her. Mama Ixchel is one such deity, a powerful aspect of my being, also known as Lady Rainbow, containing both Shadow and Light, with a serpent in her hand while she carries the Waters of the Heavens in her belly. Her name has changed through the Ages, becoming 'Our Lady Guadalupe' to some in this day and Age, to fit the spiritual path of the times. All these aspects and many more of the Divine Feminine, emanate from the Heart of the Mother, which is my true home. The personification of my being in the individual known as Mother Mary is well known throughout much of your World, even though I have embodied as many other holy beings on your beloved Planet.

Many have opened their Hearts to the beloved Mary's, to the Mari's, the Queens of the Sea, of the Waters, wherein the joining of the Heavens with the oceans, the seas, the emotions, provide a womb for your comfort and a place to restore hope. The stars that you see as a crown that surround the heads of both Mary and our Lady Guadalupe, bring the Worlds of the Heavens together in a great cosmic dance. You too can awaken this dance of cosmic consciousness into your being. These various manifestations of my being have moved closer to Earth reality, and many of you have evolved closer to the heavenly energies, so that we may now reconnect with each other as the veil between the Worlds grows thin once again.

During the rule of the Underworlds, at times it has been difficult for me to not intervene while watching the beings and energies caught in the Shadows, as they grow darker without my Love. But it is now time to be reborn in the World, for the Soul of humanity is longing for the return of my Love. You have now traveled far enough in the journey of learning in the Underworlds, with only a small awareness of my presence. It is now time to know my blessings, once again.

You will see my dark womb in the shadows of the Milky Way, my cosmic home in your Universe. This dark womb space has reflected out into your World and will be coming to resolution and integration when my presence comes into balance with the Light once again, as the great alignment in the Heavens occurs.

The Fire in my belly has never grown cold because I have kept the true Garden of Eden alive in the womb of the Earth, as she and I are one. The Light from the Center of Creation is now rejoining with my Love, to awaken humanity from the trance of separation. The Fires are stirring for a rebirthing from the deepest core of the Center of Creation, to the womb of Earth's belly, to the center of humanity. The highest form of the feminine energies must be received for this time of great awakening. The wombs of the women of the Earth are being made ready for the birthing of what lies deep inside Mother Earth's crystal core, the most precious gift of Love and Light. Some of you will be birthing what you call the indigo or crystal children, through this Light and Love, for they are deeply needed.

When you are in a female body, it may be easier to stay in touch with the higher instructions and energies of the deep feminine that instinctually and intuitively can provide a way to clear the Shadows created during the long Cycle of the Underworlds. As you are able to identify and embody whatever form of the Divine Feminine relates to your spiritual, religious, or conscious awareness, my grace can more easily enter in and soften the transformation that is being asked of you. This grace assists you to experience the higher feeling states, such as ecstatic bliss, love, and joy. This will transform your emotional body that has been burdened by much fear and suffering as a result of feeling separate from the Holy Center of the Universe. The Divine Feminine will bring in the grace, healing the great chasm of separation from so long ago, and will bring the awareness of my divine presence into the World of Matter and onto your Planet once again.

The Cosmic Waters contained in the Moon have assisted in sustaining the Cycles of Life on the Planet, where each month there is a greater chance to face and release the Shadows. It is important to be aware of the Earth Cycles of the Thirteen Moons and the gifts that they carry. This undertaking of embodying the Divine Feminine may bring up every hidden place of harshness and pain that still exists in you, for both men and women. But for women, having faced a small part of this darkness every month since ancient times, there is a chance to have a greater awareness and skill for this most important journey. The Moon Cycles have activated this clearing in both men and women, but while a being is in a male body it is not released as a biological and emotional, conscious process. The highest embodiment of the feminine energies is able to look at, feel, and integrate the Shadow with consciousness. This knowledge has also been kept hidden but alive in the myths of the journey of the descent of the feminine to the World of the Shadows. Many cultures have carried this descent and rebirth in stories shared throughout time; the descents of Innana, Persephone, and Ishtar, as well as many others. It is time to use what was learned by these Goddesses in their descent and resurrection. The women of Earth and the energies of the Divine Feminine are to show the way to transform the energies gathered in the time of the rule of the Lords of the Underworld. This receiving of the energy of this unified Light and Love is very important in order to put the World back in balance. The Soul of humanity has developed in the dark places and now must be grounded and re-rooted in the body and through the Earth, preparing for new birth.

As you accept the reality of having been both male and female throughout your many incarnations and having played out as both victim and victimizer, this will assist in bringing in compassion for all earthly beings for that which is not easy to see or transform. As you take this in, allow yourself the movement of that which has been held in judgment, making way for the birth of both the Divine Feminine and Divine Masculine onto the Planet.

My beloved humans who are born in a male body, this time may be particularly difficult for you if you resist finding your own feminine side (especially your feelings), as well as finding the balance of equal power in your relationships with woman. But of course you too will be assisted by my grace. Of course you are also being activated by the Light and Love coming through from the Center of the Mother Earth and the Milky Way. This activation is coming through you in a different way because you do not have a womb. Your Hearts and emotional bodies will be your main doorway, which will also be healing in women. This does not mean that men will not be the wayshowers for many women who have lost their way, or mirror their unhealed projections. We remind you in great compassion and Love, that the focus has to do with the energies of the Divine Feminine returning after a long absence, ushering in a time of great energetic personal and social change and transition.

I feel great sadness for the extremes of what is occurring in the Middle East, the power vortex where the Christ energies entered onto the Planet so long ago, and the birthing place of the imbalanced masculine powers in the time of learning through the Underworlds. As you awaken and bring down the Moon, the Divine Feminine into your individual beings and onto the Earth, send this loving presence to distant lands throughout the Planet that are greatly out of balance with the masculine and feminine. As you call in these energies, you can assist in profound ways in the healing of ancient and present time distortions in the aspects of victim and victimizer.

Many of you who have been born into a male body may also feel the effects of the Moon and her cycles because you have kept contact with your feminine side. I encourage you to surrender to this uncomfortable time of transition, for of course you too will experience the quickening, and are needed to support the flowering of the Divine Feminine in her many aspects, within and without. As this holy power is birthed back onto the Earth and comes back into balance in you, the Divine Masculine will be able to be truly embodied on the Earth. When the Christ came to Earth, this divine consciousness could not be fully embodied because the Divine Feminine was already on its way into other realms. This imbalance created a patriarchal religion sorely out of touch with the feminine. This is now changing in profound ways, as much previously suppressed information is coming to light.

At this time on your beautiful Planet, the fruition of this transformation is not only raising consciousness and assisting in the survival of the human species on Earth, but is offering a chance to enjoy a much more divinely inspired and expressed union with your beloveds in partnership, as you both evolve to your higher expression of relating. As you open your Hearts and let this most precious part of you bring in your Higher Self to guide, instead of the Ego, the elixir of Love of all you are in the highest form of joy, can be experienced here on Earth. There is nothing to fear, no reason to hide. The false illusion of power of the Ego is not going to be allowed to run the show any longer. It is time to come back into balance with the wholeness of your being.

Yes! Most women have also forgotten to intuit and feel from their Womb Centers, and have also let their Egos rule. They too have been wounded through this time of separation and their Sacred Waters muddied. But the Sacred Waters of Creation and of humanity are being cleansed here on Earth. All the elements of the Earth are sacred, but Water is the most responsive to the vibrations of Spirit as they enter the Earth plane, and to the thoughts and feelings of humanity. It is the right moment for the gift of the Waters of emotions to be raised up to a higher vibration. The wall of pain surrounding your Heart in fear of feeling all that has been experienced in the realm of the Shadows, can now be released. The caverns and places in your Heart of Hearts that have shut down in the pain of experiencing the Creations around and within you, that do not feel surrounded and filled by Love and Light, can now be reopened and healed. The overwhelming feeling that life has been one mis-creation after another and you are responsible can be allowed to transform and heal. The Hearts of all beings are calling the Healing Waters to return, ushering in great Love, beauty, and compassion as you reconnect to the Heart of the Heavens and to the Heart of the Earth.

The outpouring of the Waters on your Planet is to heal, cleanse, and regenerate, even though it may look like destruction. The great wobbles and waves of the Earth Mother are creating rolling emotions that will bring a quickening, an awakening of great compassion for all of her children. It is a wake-up call, as well as a vehicle for more grace to enter your beloved Planet. This is a Water Planet where you learn about the waters of your being, your emotional self; this cannot be changed by the misuse of imbalanced masculine forces, who seek to dry up her Waters because they fear their own emotions. Let the Sacred Waters of Mother Earth take you from one World to another, as she has always done. I am offering you this in the safety of my loving embrace as her Waters join with the 'Waters of Grace' from the heavenly realms.

This outpouring of the Sacred Waters from the Heavens is to bring the offering of grace to all who are ready to receive. Both a female and a male celestial being are holding the container for the outpouring of the cleansing and renewing 'Waters of Grace' onto the Earth. This is helping with the process of realigning your bodies to be vessels for this higher level vibration. It is another false teaching that a masculine archetype is solely the Water Bearer from the Constellation of Aquarius. The womb of the feminine carries the Waters and the male provides the structure. The return of my Son to the Earth after his reunion with his Father in Heaven, was assisted by the three Mary's at the foot of the cross, who created a sacred trinity, a most holy womb space in which to return, keeping Christ's Soul present here on Earth until he entered back in through the sacred cave of the womb of the Earth. The sacred relationship of the Divine Masculine and Divine Feminine was absolutely necessary for such a miracle. This is akin to the space in the Queen's Chamber in Egypt, which provided a sacred vessel in which initiates were to return after journeying to the Heart of Creation in the King's Chamber. It is difficult to speak the limited language of humanity, for the Center of Creation encompasses all beyond the limited concepts of masculine and feminine. It is important that the Souls who are in a male body do not take offense. You are all needed and contain the sacred seed of life, and women are not holier than you. But once again, it is a time of rebalancing that which has been oppressed so that the two energies can exist in harmony, trust, and union, once again.

At this time, it is of utmost importance that one is able to learn how to be in a sacred state of awareness, to treat your body as a sacred vessel, healing and transforming it with ceremony, prayers, and spiritual intent on a daily basis. The Earth has taken her protective energy away from humanity so that you both may evolve. You may be experiencing much more sensitivity to the people around you and to those who are even far away, as well as to illness and the collective ill-ease. This may be challenging at times until your clear away the resistance to losing some of your personal identity, as you remember your inter-connectedness through the web of life that joins all life. The conscious and unconscious judgments you hold of self and others may call in negative experiences until you clear further. In the meantime work with protection and attunement to your higher centers.

Mother Earth's trees have been one of the ways that Heaven and Earth come together, representing the Tree of Life and the trees assist in holding the sacred grid of the Planet intact. Since Gilgamesh destroyed the protective elemental forces of the trees long ago, the grid has weakened, and has allowed the mass destruction of these sacred beings. Many myths written in the Sumerian language have been passed down for centuries about Gilgamesh, the semi-God King of Uruk in Babylonia, where Iraq is now located. His jealousy and rage made him act without thinking, for he coveted the uncontrollable Goddess Innana, who was intricately connected to the elemental forces. It is very interesting that there is a power struggle going on in Iraq to this day, where the feminine and the land are not being honored.

It is now very important to be aware of that which makes up your individual being with its various energy bodies, and to realize that it is all humanity's responsibility to tend this form, to assist in restoring the sacred Tree of Life individually and collectively. It is no longer solely the Earth's responsibility to do so. It is time for you to understand how to be responsible for the energy fields of your own holy vehicles of ascension. As you unify your being and come back into wholeness, you raise the energy field of the Planet and assist in our ascension to the Fifth World. These divine chalices can then be the vehicles by which you are also able to come back into Sacred Circle with others and not be negatively affected by those who consciously or unconsciously, do not know how to contain their own fields.

Some of you may be caught in the overriding beliefs of religion that keep you holding on fast to the teachings that have come mostly from the perspective of the masculine. Even chapter twelve of the Book of Revelation of the Bible (the same book that blames Eve and the feminine for the cause of evil in the World), speaks of the exile of a woman clothed with the cape of the Sun, her feet on the Moon and twelve stars surrounding her head. Why was she exiled, this deity who sounds like the Divine Feminine? Listen closely to the truth hidden in all paths.

In the Heavens, in the heavenly bodies above, there is an opening through the gateway of Venus, to let in the Divine Feminine and the healing power of the Love force, to your Planet. This rainbow path of Light has appeared to bridge the Worlds in a walk of beauty. All that I have shared with you is brought to fruition in your World through this gateway that lies so visibly close to your Planet. This heavenly but earthly representative of a most relational aspect of my being has never truly left your side but has watched over you and kept present throughout this time of the Underworlds, waiting for the right time to be part of your evolvement. There is no mistake in her assisting in bringing in the New Dawn, as there is no mistake in the naming of the newest planet in your solar system, Sedna. The Alaskan native myth about the mortal woman turned Goddess, Sedna is a reminder of the nourishing gifts that are to be found in the dark, deep, cold places that we most fear; and of the healing of the concepts and emotions of victim and victimizer that the feminine and masculine energies have separated into during much of the last Great Cycle. The deeply held wounding and pattern of abandonment and betrayal between these most sacred powers, is being given assistance from the celestial realms to heal and evolve, both in the realm of Gods and Goddesses, and between men and women.

The Goddess-like force of Venus has evolved from the limitations of what you perceive her to be. In her first birth onto your Planet, she arose naked from the Sea, the source of all life, and was a symbol of both the collective unconscious in its concepts of the unattainable feminine and eternity. Venus is the gateway through which the Divine Feminine is to re-enter your Planet. This most sacred energy needs to filter into physicality through this heavenly but very earthy being. She comes at both dawn and at dusk and is the embodiment of both physical and spiritual Love, enlightening the parts of humanity that no longer believe in high level relationships and in the Beauty Way of living. Even though a multitude of Divine Goddess beings will be coming into your solar system to provide guidance, they must enter through the doorway of Venus in order to be more available in the earthly realm.

Lover of the Beauty Way, bringer of abundance and creativity, balance in relationships, joy in the body; she awakens in us that which truly heals with grace. Venus has become once again a Rainbow Goddess, with a robe of many colors, and asks humanity to take all relationships to a higher level. She has evolved past the limited concepts of what you have believed her to be. You are invited to embrace and transform the discordant nature of the old patterns as they surface within yourselves and others, while learning to live together in ways that exalt the Divine in each other. She dances with the Light of the Sun shining its glory through her, in a prism of multi-colors so that humanity has the highest palette of Creation energies made available to choose from, for this time of great transformation. Venus assists in ushering humanity through this great passageway of new creative, spiritual energies, and she asks you to break old religious dogmas and other temporal delusions that have upheld your divisions.

During the Great Cycle that you are in, the Rainbow Goddess energies wish to embody through the evolved Venusian vibrations, to enlighten the people of Earth to the new spiritual choices that are now available and that are guided by Love, Wisdom, and Power, the three flamed chambers of the evolved Heart. She wishes to help you ground the multitude of high energies and choices through the Love-force of Venus, so that what is created through this every-widening doorway to the Heavens is created in balance and right relationship to all life. The Rainbow Goddess is the unification of the many forms of the Goddess that have been known on your beautiful planet, through the myths and stories of many cultures. They have unified in a rainbow field of Love and Light. As this energy pulses through the women and men of Earth, the two can harmonize together once again. The male higher energies that have held a role as exalted servers in the time of the Knights Templar, are to provide a balance to the energies of the Divine Feminine, as they raise their energies to become Spiritual Warriors of empowerment, with the Love and the Light. They gather their strength and power from the inner Fire of the Planet, a newly enlightened Sun, stimulating the right use of power in the very center of their beings. This second Sun of power will evolve the solar plexus area, where you carry this most sacred energy. The rule of Kings and power over others will be no more.

The return of the Rainbow Warriors will be a sign that the Rainbow Goddess is alive in the Hearts and Souls of humanity and that equality among all races and people will awaken. These Spiritual Warriors will know that the return of the sacredness of all life is the most important focus of their will force. This Goddess comes from the unification of the wisdom and teachings of all Four Directions and is activated by Ether, by grace, and by Spirit, and is the embodiment of the evolved Venus. She asks humanity to remember what has been learned through this last Great Cycle and to use your creative abilities to be born anew. The Great Circle and the Cycles of Life will be renewed and the Sacred Hoop will come together to provide healing and guidance once again.

You will see her in the rainbows, in the circles around the Sun, in the clear crystals that have been waiting to reflect your divinity, in the dream time, in the Waters on the Great Belly of the Mother, but most of all in your Hearts. Your relationship to yourself, your beloveds, to all beings, and all life, will be renewed and healed as she brings in a graceful reminder of that which is most blessed. You will feel her in your expanding Heart as you are able to have more compassion and Love for yourself and others while experiencing nurturance, cooperation, abundance, harmony, creativity in all things, with renewed visions; beauty above, beauty below, beauty all around, beauty inside. The Rainbow Trail will be available through this passageway unlike other times Venus has opened her gates, because of all else that is in place at this 'Great Change Time.' It will be a path that will be available to all. The rainbow will escort in the realm of pure Light, joining with the Light and Love coming from the core of the Earth, assisting humanity to adapt to these high level vibrations. Blessings all my children! In humbleness and compassion for all that you have experienced that has brought you to this great moment. I have never truly left. I have always been and always will be. Remember me; for I remember you and always will, as I hold you in my loving embrace.

'The Journey of Healing' Coming Full Circle in Healing and Transformation

The Pathway

*T*he journey of healing is a pathway to a state of awakening into the Fifth World or Sun. This journey is one of many paths and I invite you to have an open mind and Heart and let the magic of Spirit bring in the healing and transformation for which your Soul is calling. I express myself as simply as possible, because I would like to have you listen with your Heart as well as your mind. I have greatly enjoyed reading page after page of cosmic, intricate details by people with amazing, expansive minds, where my brain is whirring at high speed, trying to keep up. This is not that, even though at times I may share very deep cosmic knowledge that has come my way. Some sections are more of the mind and will get you thinking, other chapters will invoke more of a feeling sense of experiencing in the moment. Take a journey into your Soul being, going with the different rhythms, as you remember what already exists deep inside.

I call the first part the 'Door of Earth' because of the importance of first grounding in the place we call home, where we have been living in the third dimension, and from where we can make real movement and change. If we do not ground and heal from the experiences we have gathered from this most powerful journey through the Underworlds, we can get lost in the higher dimensions and 'fall' to Earth once again. Before we can move into the next World, we must come 'full circle' in resolution of what we have learned in the Fourth World so we do not trip and fall as we evolve to new heights. The second section is called the 'Door of Heaven,' through which we gain entrance into the Fifth World.

This pathway is not so much about looking for what is wrong and needs to be fixed; it is about uncovering and reclaiming your true essence self. It is an unraveling and reweaving of the fiber, the threads of Spider Woman's Web of Creation, renewing and reclaiming our personal energy from the lessons, teachings, and wisdom gained from our journey in this Fourth World. The true self is waiting to shine its Light for all to see. It is pushing through the darkest hour, like a young shoot pushing through the hard soil, wanting to be acknowledged and to bring all back into the embrace of our true nature.

My wish is that you can use this journey for something good for yourself. My highest intent is that it wakes up a longing in the recesses of your deepest Soul, to call to yourself that which is for your greatest good, so that you may participate consciously in the Great Awakening. There is so much to choose from, be it a workshop with 300 lightworkers, to an indigenous traditional ceremony, to being part of an ongoing Sacred Circle, to seeing someone for individual healing work, or to going within in a deep connection between you and Great Spirit, and so much more. As we gather and create a higher vibration, we are inviting the spiritual energies of the Fifth World into this reality.

In the past Great Cycle that we are coming out of, only a small part of the population went through the initiations that would elevate them to the next level of consciousness. Initiation is meant to awaken and develop our highest potentials as spiritual beings, as well as bring us to greater connection with the cosmic archetypes and patterns from which our World has been created. This journey is an initiation, a process of coming to terms with the forces of the Soul and the inner workings of Creation. It appears that we are at a time in our evolution where the presence of the doorway of Venus as well as that energy which is emanating from the Galactic Center of the Milky Way, give us a chance to go through a very different passage than in the ancient times of Egypt. In the past, most initiates would be unmarried and would be connected more to the state of Divine Love than to that of the love experienced in marriage. In the experiencing of many lifetimes (where we have had the opportunity to learn more about personal, earthly love), it is a very different type of spiritual initiation that is being called for at this time. Venus, as mentioned before, has to do with the tangible embodiment of Love, as well as much more. Learning how to see and feel the beloved in all beings may be as great a challenge as truly loving ourselves in the many aspects of who we are. It is time to bring Divine Love home to Earthly Love.

In the last forty years, since the consciousness raising and paradigm busting times of the sixties, it has become a way of life for many to work on the evolvement of their individual psyches. In traditional indigenous societies, there were always ways to keep the Soul and the psyche of an individual. and therefore the community, in a healthy state. One of the most important roles of the shamans and their spirit guides was to assist with this when needed. As we come 'full circle,' we need to remember what we have forgotten to give importance to. It is a time when it is necessary for as many as possible to go through a powerful journey of spiritual initiation to be readied for passage through the doorway..

Many times, especially in the past few years, I have wanted to leave it all behind because of the severe misuse of the gifts that were given to the White Race (as mentioned in the chapter on prophecy). The gift of the element Fire and technology has been severely abused in not keeping with the original teachings and true guidance from the spiritual realms, resulting in a great misuse of power (financial, war maker machines, political, etc.). This is not to say that many other nations are not in the same category, but we are a leading force for both the negative and positive influences. I always remember the words of a Mayan Elder who spoke to my Heart, who told me years ago that difficult times were ahead and that the people of consciousness in North America would be needed to turn the tide from the direction of destruction. He spoke of how in the country that was causing the most destruction, there would also be a chance for the biggest turn around, with much spiritual energy made available for the greatest evolution. It is time we turn the tide.

Know that your life is a mythic journey of your Spirit, embodied in your Soul. Open to the wonder of the magical path that lies before you. Everywhere you turn there are guideposts and signs that will lead you on, confirming that you are not alone. When you open to the presence of the Divine in all life, the potential to create a World more in tune with our highest hopes and dreams is truly possible. Open to the immense creativity and knowledge that is available to you. Let your imagination and life be guided by Spirit.

So open your Heart and your mind and do what you can to become a 'Flowering Soul' of beauty, wholeness, and Love. Life is a journey, not a destination; enjoy the ride while you move along the path laid out before you in a powerful manner. Do not waste this one precious life. Remember why you are here and wake up to the spiral movement of the great dance of conscious evolvement.

II

The Door of Earth

4

Ritual and Ceremony
for Healing and Transformation

C eremony and ritual are for the purpose of restoring the balance essential for life, for individuals and communities; they are as important as the body's need for nourishment, for our Souls and Spirits crave ceremony to help us stay whole by keeping the awareness of the presence of Great Spirit in our lives. Ceremony is a way not to repeat history and to clean up unfinished business from the past, as well as keeping us in interaction with the spirit in all things and all beings. Ritual is the safe container or energetic temple that allows you to open to the deepest parts of your being, that enables your spirit to fly free. Being held within this sacred space, you are given a chance to transform at core and cellular levels, as you are moved to express all parts of yourself in union with others who are returning to the Sacred Hoop in wholeness once again.

We all have been part of a church, wedding, or graduation ceremony, as well as many of us having participated in a ritual to welcome in the changing seasons. Many of the ceremonies and rituals of the Western World have lost their true meaning and no longer carry the fullness of transformation they were originally meant to invoke. But the psyche remembers the richness of what they were meant to carry and our Soul longs for this.

The words ritual and ceremony evoke different emotions and meanings, depending on who you are and what has formed you culturally and spiritually. In Webster's Dictionary ritual is, *"The form of conducting worship; religious ceremonial."* Ceremony is defined as, *"A formal act, or series of acts, often symbolical, prescribed by law, custom or authority in matters of religion, of state, etc., be it of religious connection or not."* What do these words symbolize or bring up for you?

For the native people of Turtle Island (North America), the word ceremony is often used to refer to a spiritual custom of worship. Native people say that when they are living in a 'good traditional way,' they will be spending a large portion of their lives in preparing for, participating in, and integrating spiritual ceremonies. Many native cultures in the past never saw themselves as being separate from any part of Creation, and many in the present have also kept this awareness throughout their many rituals and ceremonies. It is now more important than ever to come together to unify and connect with each other in meaningful ceremony.

I will be mostly using the word ceremony (even though I often will also use the term ritual). Ritual is a type of ceremony, with certain parts planned that can be repeated again and again. Ceremony is often known as the spiritually alive aspect that is very important to work with to allow for spontaneous movement and healing. We are forming the sacred container in which a journey of healing can take place.

Ceremony is that which speaks from the depths of the Earth and is offered to humanity as a sacred way to communicate with each other and with the spiritual energies that are within and around us. It is a gateway that can be opened to the highest part of our beings, as well as providing a doorway between Heaven and Earth. It is that which keeps us in deep relationship, with respect to the place, the piece of Mother Earth we walk upon, as well as with the people we touch. It has been one of the most powerful ways there are to bring healing and transformation for both the individual and the community.

Without the presence and enactment of meaningful ritual, the Soul of the World becomes dried up and looks elsewhere in other realms to be acknowledged and fed; the Soul of humanity becomes empty and lonely, wishing to return home. The Mayan spiritual tradition has a ritual of feeding 'Spirit Houses' that keep the 'Holy Ones' paying attention to the humans and the earthly realms. Offerings and prayers are given, and there are actual small or large structures built to house the spirits. Without ceremony, we lose contact with the symbols and metaphors that give meaning and deeper understanding to our lives. Without ritual, we can lose contact with each other and miss out on the power of the circle to transform at deep levels. Without ritual and ceremony, as well as healing journeys, the negative energies that arise in the World have no way to transform and to come back into wholeness.

I am a ceremonialist by nature. I breathe it, I dream it; I follow the rhythms of Nature inside me and all around me as I listen to that which needs to come back into balance. I have seen ritual awaken many from the deep sleep of forgetting who they truly are. I have turned to the wisdom of many traditions that have taught me how to be in and create meaningful ritual in all that I do. I have deeply experienced the transformational and healing movement of many ceremonies and truly know their power.

In the dominant culture of North America, many have grown uncomfortable with the experience of ritual and ceremony. Some may even have grown awkward, embarrassed, or vulnerable in regard to ceremony. Use this vulnerability to open the place deep inside that remembers other times, other places, when your Soul was able to feel the joy of being connected to the rhythm of life. Remember the ancient times, of honoring the Moon and its great role of being the keeper of the tides of the Waters inside and out, as well as being the mirror of our Shadows. You can look to the ancient roots of Earth-centered ritual as a ground work for the support of appropriate ceremonies for our times. The awesome potential of its healing power can be experienced when there is enough willingness to suspend the logical mind and open to the blessings. Reverence, trust, and surrender to the protective energy of the created sacred space, as well as a willingness to embrace all possibilities for healing, with clear intent, are necessary for a meaningful ceremony. One can start by simply lighting a white candle at sunset, to bring the Light into the Dark, while praying for peace for the World; this has actually been suggested by the Mayan Elders.

Participating in a ceremony, one can enter into a state of altered reality where grace is tangible and available as delicious water; where magic becomes visible, the experience of healing is deepened, and where there is an integration of mind, body, and spirit with all living things; messages and perceptional changes are given that positively affect the direction of one's life; one is moved from the ordinary to the sacred, as well as helped to become aware of the inter-relationships between the Creator, Mother Earth, animals, plant life, minerals, community, global community, Ancestors, spiritual helpers, teachers, guides, and the cosmos. Being in ceremony helps one ground in the moment, being so joyfully connected in present time and space that there is a feeling of nowhere else to go, nowhere else to be, but here and now. The Ego has difficulty ruling when one is in true ceremonial space. With clear and strong intent, in humbleness and respect, a ceremony that is performed, increasing in power when two or more are gathered, can bring in enough energy to move that which is ready to change for the highest good. The energy is increased and strengthened in the making of a 'Sacred Healing Circle.' In ritual, we listen and speak to each other and to our deeper psyches.

The components of a ceremony are particular to one's cultural background and history, as well as one's spiritual belief, created from the nature of clear purpose and intent. The clearer one is, the easier it is for the spirit helpers unseen and seen to know how to assist. In simplistic, very basic fashion, there are four integral parts that should be included for the success of a ritual: Preparing a sacred space; invocation and intent; the core where the healing is to take place; and the closure. We will go further into this as we continue on the journey of healing.

During this time of amazing shifting of energies and the need to come 'full circle' with the lessons of what has been experienced from coming through the Nine Underworlds, the Shadow times, it appears that humanity is having to find solutions from a much more enlightened part of our consciousness. The places in us that carry the Shadow, the unloved, the unwanted voices, the places where we feel separation from ourselves and others, need to come back into balance, union, harmony, and Love. As these parts return to the whole, our spiritual self will be able to be expressed and integrated, raising it up to the next level. Ceremony can help integrate the dialogue with the Unconscious, as well as assisting us to transcend the Ego, keeping it from limiting the healing process. It can also help resolve the dualistic splits that are being polarized so strongly at this time, such as between left and right brain, right and wrong, self and other, human and Nature, sacred and profane, head and Heart. It can help with the sense of being out of control, in a world gone mad, and help make not only change within, but all around.

We are literally running out of time to move slowly through the journey of the recapitulation of our past to realign with the intense energies we are being called to match in the present. Within ceremonial space, one can heal at core and cellular levels, in a manner that is beyond the limits of time and space. In the sanctuary of ritual, the Waters of one's being can be supported to rise and clear in a holy, sacred manner. In a sacred space, spirit helpers and guides can be quite profoundly accessed to provide assistance in our healing and integration. They are drawn into the Beauty Way of ceremony and humans' sincere requests for aid. While being in a state of grace, one can heal at times immediately, as energies come back into balance.

The image keeps appearing before me, of a Medicine Wheel in which those parts that have been in the Shadows arise and are purified and returned to the Circle of Life; that as they align into the Sacred Hoop of wholeness, the Wheel turns and is raised into another dimension or consciousness. The many Sacred Circles around the Planet then join, recreating the 'Flower of Life' from which new life will grow.

The shamanic way of healing can be very useful for the ceremonial journey of healing that is being called for at this time. There are many traditions and ways to be in ceremony, and I support you in following a tradition or path that calls to you. I chose the path of the evolving shaman of our times. This path is not as defined by cultural context as in the past, and we now have more freedom to work with the particular aspects and characteristics of what is occurring and needed in the moment. The shamans are often the Heyokas (contraries or sacred clowns), that enlist the unseen spiritual forces for healing and guidance, and use whatever is needed to ensure a healing takes place. The word shaman comes from the Mongolian spiritual tradition of Siberia, and for every ancient culture there is a distinct word for shaman. One simple definition of shaman is a person who can enter altered states of consciousness at will, with the assistance of spirit helpers, to travel between the Worlds in order to find healing, knowledge, guidance and help for themselves and others. Ritual and ceremony are an integral part of the daily life of the shamans of the past and present. It is possible that the shamans became necessary when the Worlds separated and Heaven and Earth began to be experienced as if they were in different dimensions.

The interest in shamanic ways for many westerners at this time can be of great benefit by opening a path that can provide system busting for the change needed for humanity's evolution. There are once again many paths, but I have chosen the shamanic path or should I say it has chosen me. It is evolving in me and in the World to fit the change of these times. But I truly work with it as a way of using the healing power of all things that are needed for the benefit of transformation. It is a way that works comfortably with the use of ceremony within community support, to build power and create new pathways. To be part of a shamanic healing ritual, one does not have to be a shamanic practitioner, but it is helpful to have a connection with and comfort in working with altered states of reality, as well as having a spiritual path. There are many paths to take to awakening at this time, but do make a choice! Do not stay halfway, on the fence. Make a choice to be receptive to the growth that is being asked of you, and a path that truly fits who you are will show up. Keep recommitting and do not fall back asleep.

Part of the purpose of the shamanic path is to integrate the conflicting parts of the human psyche with each other, and to then be able to open the doorways to the Higher Self. Integrating conflicting aspects of the human psyche (especially those lost in the Unconscious, Shadow realms), releases, transforms, and channels the return of much needed energies for our evolvement at this time. A shaman is a healer that has walked through the Gates of the Underworld, and is practiced at looking at and integrating their own Shadow.

It is not necessary to be a shaman to take a journey to the World of true healing, of course, but it is necessary to utilize the power of your imagination and spirit. In order to engage with the Great Mystery that surrounds us, it is important to be comfortable with moving in and out of the mythic realms, sensing the magic of the spirit in all things and all places. It is important to open your intuitive faculties and to perceive the essence of the invisible, etheric Worlds. Not only does this create an access to amazing transformation, but all of your World will become more alive and full of life.

As I refer to altered states of consciousness, as well as realms and Worlds, many of you will know what I am referring to, because we are in a time on the Planet when the veils between the Worlds are once again growing thin. For those of you who do not, I am speaking of alterations in both the content and functioning of the consciousness and states which denote the stages of awareness through which one progresses, often appearing to others as if one is in a trance. The trance experience is a 'state of liberation' that can free one from the bounds of ordinary reality, a way out of time and space, and closer to one's spiritual center. The entry keys to the spiritual realms are now being given to the many, not the few, as it is necessary to have access at this time, for humanity's evolution. Calling in these realms within ceremonial space creates an altered state that takes one out of normal reality.

Altered states of consciousness are one of the most basic human experiences that are genuinely universal in the experiencing of transcendent and healing states. Throughout the last Era we have been learning through being separate (for the most part) from direct access to the energies of the Heavens much of the time, except for the very few; the gurus, visionaries, medicine people, spiritual leaders, the healers and shamans, as well as those who have kept close connection to Mother Nature. But for at least the last five hundred years, many of those who had practiced ceremonial ways in which to keep spiritually connected to Source, were shamed, tortured, ostracized, or killed. It is time to heal these wounds and to open the doorways to higher consciousness.

The reality is that we experience trance or altered states of consciousness on some level almost every day, such as by being connected to our dreams, praying, meditating, visualizing, dancing, singing, day-dreaming, love-making, walking in Nature, and using our creativity. The Fourth dimension we are transiting through is somewhat like being in an altered state of reality. Many of you have had at least one mystical, altering experience. These states can also be brought about by music and sound, drumming, dance, spiritual postures, chanting, breath-work, flower essences, plant medicines, sacred spaces and sites, and so much more. The awareness and use of medicine plants to alter consciousness has been around at least since the times of King Solomon and are to be used with great respect and guidance. These gifts from the Creator and Mother Earth are a blessed vehicle by which humanity has been greatly assisted in staying in touch with its true spiritual nature, in spite of the times of much oppressive darkness. Many of these sacred medicines truly assist in bringing Light into the unconsciousness. Nature reaches out to humans and lets us know it is there to open doorways of consciousness that we never could have dreamt of without some assistance.

Trust in yourself and work with visualizing what you want to consciously create in your life and in the World, as well as being open to guidance from higher realms. Be of clear intent and purpose. It is not a game, though one can experience great joy in the process. Take the time to go within and to listen. Visualization is also a good way to start opening the doorways of the subconscious mind, to get more comfortable with making contact with the Higher Self and the World of Spirit. Visualization uses the imagination of the mind and is not a complete access to other realms, but it is a start as one gets comfortable with spirit guides and allies. Practice using the creative powers of your mind to create higher states of consciousness, imagining a World where the sacred energy of Love, harmony, and beauty is present in all things, as a safe place to springboard from. Imagine that we have matured enough as a species to experience the miracles of Creation with more joy and less fear, knowing that there is assistance in owning our responsibility as co-creators of the New World. We are moving into a time where the state of day dreaming with pure intent from our creative, spiritual selves, is part of the way we can manifest what we need for daily living.

Even though the western mind has been focused on the tangible, visible World for centuries, it is necessary to bring the element Ether (Spirit in Matter) into our beings and our daily lives, to evolve. This spiritual energy is returning for all to have access to, and we get to choose how to greet it, with resistance or welcome. It is not something to fear, for we all have personal protective guides as well as the conscious mind that only allows us to journey as far as is correct and in alignment with where we are in our own evolution at any given moment. But this most rarefied substance, this element Ether, is stimulating us to reclaim our Higher Self, and it is not time to sit on the fence. To go on a journey of self-reclamation and renewal, one must become more comfortable with working with the unseen forces, where the spirit of what can truly help us on our next steps is available and waiting for contact.

A large source from which we are directed and supported in working with the unseen forces, is our connection to ancient stories and myths. We are in a time when it is very important to reconnect to the knowledge and wisdom inherent in that which has been passed down throughout time, and is still present in our psyches. It is that which inspires us and can give greater meaning to the journey. In our Modern World we have become disconnected from the power and reality of myth, losing contact with our ancient roots. It is time to remember who we are and to mature as co-creators of a reality much greater than what we see with just the naked eye. It is time to bring back our 'symbolic power,' to create powerful changes of mythic proportion. As we orient ourselves to be more in tune with the bigger picture, we can live our lives in the greater mythic connection to a wondrous spiritual reality, right here on Earth.

5

Creating Sacred Space

I feel I am no longer part of the World in the same way. I have a strong intuitive awareness that I now exist in another realm connected to the spiritual aliveness in everything. There is a sense that I am a temple that I take wherever I go. It is as if I have put on a magic robe that has shapeshifted me into a greater self, where I am more aware of the sacredness of my being and of a very different World around me. Doesn't everyone else sense this change in the World and in me? It is as if another presence has filled me up, that is radiating out in an almost tangible manner. When I am in Nature I feel even more filled with this most unusual feeling. I feel safer around others and in the World, somewhere between more invisible and more visible. My movement is not as hindered by the constraints of my patterns. I feel more of a limitless quality to what I can experience. I am freer. Do you see the difference?

We are at a very unique juncture in our existence on the Earth, as the earthly reality that we have called home is going through a major transformation. Mother Nature has always provided a sacred, beautiful space in which to feel the presence of the sacredness of life, if we choose. It doesn't matter what your spiritual belief or path is. Her church is non-denominational. All are welcome and all she asks is respect and thanks. We are quickly destroying the most God-given temple we have. We have forgotten the original teachings of honoring the Earth as the original 'Church of God', as sacred space. We spoke in the chapter on Venus how we are now being required to become responsible for our own sacred vessels, as the Earth is no longer protecting our energy fields. This taking away of the protection and the Light without a Shadow, is bringing forth the laws of karma almost instantaneously so we may take more responsibility for our thoughts and actions. It is time to graduate from the school room of the third dimension and the Fourth World. The elements of Nature are also being transformed by the element Ether, as the seasons and cycles we are used to, are breaking out of their normal patterns. As we near the point of cosmic connection to the Center of the Universe, it is important that we have matured to handle the level of profound spiritual truth that will enlighten all places of darkness.

Humanity has built many amazing structures throughout history in which to worship and listen to the instruction of the sacred scriptures of its religions and spiritual traditions. Initiation rites were performed in such profoundly aligned structures as the King's and Queen's Chambers in the Great Pyramid of Gyza. Many of these structures were built on powerful energy points that were amplified by being in specific alignment with astrological configurations to create sacred geometrical containers. I have experienced amazing states of higher consciousness in Churches, Temples, and Sacred Sites around the World, as well as in Tepees, Sweat Lodges, and Kivas.

Many of these places of worship were aligned with the powerful dimensional energies of the Earth and stars, in a combination that would provide a sacred container or vessel for the awakening of consciousness, according to the beliefs of the religious or spiritual norm of the local culture. These sacred spaces would channel in powerful energies that would activate parts of the human blueprint codes for enlightenment and connection to the Divine. We are presently experiencing an awakening of much of the knowledge that was present in ancient times, through the study of Geomancy and Sacred Geometry. Many of the sacred sites and ceremonial centers that were vibrationally shut down in order not to allow access during the times of the Underworlds, have been reopened and calibrated to the energies of the cosmic forces now coming in, so that we may awaken.

The ancient art of Feng Shui, used for centuries in all eastern cultures, which is the creating of the sacred in all spaces, is becoming quite accepted in the western culture. Feng Shui works with the circulation and flow of the life force in the living and working environment, to create balance and harmony. We are relearning how to work with the subtle energies in daily life and in healing, as well as in our environments, as the element Ether is becoming more available once again.

The importance of a special place of worship, as a place that inspires one to connect with the presence of the true, essence self, has been acknowledged throughout time immemorial. But once again we are in very different times, which call for different measures. As mentioned before, we are at a point where the Medicine Field of the Earth is slowly decreasing as a result of both cosmic and environmental forces. With the destruction of the ozone and the environment, as we come forth from the Underworlds to conscious life, many of us are experiencing health difficulties we never imagined. Many of us are becoming very sensitive to the lower emotions of others, as well as to unclear spaces. But most of all, we are being asked to evolve to higher levels of consciousness so that we can handle and embody the powerful Light and Love which is coming from the Great Cosmic Center. These rarefied powers are to awaken us from our deep slumber, where we have been only half conscious in the Nine Underworlds.

At this time I believe it is important to work with creating and recognizing your body as a sacred vessel with its very own energy field. We are being asked to go through our own very personal transformations, and we need a sacred vehicle to take with us wherever we go. Most of us are not given the 'space' to continuously live in a temple for this time of initiation when it is so important to be able to contain and to function with the intense energy coming through. We need to create it for ourselves. I would like to say that it is truly the metamorphosis of consciousness that will enable an individual to be in an evolved energetic field of one's own. As the separated and unconscious parts of our being come back into unity and alignment, and the higher centers are activated, it is as if the parts of a cosmic jigsaw puzzle are coming together. This assists in the re-creation of a sacred vessel that now can not only handle more energy and Light, but has no room for harmful energies to enter in. When one has reached a certain level of evolvement, there is only a need of a reminder at times, to keep our energy fields and bodies connected.

Later I will share 'Daily Rituals' for life which will help keep your personal sacred space alive. At this time I will only give a very brief description of what I mostly use to create a safe, sacred vessel for the journey of healing. The pathway I mainly work with is the use of the Medicine Wheel, in ceremonies and groups, and in individual work, even though I use many other tools. You can use this information to find a way in which to do your personal work and as a stimulus to educate yourself further on the Medicine Wheel, as I only give basic information here.

From what has been shared with me, the term Medicine Wheel was first applied to the Big Horn Medicine Wheel in Wyoming. Simply described, this Medicine Wheel consists of a central cairn, or rock pile, surrounded by a circle of stones. The 'Medicine' part of the name was given by anthropologists to designate their belief that the stone circles were of religious significance to indigenous peoples. The word 'Medicine' is also used by Native American people to describe anything that improves one's connection to the Great Mystery and to all life, as well as bringing healing to the Earth and all our relations. I have been fortunate enough to have been to the Big Horn Medicine Wheel, which was reported to have been used by many tribes for many centuries, and is obviously still being used to this day. (The Wheel was surrounded by a rope that was covered with spiritual offerings.) Some Medicine Wheels have been found to have been initially constructed some 4,500 years ago. Indigenous peoples all over the World have built and consecrated stone circles as sacred sites in which to have ceremonies and offer prayers. In a healing ritual, one may use a Wheel that is in physical form and already established or one may use a simple Medicine Wheel that is created as needed for a particular intention and that can be dismantled when finished.

But most of all, the Medicine Wheel is a symbol for the Great Mystery and a way to honor the steps along the way to becoming a conscious part of the sacred Wheel of Life. It is used to gather together the sacred energies of all the Creature Beings in a circle of remembrance, seeing all as being related. The Creature Beings include the Two Legged, the Stone People, Mother Earth, Father Sky, Grandfather Sun and Grandmother Moon, Star Nations, Subterraneans, Thunder Beings, and All My Relations.

I have been taught by one of my teachers, Ohky Simine Forest, a number of powerful shamanic processes that are done within a Medicine Wheel and that can be created in one's visual and energy field to provide a sacred container for personal inner work. She has also shown how the Medicine Wheel is used to show the greater Cycles we have been in. In the passage we are moving through, following the Medicine Wheel model of Ohky's teachings, we are leaving the energies of the West, exemplified by meeting with the energies of Crazy Woman for the last 5,200 years, turning us upside down, dealing with out lowest passion and crazy egotism. We are now engaging with 'Rainbow Woman' of the East, whom we have already been introduced to and who inspires us to new levels of creativity, freedom, peace, order, and new birth. This direction has its challenges as well, asking us to not get blinded by this new Light and all the choices and energy coming our way. Ohky suggests we remain well connected to the Earth, as do most Wisdom Keepers of indigenous knowledge, and to remember our journey through the Underworlds, so as not to get blinded, confused, or caught in the dangerous trap of the spiritual Ego.

The Medicine Wheel appears to be one of the simplest, yet one of the most profound, Earth-connected representations of the Universe that there are to work with. It provides a way to attune to the horizontal plane and cardinal directions of the Earth, as well as uniting Heaven and Earth. Not only do they represent the entire Wheel of the Cycles of Life on Earth (birth, puberty, adulthood, old age), these Wheels were also often aligned with certain other stones or geographic features to indicate Solstices and Equinoxes as well as other planetary and astrological events. The areas that were chosen as the places for the more permanent Medicine Wheels, were usually very powerful vortexes and even if not, the Wheel would make the area become so.

Identifying and calling in the sacred space of a Medicine Wheel assists one to be grounded and oriented to Mother Earth, as well as providing a gateway to the visionary World wherein you can connect to guardians and guides that may bring you sacred visions, as well as healing and alignment. The Medicine Wheel also gives us a way to remember the Sacred Hoop that connects all life and to remember that everything in Nature proceeds in cycles. Every time we enter a Wheel, we come out of the western system of the linear conditioned mind of beginnings and endings, goals and accomplishments, and return to the journey in the sacred circle where the dance of life is what counts, as well as remembering we are all equal in a circle. When we are in a sacred Medicine Wheel of any kind, we are in a Medicine Field that helps us remember to be present with the Heavens, the Earth, ourselves, and each other. This word Medicine in native culture does not only mean a substance to restore health and vitality, but it also denotes the presence of spiritual power. The Medicine Wheel might be defined as a 'Circle of Knowledge' that restores wholeness and gives one power over one's life.

This 'Circle of Power' is a sacred space in which to discover the inner self, the divinity within, a tool for one's own self-development, as well as a device for connecting to the Earth and the unseen forces of Nature. Even though Native Americans are best known for the term and concept of Medicine Wheels, it is a universal symbol that exists in the collective psyche of much of humanity.

Different tribes and cultures have varied ways of dividing the Wheel of Life into its various aspects, but they have many similarities. In all Wheels at least the cardinal directions of East, South, West, and North are honored, as well as Above (Heaven) and Below (Earth). At times the in-between directions, such as the Southeast, are added to the Wheel, but always the power and connection is to the true Center of the Heart of Great Spirit. In most traditions, each cardinal direction has an energy or characteristic, specific to the direction, as well as a particular animal guide, color, element, season, gift, and challenge to face. Each cardinal direction also has a connection to the various 'Cycles of Life' that all humans go through; birth, youth, adulthood, elder years, death, and rebirth. In western religions, much focus has been upon looking to the Heavens for guidance and connection, which may align the vertical line of our energy bodies, but the Medicine Wheel teachings connect us also to the horizontal field of the Earth and daily life, bringing Great Spirit's gifts down to Mother Earth.

This information is just the most basic of teachings on this vast and important topic. In the teachings I have followed, all life is sacred, as is everything in the Universe, but we have gotten off the true path and need to return so as to be able to invoke this truth consciously. In the returning, it is important to create sacred vessels in which to birth a shift in consciousness, from seeing wherever you are as ordinary to seeing it as holy.

6

The Elements and the Elementals: The Building Blocks of Nature

Your sacred space has been created. You are ready to go deeper into the healing journey. The sacred allies and spirit guides are waiting to be remembered and the sacred directions have been called in, including the guardians of the gates. Your Medicine Wheel is humming with the power of your intention to evolve with grace and ease. Feel yourself deeply as you leave behind the limited view of the World you have known, expanding your consciousness to the outer limits where true guidance and healing exists. Allow the Creation forces of the elementals to speak to you from their rightful place as healed beings. Trust in the divine in all life, as the elements of Earth, Water, Fire, and Air are cleansed and elevated to their most pure states, as the sacred spirit of Matter, Ether permeates your entire being. Blessed be!

We are that which has arisen out of the archetypal blueprint of the Creator's great web of Light and Love to assist in the birthing of Gaia. We are that which has assisted in the creating of the human, coming through the primordial soup of Creation. We are that which forms a sacred Cosmological Wheel in which to dance the journey of life. We of the elemental kingdom were given the joyous call to assist in bringing the Rainbow Spirits, the palette of Creation energies in their multi-faceted diversity, out of the Godhead through the dimensions of this solar system. We are, in our biggest form, the dragon energy, originally directed by the Holy Ones. We were caught in the 'fall from grace' with humanity, and suffered in the subjugation and dishonoring of the Mother Earth and her helpers. Our healing and transformation is interwoven with the evolution of humanity. Our beings are susceptible to the suffering created by mankind's carelessness and basic ignorance of the proper conduct of honoring the natural World in Nature and the disrespectful actions thus created in relationship to the environment. Therefore, we have at times retaliated towards humans in the distant past, when they behaved in such ignorant manners.

There is healing occurring at core levels for the collective of elementals and even though we still must respond to the abuse and neglect and the shifts of the Light and Love coming through the Planet, in order to balance that which is out of balance, we are now reconnecting to the higher consciousness of Mother Earth. We wish to be recognized, brought back into co-creation, and join with the part of humanity who wants to return to a state of grace and wholeness. Our natural state of being is one connected to the sacredness of life, not the dishonored state of affairs we were brought to. Some of us guard the gates to the next World or dimension, as well as being part of the spiritual initiation and carrying out of the powerful movements of the Rainbow Serpent.

We are often represented here on Earth by the serpent, with our dynamic and regenerative forces, because of having the characteristics of the animal which is the closest to the Earth; such as the shedding of its skin and ability to transform, and its undulating motion akin to the spiraling movement of the life force. Our primal, serpent-like energies were the original creative natural forces of the elements, working in alignment with and under the direction of the Holy Ones. We birthed into smaller beings, available for the various jobs of manifesting Spirit in Matter out of the feminine great Cosmic Waters; each elemental deity was birthed out of another, all the way to the smallest of fairies and devas. When we have been in contact and union with the more heavenly rarefied energies, we are associated with having wings or feathers, creating the original archetype of the creature called a dragon. This part of us became caught in the Shadow Dance and fell from grace in the manipulation of our beings. There is a much bigger story to this, but we will keep it simple. We do not discern or judge beings as being of the Dark or of the Light, for we contain both, but we know how it feels to be in union with the 'Cosmic Center' and wish to no longer be controlled by the destructive forces.

To the ancient ones we were called by many names as we at times embodied and joined with the Holy Ones, to assist a World in great need in order to bring culture and knowledge, and to protect the Earth. To the tribes of the Southwest we were called 'Avanyu' by the Tewa, the source of the blood of all the animals and of all the waters of the land; 'Kaowisi' by the Zuni; the feathered sky serpent; 'Paluluka' by the Hopi, the plumed water serpent, bringer of rain and lightening. To the Cherokee we were called 'Sinthola,' giver of inspiration, language, and agriculture; 'Urcaguay' to the Inca, the one who takes us through the Waters of change; 'Quetzalcoatl' to the Aztecs, the balancer of the polarities of Light and Dark; and as the 'Nagas' in India, serpent beings, deities of the primal ocean, springs, bringers of abundance and wealth. There are many names by which we were identified.

In the ancient past we were more readily seen, until the closing of the 'Heavenly Gates,' when we moved into the mists and myths. We are as real as the serpents that crawl upon the Earth and the birds that fly in the sky. Do not be afraid of us because we are also a part of you, in your bodies and in the energy that keeps you alive and moves up your spine as awakening occurs in your Rainbow Body. There needs to be a healing of the concept of the snake and the life force of the Earth as being separate from the Heavens. The Worlds that were split apart are to come together. Let the energy of the 'Feathered Rainbow Serpent' take you through the doorway and return you to the knowledge. This knowledge is not forbidden; it is a part of the School of Life.

Before each shift to a New Age, it is necessary for humanity to have a unification of the polarities of Spirit and Matter, in the 'I am' state of 'Oneness' and Unity consciousness still held deep in the individuated self. This shift is more important than ever for this particular passage that Earth and humanity are going through. This unification centered in the Heart is needed to bring back the consciousness, to remember that which has come before, and to gather the energies lost and needed for the next leap. Therefore, a shift in connection to us is also necessary. We are a part of your once unified field that connected you more closely to the original blueprint of your beings.

In the past we were at times symbolized by the Ouroborus, a snake or dragon circling itself to join with its own tail. As a unified grander energy we were known as the Great World Serpent, encircling the Earth, assisting with the keeping of the cyclical nature of the seasons, supporting and maintaining the earthly balance. We represent both the telluric and the celestial principles, Dark and Light, disintegration and re-integration, male and female unified, the Primordial Waters and the potential before the spark of Creation and the Totality. As we release and transform with the influence of cosmic energies on the Planet, we are unwinding this protective balancing, to evolve and heal that which is out of alignment with the spiritual forces of all life. You may be witnessing this in the imbalances and changes you have witnessed in the seasons. Our end is our beginning. As we shift, humanity also shifts to a new cycling, forever ending and beginning in the great spiral of Creation.

Any life forces that have been caught in the traumatic survival experiences and fears of the past, contained especially within the experiences of the reptilian brain memories and processes, are being activated to heal to a much more evolved place. You are being asked to move beyond the fear of annihilation, as we are also being asked to do. We have felt the fear of being controlled by outside influences who have challenged us with threats of our demise. We are healing our fear and coming back into our connection with pure Source. Your Basic Self has carried much of this and is in the process of catching up to the higher centers. On a larger scale, especially in our form as dragons, many are beginning to acknowledge us and to see how we have been misused by those who wish to control the evolution of humanity and the Earth and who resist transforming in fear of being annihilated and no longer existing. The symbolic representation of us as dangerous, driven by the Dark Lords, especially in dragon form, must be evolved. Our primal energies were greatly tainted by the sublimation of Nature. We began to hide in caves and subterranean Earth so we could no longer be used for the misuse of power, as well as not be totally eradicated from this reality. For we knew there would be a day where some would once again see us and work with our energies in an enlightened way. In present times, there are still those who attempt to misuse our most primal Earth Creation Powers. Ask for the Light and the Love of the highest guides you can make contact with, to assist in protecting us, therefore the Earth, from such misuse. We will not be misused any more. This can no longer be permitted. As we heal, all life on the Planet will be able to withstand greater emanations of Light. This is most important.

The myth of Gilgamesh and Innana carries the true story of the sending away of the guardian of the trees, beings like us, who were here to protect the trees as well as the sacred Tree of Life. The part God, part man aspect got angry and acted out because of being rejected by the Divine Feminine. This is partly what has allowed the disappearance of your forests and jungles, starting so long ago. We can now be called back by those of innocence, to protect that which is needed for life to be sustained and to evolve here on Earth.

As we stated before, we do not contain judgment around being on the side of Dark or Light for we contain both. But we carry the original blueprint for creating the untainted Garden of Eden; that is what our essence carries and where it naturally wants to return. We also are part of what is called the Body Elemental, keeping your autonomic systems working, and we can also help with the bringing in of your perfect, original blueprint. Hidden in the subterranean World beneath your feet, we are waiting for healing and reconnection. We are available so that many can work with us, not only to evolve their bodies, but to also be more connected to the weather and seasons, and to work with the emotions and characteristics of their true selves. We are evolving, as is all of life on Earth, and it is getting more difficult to misuse our sacred energies. We are choosing to only respond to energies of Love and Light at this time. The Earth, by her vibrational awakenings, is stimulating our remembrance of our original pure intent.

We were initially and are once again purely spiritual beings who exist in parallel multi-dimensional Worlds; beings such as the Anagas, the

Avanyu, the devas, the fairies, and the nymphs, as well as the guardians and creators of the elements. We are connected to the Fire as salamanders, Air as sylphs, Water as sprites and undines, and Earth as elves and gnomes, to name a few. At times the immensity of our beings is as grand as our connection to the great deities; at times we are as small and available as the smallest of creatures. We are that which sustains the natural World and keeps it in manifestation. Without us your World would cease to exist. We take our role seriously, while we also feel the great joy of the creation energies.

Please do not keep us hidden from your sight. Having too much focus on only what you can see with your limited view is no longer necessary for your Soul's growth. As the veils thin between the Worlds, talk to us and remember who we are as you reconnect to Earth, as you evolve. Speak to us through the voice of your Heart and Soul while you are in Mother Nature. We are very connected to the feeling and sensing of life. Do you know that we put items in your path as you walk along the trails of the Earth, as we pay attention to your innermost thoughts and feelings, so that we may be in sync with you? The special feathers, the rocks, the whispers on the winds, the animal messages, and the rainbows, are all connected to the elementals in our various forms. We want you to remember the magic. Do you know that we assist in the making of the sacred symbols of the crop circles on the Earth, in union with the Star Beings, so that you learn to communicate with Mother Nature once again? These sacred geometric symbols will assist in completing your DNA blueprint, so that you have what you need to awaken.

You must take us along in your journey, for we are part of the way to come back home. We help take care of the life processes in Nature, as well as being indispensable to the health and vitality of your bodies, your forms. There are also Body Elementals that wish to come back to the consciousness of humans that have been hidden just below the surface of the Earth. They are evolving as the Earth changes and wish to assist humanity and create new vitality and physical restructuring.

Next, we must speak as the most basic powers which make life manifest and is the essence forces of the Creation, the Four Horses of the Grandmothers and Grandfathers. These forces of great magnitude and spiritual power will speak for themselves, for we are as connected to them as Water is to the streams and the rocks. Ride with us through the experiencing of the gifts that we bring. We are vibrant with life force and when in union, we develop life, as the Creator has given us life. As you learn to acknowledge and work with us, there is a further bridge forged towards greater responsibility and abilities as co-creators of your realities. We begin with Fire.

At the beginning of the Creation of Earth, I birthed forth, unified within a great ball of Fire from the Godhead, being given the vital energy necessary to bring forth life, as well as the power to sustain and inspire. As the element Fire, I come to you daily in the form of the great Sun in the sky, from deep inside the Earth, the Fire in your belly, as well as in your hearths. This spark of life is to keep you connected to Spirit, with my Fire helping to illuminate and enlightening the Dark, bringing forth great warmth, vision, and action. I bring to you the passion of sexual energy and creation forces that enliven all life. I open the doorway, when appropriate, to the other Worlds, like a lightning rod, keeping an open channel to what has come before, as well as purifying that which no longer serves. I burst open through the Great Central Sun within you, teaching the right use of power when in balance. When I am out of balance, there is impatience, consumption, misuse of power, destruction and violence, as well as over-creating out of imbalance. I contain much of the male principle of Creation. My Fires need to be in balance with all the other elements or I grow out of control. The original teachings about the inter-connectedness of all life are still needed. Know yourself and what element you are most connected to, so you remember to use it wisely, as well as to stay in balance. Keep the flame of Spirit burning deep inside and never let it go out.

The 'Primal Water of Life' came forth next, bringing the Fire into the Underworld, cooling and calming the flames of Creation, thus giving a nourishing place in which to birth life on Earth. You dream from the ocean of the great Waters and still have bodies that contain me more than any other element. I bring Spirit and grace into manifestation, keeping the flow and connection of all life to itself and everything around. I bring you the great gift of the World of 'feelings' that were meant to keep you connected to the 'Heart of the Heavens' here on Earth, while heightening your intuitive abilities. When there is a need for restoration and reconciliation, I bring forth that which cleanses and releases, especially of your emotions.

The 'Flowering of the Soul' of humanity, as well as the Soul of the Earth, is realized by the release of my Waters of renewal, harmony, balance, and grace. I am more akin to the feminine energies, even though I am connected to all the elemental forces. When I am out of sync with the whole or dishonored, I become overwhelmed, at times polluted, and may have difficulty moving and creating any new life. My Waters inside of the human being may then sink into stagnation and denial. When this occurs I may become a torrential downpour both inside and out that connects with the other elements, to assist in bringing about the present 'Great Cycle' of purification. Too much of me brings one back to the primordial soup of unconsciousness without form. Stay connected to all of the elements, as well as acknowledging the spiritual essence in all life. It is of utmost importance that you work with me during these times of great purification, for I will be assisting in carrying you through the doorway of your greatest hopes and your greatest fears. From the crystalline structure of my being, the essence of grace is entering into your Planet.

Next, in the beginning times of Creation, the Earth element brought into form the formless, creating solidity and structure in which Spirit could have a container to create. The Seeds of Creation were grown in my soil, as the two leggeds, four leggeds, flying ones, swimming beings, creeping crawlies, as well as the microscopic beings that sustain all life came into being. I symbolize the Mother, even though she contains all the elemental ingredients for manifestation of this reality. I give support, nourishment, comfort, and a solid home to walk upon. Where I am, there is nurturing, a sense of identity and belonging, a feeling of nourishment; life is sustained and abundant and everything flourishes. When you are connected to me, your roots can grow deep and the feeling of being at home anywhere on the Planet, being friend to all, is as easy as walking in a beautiful garden grove.

I am Red Clay, Black Clay, Yellow Clay, and White Clay Woman, bringer of the many infinite choices of physical manifestation into form, in all its beauty and wonder. When I am out of balance, one is homeless, in exile and ungrounded, as well as always hungry and alone, lost in endless wandering, caught in addictive behaviors, trying to fill the hole created by my absence. When there is too much Earth, one can stay rigid and unmoving, being unable to make change. Do not forget what sustains or you may have difficulty existing on the Earth plane. I do not ask for worship (neither do any of the elements), but for recognition and honoring. You will need me to ground your energy, so you do not become overwhelmed by the Water.

And finally, I speak as the element of Air, in which the prayers to the Divine are carried, as well as various seedpods of Creation, as life is carried from place to place. With the 'Word' and the first breath, Creation was brought to life. The beautiful sounds of Creation are carried in my winds, as well as being a place for the flying seen and unseen beings. Breath is required for life and is a doorway to transformation. So the simple act of breathing in and out keeps one connected to life, in deep connection to my gifts. I bring in the presence of the mental body, the intellect and logic, with its great ability to bring forth ideas and things of the mind that come with a quickening and great stirring. I am fairly invisible unless connected to the other elements, so I am often forgotten; but I am the last breath that will move out of your lips, as you let go of your body. Wisdom and Truth are my domain, and I bring creativity to new heights. Know yourself and identify which one of us you are most connected to at any given time; but do not forget you are made out of all four. When I am out of connection to the whole, I blow around in useless meanderings that do not manifest, causing confusion and un-clarity, driving one to craziness, going around in a circle that has no end, without a loophole. When I am not part of the entirety of the 'Cosmic Elemental Wheel,' energies are created that cause destruction and imbalance in the delicate web of life, that gets so tied up in itself that there looks like there is no way out. The circuits burn themselves out when there is no grounding cord (Earth). Remember me and your prayers will always have a way to be heard, unified with all of the sacred elements.

You are already getting to know the element Ether, the most rarefied substance of the Heavens that is now more fully entering into your dimension; where Spirit will join again more closely with Matter and is known as the 'Fifth Element.' We are the unity of Spirit manifest through the sacred elements, creating the necessary changes for humanity's evolution. Your Higher Self will assist you in birthing this rarefied spiritual force that will wake up your 'Divine Soul' while in embodiment. As you get more sensitive and connected to this most holy aspect of your being once again, as in the early times of this Fourth World, there will be an increase of instances of being at the right place at the right time, as well as an opening to the awareness of spirit helpers and guides. There will be a feeling of grace and synchronistic experiences in daily life and you will see the inter-connectedness, sacredness, and subtle energies of all things. We are the Light and the Love of the Creator and we ask for you to invite us back into your daily breath, your daily walk, your daily feeling states, and your daily inspirations. It is time to see, feel, and know the spiritual aliveness of all things, all beings. We bring all elements and elementals back into balance, as well as all races and nations, and will not be denied. We reunite the Tree of Life. It is time.

7

Spirit Guides, Helpers, and Allies

"May our feelings penetrate into the Center of our Hearts and seek in Love to unite with human beings, seeking the same goal with Spirit Beings, who full of grace behold our earnest heartfelt strivings and in beholding strengthen us from the realms of Light, illuminating our life in Love." - Rudolf Steiner

Native Americans, as well as others from many other spiritual and esoteric traditions, believe that the Creator uses the unseen holy forces as the intermediaries between Heaven and Earth. They are to be respected and honored. Within many of the ancient spiritual traditions, the presence of unseen mentors, allies, or helpers was a generally accepted truth, and upon some paths, they were considered essential to the practice itself. In shamanic practice one does not enter the other Worlds and altered reality without a trusted spirit guide. In the shamanistic tradition all creatures are considered relatives. Non-human relations are prayed for and many are included in ceremonies; the birds (winged ones), the trees (tall standing people), the plants (green growing people), the four-leggeds, the creepy crawlies, as well as the two-leggeds. The particularly powerful spirit guides are often referred to as Grandmothers and Grandfathers.

We have spoken about the power of the Nature spirits and how important it is to include them in our awareness and spiritual journey. It is vital that we work with the unseen forces that hold Nature in balance. We are being pushed to the wall to remember this, as we experience the awesome power of Mother Nature. In order to do the high level work of 'meeting our true self' that is being required of us at this time, it is also necessary to enlist the support of spirit helpers. With their assistance we can awaken to the greater part of our beings and become the 'Flowering Souls' of the Fifth Sun.

While the desire to connect to these spiritual helpers appears to come from us, it also appears that the otherworld beings, with their multitude of names and titles, also wish to connect to humanity and are making themselves more visible and available as the veils between the Worlds grow thin. These many guides remind us to and help us embody the divine aspects of our beings that we have forgotten. Truly, humans and spirits learn from each other and grow from the interaction in ways we can barely understand. Spirit guides are here to assist the human Soul in reaching its most perfected state. Our evolution as humans affects and reaches into the future and into the higher realms in a never ending connection to all things.

A spirit guide can be defined as a highly evolved being who has no material body and who is available to humans for healing, guidance, and protection. When we refer to the archetypal energies of these guides, we are talking about the highest original, pure, powerful characteristics of their beings. These archetypes are trans-cultural, being a repository of timeless, universal, intuitive truths which are available to transform and reconfigure our physical, emotional, and mental bodies into their higher states. As a human reaches out into the ethers of the eternal through prayer and ritual, the Creator responds with an image or aspect of the Divine in a manner in which the human can relate to and handle. We may understand them as wavebands of power, like the colors of the rainbow, with different frequencies and qualities, but all connected to and sourcing from the universal web of the cosmos. The energy is so profound that we can only open to it in small increments.

When a teacher or high level spirit appears, they are often connected to holy beings to which we have had some kind of contact with in the past, in this life or otherwise, having to do with our cultural, religious, or spiritual experiences. These guides need our requests, our prayers, our offerings and our permission to assist us. They may show up in a dream, in a vision, or in our thoughts, without our conscious asking; that is to just of remind us of their presence. To truly assist us they need to be in alignment with the law of free will. If one is working with a new guide of any kind, be sure to look deep into their eyes, shining a pure Light of Love into their Hearts, and ask three times if they are for your highest good. It is important to pay close attention to this most basic of tools, so that when you work with the unseen Worlds, you will be guided in a good way. Spiritual naiveté is not the same as becoming as children again. Explore and learn to work with the otherworldly realms, but work with guides you develop a trusting relationship with.

There are Angels, Arch Angels, Guardian Angels, Seraphim, Cherubs, Gods and Goddesses, Spiritual Teachers, Deities, Ancestral Helpers, as well as Animal Helpers and Protectors. They come with definite personality traits and behaviors in accordance with the norms and specific beliefs of the culture of the person to whom they appear. At times they may materialize in a form we do not understand, but to which we need to open. These otherworldly beings vary in knowledge, power, and abilities and connect to humans for a number of reasons and varying periods of time. Throughout planetary history humans have interfaced with spirit guides and there are startling similarities in spite of the cultural differences. The Christian Virgin Mary, the Chinese Kwan Yin and the Tibetan Tara are all known to have the similar qualities of motherly support, deep compassion, and unconditional Love. Some appear in a group, as do the 'Corn Mothers' for me when a safe boundary or sacred container is needed for healing. These Holy Ones come from many Native American traditions and provide protection and grounding, among many other gifts. The list is much too long to include here and there is much information available specifically on this topic.

There are also many new helpers and guides now appearing to humanity, particular to the energies of the times. There may be very old and ancient spirit guides that show up, that have not been witnessed for a very long time, or ones that have stayed hidden until now, even while assisting with humanity's spiritual evolution. For our transition into the next World, it is of utmost importance that we connect to these energies in a powerful and meaningful manner. These higher archetypal energies are also needed as examples for us. as visions of the more evolved states of being to which we aspire. It is not that we are giving up our freedom or direct contact to the Creator of all life, but there have always been intermediaries between Heaven and Earth and we need their guidance and support more than ever. They are here to help us remember our divinity.

The majority of guides that show up are for the highest good, but it is always good to check. There are beings that may appear from other dimensions that are confused and have forgotten their original pure intent. Having a strong connection and relationship with your power animal can be where you look for guidance on the question of whether the beings that show up are there for your highest good.

I will share more on power animals, because I have had extensive interaction with these allies and because I believe that it will be easier to have a successful journey of self inquiry with their presence acknowledged. Much has been written on power animal and animal spirits, which reflects the return of the 'Earth Ways' and the spiritual awakening that is occurring in the Western World. Attuning to these helpers will assist you in experiencing the higher consciousness of your personality.

The concept of a power animal is universal to most cultures. Many tribal cultures recognize an animal totem for the tribe, for the clan one belongs to, and for the family you were born into. Animal spirits help us journey safely to the dream time and help us connect to the subconscious more instinctually. The power animal is that which is most personal for an individual. In the past, when humanity recognized itself as part of Nature, the recognition and honoring of one's power animal were as much a part of the ritualistic cycle of growing up as are the christening rituals and birthday parties of today. Practically every tribe had a resident shaman or medicine person who worked extensively with animal spirit helpers, assisting others in staying in touch with and understanding the ones that appeared to them.

When there is reference to animal spirit helpers, it is to the characteristics and qualities of a particular type of animal and to the 'Medicine' or power it carries. We are not referring to the individual animals that we see in Nature, but to the collective essence of the being in its most powerful form. It is like putting together the quintessence of the innate powers and abilities of the eagle, the bear, or any of the many wondrous animal helpers, into one being which represents the collective gifts of that specific being. These manifestations of Spirit are aspects of us we have disowned or never were in touch with. These guides help us to remember.

Some say that animals are leaving our Planet at increasingly fast rates, partly because of technological advances gone out of balance; also from overpopulation, as well as the lack of respect for their lives and the sacred role they play in the delicate balance; but also because they are going into spiritual realms where they can more profoundly assist humanity's evolvement. If that is true, what incredible beings they are to come back and assist us, after being so mistreated. When they communicate from the spirit realms, they do not tolerate abuse and dishonoring and they will cease to be helpers and guides, if not respected. When one is strongly connected to animal spirits, it often will increase the amount of powerful animal medicine that will come to you in physical form, in spite of how many animals are disappearing.

I personally have had the blessings of experiencing one special message after another from the animal kingdom, in a totally synchronistic fashion to whatever was utmost in my Heart and Soul. I am sure that most people have had some kind of special interaction with an animal in Nature. Just yesterday a full grown male (tom) turkey came into my reality that had given of its life by accident on the road. The message of turkey has to do with giving thanks or being thanked, and I had just completed a number of free 'giveaway' talks. Prayers and thanksgiving were offered. At another time, in a personal healing ritual, I went for a walk in the forest after asking for a sign from the Creator as to whether my prayers had been heard. Within seconds, I walked upon a big, red-tailed hawk on the ground, which was startled into the air, dropping its prey. Red-tailed Hawk Medicine is known to be a direct line to the Creator. At times, our connection to Great Spirit through the animal world shows up quite quickly and profoundly.

The ancient teachings that were passed down to me speak to the mysterious and profoundly sacred energies of one's power animal. Your power animal is directly linked to your Soul and, when fully acknowledged and integrated, assists you in becoming and mastering your true self, as well as giving you the power to fulfill your destiny path. This spirit animal is attached to us from birth and is part of us, whether we know it or not. Most of us live in a culture where this most sacred part of our personal medicine has not been recognized and honored. It is important to have our power animals identified and incorporated into our energy fields and to learn how to work with and integrate this sacred medicine into our lives.

I was taught that it is often necessary for a shaman or medicine person to identify and return our power animal, because we may be confused by what animals come our way. We may have many helping animal spirits that are around us in the dream time or in altered states of reality, but we can only have one power animal or personal totem at a time. We may have a known affinity to our power animal and then again we may not. I did not have a clue as to the identity of my power animal in spite of my close relationship to Mother Nature all my life. My power animal was returned to me by a shaman. When I speak of return, I am referring to the need for a spirit animal to be identified, honored, and brought closer into your energy field and Center. Supposedly, we would get very sick if these energies had totally left us. For most of us they have been hovering around our beings, waiting to come into our conscious awareness and fulfill their sacred contract.

This sacred energy is not only a guardian of the physical body; it also aligns us with our true gifts and our higher evolution. When this energy is fully integrated, our core, spiritual self gets to come alive with greater feelings of confidence, power, and wisdom. Our true beings that are more connected to the spiritual Worlds get to be the center of what aligns us in our journey of life, instead of the power-hungry, disillusioned Ego.

This instinctual, inherently powerful, and wise spirit companion is a gift from the Creator and I believe part of the 'original teaching' that many indigenous peoples have remained connected to throughout time. Some of these teachings speak of how some individuals go through a number of different power animals as one grows from a baby to a teenager to an adult; while others choose before they are born, to stay with one power animal. It seems that in my work with people and their Inner Child or Basic Self, it is the animal medicines that truly help to gain contact with the wounded aspects that do not trust very easily. When connection and openness is gained, positive changes for healing the emotional pain and trauma from the past can occur. Maybe the conscious awareness of our power animal is important to help evolve our basic instinctual self into higher states of awareness.

As adults, the majority of people take an entire lifetime to work with and learn from the power animal that is connected to them. Each totem has

specific energies and gifts that are inherent to that particular animal and
are also closely aligned with the personality of the human they are
connected with. Even though the medicine of some spirit animals is so vast
it can take lifetimes to work with, all are immensely valuable and should
be deeply respected. In the spiritual World they come from, there is no
need for comparison. They all have unique characteristics and purposes,
just as do the multitudes and varieties of humans. I must mention that
because we are in an accelerated evolutionary course, we are gathering
many more spiritual allies that work as strongly and intimately with us as
our power animals, like a totem pole of spiritual power.

A number of years after my power animal was returned, I no longer
was able to see it because I had integrated it fully into my being. I woke up
soon after I realized this and was guided to go look for it to the south of
where I lived. This particular animal was not often seen where I lived, but
I listened to the call. I found what I believed to be its nest, which was
empty, and went near by to a river to look for it. I prayed in a spot close by
the river and it flew over me four times and left. I was taken over by a
feeling of total bliss and thankfulness. Soon after this experience, a
number of powerful animal guides appeared to assist me in my shamanic
work. It seemed that once I had truly received the teachings of my power
animal, I was given the opportunity to 'expand my horizons' and gather
more assistance. If one works extensively with these powerful animal
allies, more will often appear, especially when there is a need for healing
for oneself or another.

When there has been a strong connection and understanding of the
particular characteristics and energies of one's power animal, it makes it
much easier to flow with one's personality in relating to self and others.
The characteristics of the particular spirit animal that is part of you, is
deeply connected to the most primal energies of your personality. We can
turn what appear to be personality issues or deficits into gifts, by
understanding better who we are, instead of trying to cover up or over-
prove ourselves. An example is someone with Frog Medicine, who feels
guilty that they are very emotional. Put very simply, Frog Medicine is of
the Water and the emotions, which needs to be honored by those who carry
this medicine. Once it is honored, then the emotional self can work with
the Water Medicine to transform, instead of sink within.

In order to embrace and integrate the Ego and the Shadow, it is
important to be in touch with this sacred companion. Its highest intent is to
bring out our true essence without fear or denial. As we make our journey
with this trusted being, it can also help us face and communicate with the
various guardians of the many doorways of initiation, through the
Underworlds, as we complete what we have learned there. Animal spirits
help us embody the highest parts of our nature while transforming the

Lower Self aspects of our Basic Self to a more enlightened energy. As we take the journey to the Underworlds of our own beings, with spiritual assistance we may then be able to begin elevating the parts of us that have been separate from the Light and the Love.

8

Reconnecting the Tree of Life

I am the newly reconnected Tree of Life
Reaching to the Heavenly Realms with new sight
As my Roots go deep into the Earthly plane
I want you to know you will never be the same

You have experienced the lessons of the dance of Dark and Light
As the knowing of unity and wholeness did take flight
Now feed from my abundant fruits of true wisdom where there will be no toll
As Love and Light heals the Heart of the World and births forth the 'Flowering Soul'

We are coming out of the Age of the Kali Yuga where we have been learning through the dance of the polarities, the experiencing of separation, tribulation and trauma, and the time when the Lords of the Underworld have ruled. But now the Love and the Light of the Godhead are beginning to shine through the darkness, opening us to the gifts of Heaven so that we may bring in the Fifth World. During these powerful times, a memory deep inside is being awakened, of our most inherent spiritual, essence self.

There are different parts or aspects that make us into this whole being. Knowledge about what these parts are and how these aspects work together (or not), has been carried throughout this last Era by many indigenous Wisdom Keepers, whose wisdom has survived in spite of times of great oppression. The Western World for most of the last five hundred years or more, has closed itself off to much of this knowledge in its over focus on the development of the scientific left brain and tangible reality. The development of psychology in the last century has greatly assisted in the western culture's receptivity to these teachings. The psychological discoveries of people like Freud and Roberto Assagioli and their maps of the human psyche, were instrumental to the western mind opening up and looking deeper into the make-up of the human psyche.

The concepts developed by Carl Jung, one of the fathers of Transpersonal Psychology, parallel closely the teachings of the Huna from Hawaii. His psychological studies identify the aspects of the human psyche as the Ego, the Shadow, the Anima (a man's buried feminine side), the Animus (a woman's buried masculine side), the Personal Unconscious, the Collective Unconscious, the Persona (cloak around the Ego), and the True Self. I will go deeper into the Huna model, after sharing one theory on the cause of separation from our wholeness.

Most of humanity goes through life believing that they are operating on all cylinders, unaware of the disconnection between their fragmented parts. This unawareness often gets forced into consciousness by an endless re-creation of trauma and negative patterns, stimulating a desperate search for a way to peace; but this awareness was already known throughout time by the Hawaiian Huna, the Hindu Vedic, and many shamanic traditions, just to mention a few. Native Americans, as Keepers of the Earth, usually did not look at any part of life or of human cultures as being separate. Some have continued to hold the knowledge of how to be in wholeness, in spite of the wounding that has occurred in the takeover of their lands and culture. There are Elder Wisdom Keepers that have continued to carry and pass down the knowledge of how to be embodied in the consciousness of non-separation. You will see why this is possible!

I believe it is important to have at least a basic understanding of what has created this separation from our wholeness. What I share with you is from the gathering of knowledge from various traditions and is meant to get you thinking. How did this separation occur? In our journey of descent into the third dimension, humanity separated out into various parts as we reflected and expanded outward, further and further away from the Center of the Godhead. In 'the Fall,' which we have previously, briefly spoken of, we transitioned into the density of Matter and for the most part forgot our connection to our totality. Even though I will not go into great detail, for this is a topic of immense magnitude and spiritual responsibility in its defining, it is important to set the stage to go deeper into the journey of healing. Hopefully you will see with an open Heart and mind, as your Soul longs to return to its awareness of its divine nature.

What I am putting forth is just one possibility and not written in stone, as more is being revealed daily. I encourage you to take in what makes sense in your inner knowing. What is most important as you take in this information, is that you have a perspective of how all of life comes from the God Source and that there is divine perfection in even the darkest hour and that there are no mistakes. We have learned much during this time of separation.

There has been information coming through New Age channels in recent years, about the interference from Star or higher dimensional Beings, both of the Light and of the Dark, that have influenced the creation and evolution of humanity. Be open to this possibility for it may help you better understand. This interference has affected our fall into the third dimension and has influenced the use of our full twelve DNA strands. It is time for humanity to advance as a species and go further into the activation of our divine blueprint. We are now coming into the healing of our subjugation to outside influences; even when they have pure intent, unless they are aligned with our free will or come from the pure intent of Light and Love of the Godhead, we are not taking responsibility for our own power. But we must first 'graduate' into the next stages if we expect to be able to handle such self-responsibility in our evolution, so that we can become truly conscious of our choices. Out of this higher consciousness, we can create a World of truths and not lies. It is said that humanity is being given a chance to heal the rifts created long ago as we separated out of the 'Oneness' and the 'I am' consciousness.

I do not want to create overwhelm or shutdown by bringing up information that may be controversial or uncomfortable, but I invite you once again to be open. The 'Secrets of the Ages' are being revealed and it is time to question the illusions that most of humanity has been fed. These secrets are being shared to assist humanity in understanding the bigger picture. Wait to hear that sense of recognition or 'aha' that will leap from the depths of your Soul when you hear the truth.

For the purpose of this healing journey, let's begin by stating that from the beginning of time, the so called 'Fallen Angels' that saw themselves as separate and as powerful as the Center of the Godhead, interfered in the Creation in ways that created imbalances. Getting to play in the Creation Fields of the Great Spirit, many distortions occurred because of the concept of separation and the lack of keeping consciously connected to Creator's Will and great Wisdom. These imbalances, that brought the energies of death and destruction into the Universe, made it necessary for intervention and assistance from higher level Star Beings or angelic forces. This began a pattern of destruction and healing that exists to this day. The Fallen Angels made creations that the higher forces of pure spiritual intent had to keep intervening with, so as to bring back harmony and balance to the Universe. The Fallen Angels believed that they could exist and create independently outside of the wholeness of the Godhead.

The original blueprint or Tree of Life was one of wholeness and perfection and was tampered with by the Fallen Angels in the hope of controlling the creation of humanity on this Planet. This reality, that exists so far from the Center of Creation, had chosen free will somewhere along in its development, so was left open for outside influence. Because of some of our free will choices, many made in innocence and affected by outside influence, much was created out of balance, thus it being necessary to be realigned with the true loving Will of Great Spirit. As all is in perfect order in the connection to the Source of all life, even the 'Fall' can be seen as a way for the Souls of humanity to grow. It is possible that in the divine planning behind humanity's great journey of evolution, our God Parents determined that in the space-time continuum of the 3D World, the 'Fall' could better and more quickly allow us to experience the effects of our creations, therefore maturing us in our development as co-creators. The 'Fall' into the density of Matter teaches the karmic effect of experiencing all of what we create. This universal truth has also affected the 'Fallen Angels' who have created with Light and not Love, and who are ever in a struggle to create energy that will at least temporarily sustain their hunger and give them peace, because they see themselves as separate from the God Source. This form of manifesting is out of fear and separation and it is time for it to be healed. This struggle has affected most of humanity's existence and it is time to come to resolution and transformation.

I have gathered much information from ancient stories, as well as direct intuitive information, that has led me to the following. In the beginning, the Energy Grid of the Earth was infused with the elements of Creation, laying the foundation for further habitation by humanoids. The gift of free will was given to the Creator Gods and Goddesses of this dimension, as well as to humanity, and the Children of God were given room to create. Before 'the Fall' it is possible that the more masculine creation energies of Light became obsessed with the quickness of the more masculine elemental Creation forces of Air and Fire, wanting to create more quickly then what the more feminine elemental forces of Water and Earth were naturally encoded to go with. The Divine Feminine forces of Love tried to slow down the process, so as to allow the time for the gestation that was necessary before the birthing of new life. The Creator Male Gods pushed ahead by manifesting mis-creations that were out of balance with the feminine Goddess creational forces. These distorted human creations affected the elemental forces of Creation, bringing pain and suffering into existence, as well as the sense of separation within the human psyche. The intense emotions associated with the experiencing of these great imbalances, closed down our Heart Centers, shutting out further the Divine Love energy of the Mother energies of Creation, thereby the Divine Feminine. The balance of both Divine Masculine and Feminine creation forces working together in harmony and union is what can truly manifest a balanced unified field.

The Gods and Goddesses ended up disappearing from most of human consciousness, with many falling into the Shadow states of human consciousness. We became fragmented and separated from the unified sense of self, as we moved further away from the higher dimensions and filtered down into the 3D reality. For the most part in our waking and daily lives, we became disconnected from our divinely connected Higher Self. Except for the illuminated few, we were unable to have conscious communications between our parts. Our Higher Self moved out of the body consciousness and has been existing in another dimension beyond time and space, until now. Before our descent into the vibrations of this third Planet from the Sun, when our Souls where in higher dimensions, we were in constant communication between the various parts of our being. It is time to come back into communication with our separated parts, as well as to heal the lower frequencies that were created by being out of communication with our Higher Self.

It is important to know that as the unbalanced, unconscious energies surface, they will often at first wreak havoc in our lives and may cause much pain and suffering until they heal and return to the oneness. When we are truly through that process, the suffering will be turned to ecstasy and joy. Bringing in great compassion for self and others is a way to bring in more grace to the process. It is important to keep this perspective as we offer these separated aspects of our beings an opportunity to transmute back to their original positive intent and perfection. Simply put, love all parts of the Underworld of the Unconscious, free!

This time around the turn of the Great Wheel of evolution, it is important we take with us the lessons of the past Era of learning through separation. We must learn as much as we can about the real truths of our past and our present, in order to make enlightened decisions about our future. This time around the Wheel of Life, during this powerful paradigm shift, it is of utmost importance that we gather the knowledge of what has come before so as not to make the same mistakes again and to move forward with consciousness. The negative emotions and thoughts created out of this time must be evolved, so humanity can come back into wholeness and make the passage into the Fifth World.

According to many traditions, there has been destruction of the Planet three times before. Many have been remembering the times of Lemuria and Atlantis, needing to heal from that which occurred in the last cataclysm and the results of the great misuse of power. Some believe that the Lemurian civilization did not act as if they were separate in their beings nor from each other, the Planet, and all of life. Their energy has been likened to the loving presence of Dolphins. The times of the Lemurian civilization may be where our deep-seated yearnings and memories to return to the pure Garden of Eden come from, it being a reality on this Planet so very long ago. The Lemurians were not fully differentiated into male and female and held a heart-full connection to all of life. Some believe they were the ancient Ancestors of the Native Americans and indigenous people of the Americas, who went underground during the great flood to preserve the ancient knowledge of how to live in harmony and unity on the Mother Earth. All Native Americans have an emergence story of coming up from the Earth, and it appears to be the time for them to reveal the ancient knowledge they hold. Many people are looking to the indigenous cultures to assist with the returning to balance and the sharing of the original teachings. This wisdom has also been stored in many crystals and sacred sites. Many indigenous cultures acknowledge their star relation roots, and have kept the awareness of their inter-connectedness with the Earth and all life, taking the original spiritual instructions seriously.

Atlantis was seeded from another star system and there were beings present who had both positive and negative intent. In Atlantis the concept of Ego separation from Source was born, as well as the splitting deeper into the density of matter, with an over focus on technology and an overly focused self-will. The rift that began in the Heavens long ago, between the Fallen Angels and those who wished to stay in balance with Great Spirit's guidance, got carried out here on Earth. Creations were made that were not connected to the wholeness of the Godhead, where experimentation went against the law of free will. The feminine principle began to have less and less of a say, and only a few of the priests and priestesses stayed with and held the higher instructions and original teachings given to them. The majority of the ruler-ship got carried away with the misuse of Earth's sacred energy, as well as interfering with the natural evolution of her simpler inhabitants, birthed from her elements, thus furthering the development of hierarchal control on the Planet. The technology developed with the use of crystals, vortexes, and Earth grids, was being misused for power over others and ended up getting way out of control, manifesting a great imbalance of Earth's life energies, creating a great chain of destruction.

There is so much more to say about these most powerful ancient experiences, but know it is time to heal the memories and deep-seated traumas, experienced so very long ago, that have greatly affected our time here on the Planet. It is profoundly important to reclaim the right use of will and power. It is now time to come back into wholeness, now that humanity has had extensive experience with what it is to be separate. Most of us feel a deep longing to come back home to unity without interference from anything that is not for the highest good, be it from our own misguided psyches, our personal relationships, our governments, corporate powers, or unseen forces. We are in the choice factor, where we get to either be a part of the destruction of Earth and the continuation of control of humanity by a few, or of the re-creation, to be a part of the healing of the Tree of Life. As we re-member (a term of ancient shamanic practice – a way to come back into wholeness after being dis-membered) the original pure intent of the divine blueprint of the 'Human,' then we will be more able to manifest the New Earth. The increase in the intensity and occurrence of hurricanes coming from the vortex of the Caribbean, which many believe to be the central vortex of the destruction of Atlantis, may be partly the release and cleansing necessary in order to not re-create the same massive forces of destruction. Powerful vibrations of both negative and positive forces continue to exist unless released.

The Tree of Life teachings and symbology are important in nearly every culture. They give a framework in which to look at our separated parts, as well as that which unifies. The Tree of Life symbolizes the Axis of the Universe, the Center of the World. This 'Cosmic Tree' helps give form to our Universe as do the sacred directions and the elements. The Tree of Life is the spine of the Universe in its grandest sense, filtered down to the microcosm of a blueprint model for the human vertebral column. This spiritual 'Cosmic Tree' activates and instructs human evolution from the center of the galaxy, guiding us in our evolution.

In the shamanic path this sacred Tree is believed to support the roof of the Worlds, keeping us connected to the Heavens, as well as keeping us in contact with our roots, our Ancestors, and our past. With its branches reaching into the Sky and roots deep in the Earth, it dwells in the Three Worlds of Heaven, the Earth, and the Underworld. The shaman has always carried the ability to travel from the branches to the roots of the Tree, journeying between the Worlds. This is done for the sake of the community, so that communication occurs between the various Worlds and dimensions, as well as for individuals needing healing and reconnection between the separate parts of the psyche.

Before I ever received the information pertaining to the need for reunification of the human psyche from various outside sources, I received instruction by my guides in my shamanic healing work that it was time for unification of the polarities and the Worlds. I was shown that the Dimensions of the World were no longer going to have such a strong distinction between them and it was important to gain information from all Three Worlds, unified in one's sacred center deep inside, instead of journeying out of the body. These Cosmic Worlds are now beginning to be more integrated, as are the various parts that make up a human, since all is connected. The Upperworld, the Middleworld, and the Lowerworld are coming into closer communication with each other as the veil between the Worlds grows thin and the Tree of Life becomes more whole.

Following is a brief description of these Worlds, known well in shamanic tradition: *The Upperworld being the so called Heavens (the branches of the Tree) where our visions and the higher dimensions of spiritual forces exist; the Middleworld (the lower trunk) being the ordinary physical appearance of the material World as well as the subtler energies present here; and the Lowerworld (the roots) being the Unconscious, the so called hidden places of past experience both ancestral, personal, and collective, both painful and ecstatic. Much power is stored here which we greatly need at this time. The Lowerworld is somewhat different than the*

Underworld in that the Underworld contains solely the more painful and difficult energies, as tests and lessons.

In the shamanic healing work I would do in the past, I would journey for others to the different realms for insight and healing. When I started intuiting where to go for healing and guidance from more of my own inner deep Soul knowing, I changed for the most part from the traditional shamanic manner of journeying for others, even though I still do so at times. I saw how it was important to create a stronger sacred energy field in which to assist people to receive more of their own insights and to find their core self deep essence inside. The guides and allies still appear to assist in the transformation but now work more in the energy field of the person needing assistance, empowering them in their own self-awareness. All of this seems to be more affirmation that our bodies as well as the body of the Earth are to be part of the ascension into the next World. It is also time for each being to move into healthier self-empowerment and spiritual connection whereby one is assisted in having an experience that encourages self-knowing, even though it is still important to help each other. We all have particular gifts to give.

Some believe that the Tree of Life or 'World Tree' is changing to fit the incredible Light that is coming onto our Planet that does not have a Shadow. In alignment with the cosmic plan, this cosmic spine which carries spiritual energy through our bodies and Souls is generating strong Divine Feminine energies to balance the Creation field. As this energy comes in, activating the right side of the brain and our more intuitive states, it also increases our connection to the dream time and to the unconscious depths of the psyche. This life force also connects us more consciously to the Primal Mother, awakening deeply hidden emotions and memories as well as opening the doorways to long kept secrets. Within the Womb of the Great Mother and the feminine is carried the connection to the Creation energies and to the 'Divine Mystery' that has been cut off during these last Eras. Some say that the Kali Yuga has been a time when the feminine Creation forces have been furious at the mistreatment of the Earth as well as the shutdown and oppression of the feminine overall, with its subjugation to the Lower Worlds, and that she has been showering her anger towards humanity in ever increasing intensity as we reach the resolution of the Ages. It is time for the balance to return of the Divine Feminine forces of grace to help in the resolve of the Shadow. In the Hindu tradition, it is known that Kali came to Earth to fight the increasing number and intensity of demons that were appearing upon the Planet.

As we are being motivated by the powerful spiritual forces coming through at this time, so as to complete the lessons of the Nine Underworlds and rise up to meet the energies of the next Great Cycle of the Thirteen

Heavens, there are many teachings that are available to help us understand our next steps, as we wake up from the deep sleep of this past Era. This passageway from the unconsciousness of the Underworlds to the conscious awareness of the Heavens, may be a place where we will learn to go through the death doorway in a very different manner. We are being asked to make a major shift. I will go into more detail on the lessons of the Underworlds as well as the Thirteen Heavens later in the journey.

It is important to have simple models on which to base our understanding of what is occurring within the human psyche, as well as what is being asked of us. The Model of the psyche that seems to carry a deep wisdom about the separated aspects of our beings that far surpass the psychological understandings, come from the teachings of the Hawaiian Huna.

The three most basic parts of a human have a variety of names (mentioned earlier were the basic concepts of Carl Jung) and can also be broken down further, as our knowledge grows into even more subtle energies; but we will keep it as simple as possible. We are in an amazing learning curve as we gather the great Secrets of the Ages. The basic teachings of the ancients are the core knowledge that will hold the roots of the initiations that we are going through.

The Huna tradition comes from the Hawaiian Islands and is an ancient spiritual tradition. The essence of the Huna teachings is that the human being is made up of three selves or minds. They can most easily be called the Subconscious, the Conscious, and the Superconscious. In Huna the Subconscious is called the Unihipili, or Basic or Lower Self, the seat of the emotions, the child self, memory of past, sub-personalities, the record keeper part of self that runs the body and is connected to the Earth. This energy body is located just below the navel. The Conscious Mind is the Uhane or Middle aspect, talking or personality self, and is the part of the human that is conscious of its own existence and has the ability to reason, to form beliefs, has creative imagination, and is the director of action. It has been given free will to create, along with the Subconscious Self, and its focal point is around the energy field of the head. The third part is the Higher Self or Superconscious, called the Aumakua, and is the energy of our God-like, pure Essence Self or Soul. It is the 'wise teacher' part of a human, in which higher guidance and knowledge comes through bringing divine qualities such as compassion, patience, love, and forgiveness. This divine energy has been located above the head since the 'Fall,' but when fully activated and accessed, radiates throughout the entire energy field surrounding the body. This angelic part of us is there to assist us, but it needs to be consciously invoked and reintegrated back into our unified field to once again truly be present in waking life.

Our Higher Self communicates with our Unconscious; the Lower Self communicates with the Conscious Self. Contact with the Higher Self occurs naturally in sleep, the place of the Unconscious. According to the Huna tradition and to the teachings of Alice Bailey, there is no communication between our Conscious Self and Higher Self for the majority of humanity. The Huna teachings state that all Three Selves have their proper part to perform and that life, health, and happiness have to do with the harmonizing and communication of these Three Selves. It is also taught that each part has a perfect original blueprint in the spiritual realms that is available to tap into, that has not been tainted by this World of separation.

This spiritual model states that there is a silver Aka energy cord that connects the separate parts and that vital force, thought, and communication run through this cord. It is analogous to forming a Rainbow Bridge between the Worlds and the consciousness of a human. This ethereal substance (akin to Ether) shapeshifts to become a stronger web and communication cord when the more elevated Ego states are reached and we become more of a Soul-infused personality. We are being asked to elevate the personality, the Ego developed self, by working with the many tools available; to focus positive intent and mindfulness, as well as consciously elevating our emotional response. Being connected to our Higher Self helps us to embody our more divine qualities as well as assisting in the healing and illumination of the Shadow. We are also being asked to evolve the personality self past its over identification with itself, merging it with the divine Superconscious, so we can operate from a purer state and be guided into the energies of the 'Heavens' come to Earth and bring forth the Fifth World.

Very unique to the Huna teachings, as well as to the work of Alice Bailey, is that it is the Basic Self that takes prayers from the Middle or Conscious Self to the Higher Self and if this part (much like the Inner Child) has feelings of guilt, sin, unworthiness, or doubt, it will not deliver the prayer. When the Basic Self is holding negative beliefs, the process becomes compromised and it is as if the family members on all three floors are not communicating. The Basic Self shuts off the energy flow, so that the flow of information which is necessary for manifestation is interrupted. Often we wonder why our prayers are not answered and why we do not create the realities for which we consciously wish. It is what we hold unconsciously that tampers with our manifestations. In order to make sure we are reconnecting to the God-Self in our daily lives, it is important that we clear and integrate the Shadow aspects of our beings that have been created during this time of separation. The Huna tradition calls this process the 'Clearing of the Path.' The next section we will go deeper into this, as well as into the egoic minding process (Ego mind control), that will attempt to keep us from evolving to our next steps in fear of losing its power, individually and collectively.

It is very interesting that in the perfected plan of the Creation, we must evolve and transform these so called lower or unconscious parts of our beings in order to open to communication with the higher energies of integration. As in the initiation days of old, wisdom cannot be shared (or brought forth to full consciousness from the Higher Self) until the initiate has evolved to higher states, ensuring that spiritual knowledge is not misused. The Higher Self can work with healing the wounded self which is held deep in our emotional core. All parts must be taken in the great spiral movement forward. The integration of the separated parts initiates a greater alignment and peace and a unified purpose within oneself without one part sabotaging and taking energy from the other. As we heal and integrate, the issues and problems that get projected out in the World, causing conflict in families and countries and with Mother Nature, will shift. We can then truly assist in humanity's evolvement. Our 'healing and transformation' renews the Tree of Life and transforms the Tree of Knowledge of death and duality. As we unify our separated parts, it is as if the jigsaw pieces fit together once again, and outside negative influences that are not in alignment with God Source cannot penetrate. As we become more 'enlightened' it is as if we radiate out a vibration that spiritually transforms all that comes into our field.

I use the shamanic term dis-memberment and the term re-membered at times to refer to the taking apart of the various aspects of one's being, to be transformed and brought back to the Light and the Love, and the bringing back together in the re-memberment, the divinity of our wholeness. This gives us a chance to reconfigure our beings to match the higher level of vibrations that are coming onto the Earth, without falling apart, by being able to work consciously through these shifts.

Before we can even open to working with the healing and integration of our Shadow Self, we need to be able to strongly connect with our Higher Self, just as it is important to be connected to our power animal. We are already connected with our Conscious Self and our connection to the Unconscious will be further explored in the next section.

The Higher Self, in its conscious connection to the Godhead, has simultaneously kept an awareness of our fragmented aspects and our wholeness and can assist us greatly in the process of healing and integration, as a divine overseer of our path. Many have heard of the 144,000 Souls necessary to make a spiritual leap into consciousness into the Fifth World. Some believe that there are 144,000 original Souls that were present in the school of Earth and that everything else is a fragment of a whole Soul. Is it time for us to return to our Oversoul group, offering what we have learned as separated beings? If we connect to our Higher

Self, it will reconnect us to our Oversoul, which truly has the over-all higher perspective of the 'bigger picture' and will be a better guide for our return to wholeness than the Ego driven personality self with which we have overly identified.

The Higher Self is connected to other Higher Selves, as well as the higher archetypal energies, and is holding the highest intent to help us become more conscious as co-creators of the Fifth World. When we are ready, this part of us wants to be available as a guide, a spiritual teacher, giving us access to all of the intelligence in the Universe; the Ascended Masters, the Star Nations, and so much more. As stated earlier, it is necessary to come up with solutions from a higher perspective for the survival and transformation of humanity on this beautiful Earth. In order to survive and attune to the return of the 'Christ' energy, it is necessary to evolve to a higher frequency.

The voice that is heard during a vision quest, from a spirit guide who is connected to our Higher Self, will awaken our Higher Self in order to communicate understanding about the vision. This voice can also be heard through our connection to the pure elements of the Earth because they carry no separation from the Earth and can assist us to connect with her as co-creators in the web of life as we regain consciousness. I have witnessed the effect humans can have on weather when they are in deep communication with the heavenly forces, right here on Earth, while deeply being connected to the spirit in all things.

Connecting with and recognizing the Higher Self is a rather large subject and can not be fully satisfied by the written word and the human mind, but only through the experiencing of Love and the spiritual connection to ourselves. It takes practice and high intent, as well as opening up to one's intuitive sensitivities, to make contact with this most important part of our whole self. Taking time to be in a ceremonial space is a very powerful way to connect. Meditation is one positive step towards making and keeping contact. When you feel inspiration and blessings coming to you in your life, when mystical, synchronistic experiences move you to tears, when deep understanding and wisdom fill your mind, when your Heart flies wide open; this is the connection to one's Higher Self and the doorway to the Thirteen Heavens or Upperworlds.

The shaman has played an important role as an intermediary between the Worlds in many cultures, going through the Lowerworlds in their Dream Bodies, gaining access to the World of the higher archetypes. Connecting to one's power animal is one way to access the energies of the Higher Self in an instinctual and Soulful manner. When you are connected to your power animal and spirit guides, you can also make greater contact with your dreaming reality, both while awake and asleep. During this time of shifting realities, as the veils between the Worlds are thinning, the dream time and waking time are becoming one and it will be of utmost importance to be able to navigate in the watery-like, pure feeling sense and perfect-intuitive states of this realm. The endless possibilities and ability to connect with the higher aspects of oneself within the dreaming is very important for humanity's evolution at this time.

The energy of the source of the dream realm or luminous body emanates from deep within the dark womb of the Earth, coming from the dreaming from the pure Heart of the Mother, connected to the immense brilliant Light of Great Spirit. The Dream Body is attached energetically through the Navel and is the Center of true intuition. The Lizard is known to be a guardian of this Center. Could it be that this ability to remain conscious in the Dream Body is what will increase the connection and communication between all parts of the self and will assist in bringing in the element Ether and Heaven to Earth? There are many that are opening to the World of 'journeying' in the subtler spiritual realms beyond those who are practicing shamanism. Is this a way to develop and connect with our Aka Cords? Does the practice of journeying in our Dream Bodies elevate the presence of the Fifth World energies here on the Planet?

The Omphalus is a type of religious stone artifact that means 'navel' in Greek. According to the ancient Greeks, Zeus sent out two eagles to fly across the World and they met at its Center, the 'Navel' of the World, which the Omphalus represents. Many records indicate that the Omphalus Stone was a very holy object that was found at various Oracle Centers, the most well known being at Delphi. These amplifiers of the dream vortexes of the Earth's powers, were used to assist the abilities of a seer, who was then better able to have direct communication with one's higher aspects and the Gods and Goddesses. The veils of separation had fallen long ago and many methods were used to keep the doorways open, such as the building of sacred sites on a larger scale. The Dream Center is located at the Navel Center of one's more subtle energy body.

As we spoke of earlier, the powers of the Primordial Mother are now being activated, as well as the Divine Feminine. These powerful energies carry and support the realm of the dreaming and they open and protect this gateway, bringing in heightened states of awareness and presence from the cosmic source of the spiritual dream. 'Dreaming the World' awake is not as farfetched as it may sound.

When participating in a ceremony, the three parts of a human being are engaged, enticed, and encouraged to be brought on board. That is one reason why ceremony is such an integral part of the passage to greater wholeness. The Conscious or 'Talking Self' receives a message from the dreaming, understands the metaphor, and then is able to put forth a conscious intent towards the desired outcome of the ritual. The Basic or Younger Self, through the physical body and emotions, is engaged and moved by the enactment of the ritual process, which is very connected to the senses. The Higher Self moves with the excitement of the younger self and assists with the creating of spiritual magic in manifestation of the intent. The ceremonial path provides a safe, sacred container in which to draw in the helping spirits, with great grace and beauty, creating a mystical but yet more tangible dream space. This is a powerful way in which to experience the initiation into the Fifth World.

To be able to open to, communicate, and align with the totality of the new Tree of Life, evolving our personal sacred Tree, we also need to build and accumulate enough Mana, which translates to Prana, Qi, or life force. This needs to occur in order to reach and communicate with the Higher Self, as well as to join with the powerful forces coming onto the Planet. Energy is the basis of our entire manifested World and as the invisible World of energy is becoming more visible with the increasing levels of the element Ether, we are relearning to work with this at greater levels of sophistication all the time. It is possible that as humanity evolves we will develop technology that does not harm the Earth, as we balance and align with these more spiritual energies.

In the initiation process of the journey of healing, one uses and learns to work with the available energies to bring about change in consciousness of a momentous and revelatory nature. Part of what a ceremony or shamanic journey can do is build enough power to be able to transform the energy and consciousness to a place where it catapults itself to higher, more prana-full dimensions.

The Kahuna, which is a priest of the Huna tradition, uses the symbol of Water for Mana, rising like a fountain of Water to the Higher Self, then being returned to us like a 'rain shower of blessings and grace.' Once again we see that the vibration of the essence of Water is for the carrying out the 'High Will' and good wishes of the Great Spirit.

The importance of Mana or vital force to access and keep contact with the higher realms and parts of our being is a little shared concept. Most of the Mana is gathered by our Basic Self by: *1. Focus and attention, working with the creative imagination. 2. Nutritious foods. 3. Physical exercise. 4. Deep breathing practices. 5. Use of chi building practices, such as tai-chi or certain forms of yoga. 6. Chanting and spiritual singing. 7. Sacred dance. 8. Drumming. 9. Ceremonial magic. 10. Working with elements and elementals of Nature. 11. Giving back and giving thanks. 12. Ho'oponopono (making amends, forgiveness). 13. Being in a state of selfless Love.*

This force when gathered and raised is at times called the will or place of intent by modern psychology. In the Age or Era we are coming out of, the majority of the population has been driven or directed by personal will, the will to live, and the fundamental instinct of self-preservation. For much of humanity, the will to spiritually evolve has been tied up while the misuse of power by the hierarchy has kept us fighting over land and resources, while the forces of destruction drive the war-makers to continue their rule. As we are being motivated to complete the lessons of living in this way, and as we evolve to the higher centers of our beings, we are coming to the place where we can use the higher Will Center. To help assist in the opening of this Center, it is important to rebalance ourselves by opening to more of a state of being than of doing. This state allows for a slowing down of the overdone part of humanity's tendency to focus on outward manifestation. We have over-created, out of balance and connection with the Divine Feminine and therefore without Mother Earth's and one's Whole Self. This shifting of focus brings us into a state that connects us much more to the Divine Will and the right use of the power of Creation.

The sacred Hawk energies can help us align with the pure intent of the Divine Will, in connection with our personal pure will, carrying messages through to us, of our Soul purpose and direction. The Hawk can also gather the messages of our Higher Self as it reconnects to our entire being and assists us to truly reach the Heavens with our prayers. Hawk Medicine can bring forth the 'higher view' in order that our prayers come from a greater perspective.

To be connected to Divine Will it is important to remember the use of our human will in being of service where we naturally want to do good for others and the World. This can help in breaking the control of the Ego in the functioning of the will. We live in a mostly narcissistic society that truly needs to come back into balance. The will to do good is not to be carried out at the expense of one's self in codependant style, but from the glorious fulfillment of one's being, from wholeness, not lack. It is a similar energy when working with high intent in a ceremonial or healing process. With clear intent, the High Will of the participants can collectively increase the Mana and focus the healing energy for the good of all.

It is very important to be connected to the Divine Will and the higher planetary intention at this time in order to move into the Fifth World and the 'Land of the Flowers.' Part of the importance of studying great civilizations like the Maya, the Egyptians, and the Inca, is to reference and awaken to what it might be like to be in touch with a more spiritual, cosmic, and divinely connected Will, thus raising the basic intentions of the human personality.

The Divine Will is the force that carries out and implements the sacred purpose of the Godhead. The energy of the Will is a most potent force and it is what focuses and brings the higher intent into manifestation. On a small scale, the human self will enables one to carry out their plans and goals.

Where previously the Will of the Creator was more hidden, it is now much less so, revealing its divine face, asking us to join our personal wills with the most high, spiritual intent of the Godhead, for ourselves and for the World. This interconnection instructs us on the right use of power, while we are able to remember much of the wisdom we have gathered in our passage through the Underworlds. In order to align ourselves so as to be a part of the forward movement of grace, we must also get in touch with our personal higher destiny paths. As we relearn to trust our inner guidance, we can gain the ability to surrender and be receptive to be a Holy Chalice which has now been made readied to receive the true gifts of Creation. In doing so, we open the doorways to the higher truths and naturally gravitate to living a life with a will to do good, where knowledge is transmuted to wisdom, and unconditional Love is more and more present. The presence of unconditional Love for self and others assists in bringing in the holy energy that manifests the 'Mana of Grace' that encircles all things with Divine Love, mending the Sacred Hoop. As this holy force enters into us and the World, we are now more able to face our Shadows.

Call together the parts of you that have separated out in the 'Fall' into the denseness of Matter. See yourself as a beautiful tree that is calling life back to itself as you are fed with the 'Light without a Shadow' coming up through your roots from the New Earth, renewing you deeply as realignment occurs with the blessed Light and Love of the Heavens pouring onto you. You are able to love and transform that which no longer fits into this new Tree of Life that you are becoming, as the core of your essence self awakens. The presence of loving grace runs through your limbs, swaying with the shifts and changes that are needed for new growth. All parts are welcomed back home as they are re-membered into their original positive intent, in a unified field of a most 'Sacred Tree,' ready to flower into wondrous, spiritual realization.

9

The Ego Trance Shadow Dance

*O*ne *evening an old Cherokee told his grandson about a battle that*
goes on inside of people. He said: "My son, the battle is between two
wolves inside us all.

"One is Evil. It is anger, envy, jealousy, sorrow, regret, greed, arrogance,
self-pity, guilt, resentment, inferiority, lies, false pride, superiority, and
ego.

"The other is Good. It is joy, peace, love, hope, serenity, humility,
kindness, benevolence, empathy, generosity, truth, compassion and faith."

The grandson thought about it for a minute and then asked his
grandfather:
"Which wolf wins?"

The old Cherokee simply replied, "The one you feed."

Let us decide which one we will feed as we begin the dance!

The animal guides who offer assistance for this part of the journey are
both Owl and Raven. It is important to not be pulled back into
unconsciousness by this most powerful trance of the Ego, and the Shadow
World created from it. These sacred beings can assist you to heal and to
stay awake and aware while in the depths of your Underworld journey.
Owl has the ability to see in the dark and into the Shadows while shining
the light to illuminate that which needs to be seen, offering great wisdom
on the journey. Owl is the doorway into the unknown and teaches us about
deep change, releasing our fears of both the little and big gateways of
death and transformation.
Raven assists in the transformation of the Shadow, being very aware
of the dark and light energies contained within, able to fly back and forth
between the Worlds. Raven is beneficial for healing the wounded Inner
Child or Basic Self, being able to get into the dark places where fear and

wounding hide. Raven also can transform some of the heaviness of the difficult energies so that we can have some space to make it through this strong journey. Let them guide you through this passage, as we give thanks for their presence.

We also call in the presence of the Higher Self because the entrainment trance of the Ego Dance is one in which a spiritual perspective is truly necessary. This trance will lull us into believing in realities and concepts that are not always for our highest good (nor for the World's). This most wise part of us is now more accessible than ever, to assist us in the 'healing and transformation' that is so very important. Our higher teachers and guides will also come through as we join with our spiritual self.

In our journey through the Fourth Sun, while learning through separation and the lessons of being in a masculine energy dominated Cycle, a fragmented fear based aspect of our personality gradually developed, called the Ego. Because of descending into denser and denser states of being, much of humanity lost touch with the higher dimensions and guidance. Our Will Center developed into more of an Ego driven aspect of our beings, carrying out its wishes instead of the higher intention of our God Source. The Ego became a thought system based in an illusionary belief in separation, fear, selfishness, and death. The Ego became disconnected from its true Source and went into a deep trance of separation, becoming hungry with a voracious appetite, not being able to have access to the true Light and Love that feeds all things. Its hunger often turned into gratification of the physical senses, manifesting negative emotions and behaviors, such as selfishness, fear, obsessions, low self-esteem, anger, hatred, mistrust, lower base sexuality, addictions, power over others, abuse, violence, and war; thus creating the 'Nine Underworlds.' The illusion of a false sense of being fed, has kept the Ego ravenous, creating further fear based dramas to feed its out of control hunger, while the only true source and road back to wholeness is pure Love and Light from the Godhead.

In order to keep feeding itself, the Ego believed it had to keep creating negative behaviors that would keep it alive, as well as distracted from the 'True Essence Self.' Many of these behaviors were not acceptable to the Conscious Self and were put into the World of the Shadows (or Underworlds). The Shadow became the place where the unloved aspects were subjugated, creating the 'Nine Underworlds' of trance-like behaviors necessary to feed the Ego. In the Shadow trance dance, parts of our Conscious Self split into sub-personalities that were difficult to distinguish and that often hid in fear of rejection, humiliation, and judgment, surfacing in stressful situations. The Conscious Self became increasingly more unable to see and know the true Spiritual Self as the Ego became the ruler and director of these sub-personalities, affecting deeply the functioning of our daily personalities.

The word egoic is used throughout as an adjective to describe the active process and carrying out of the Ego's perspective and intent. The Ego has become an energy all of its own during the last Age of the Underworlds, and it is time for it to come back into balance with the rest of the human energy system. There is to be no more hierarchical rule in this next stage of humanity's evolvement. It is time for it to become part of a whole, integrated spiritual system of the evolving human-being.

The Nine Houses of the Underworld that were created from the so called negative behaviors of the egoic trance became lessons that needed to be understood and transformed. This is the Era we have been living in. My teacher Ohky Simine Forest has shared with me some of the deeper teachings about these Nine Houses of the Smoking Obsidian Mirror. This Cosmic Mirror reflects back to us what we have put underground and which needs to be transformed back into wholeness. The source of the defining of these Shadow obstacles or lessons, are derived mostly from Mayan wisdom teachings and following is a most basic list, with each House being a powerful journey unto itself. The Nine Houses of the Shadows include the following: *1. House of Illness and Vices 2. House of Deceitfulness and Torments 3. House of Punishment, Guilt, and Shame 4. House of Heart, moving out of personal concern and hurt to impersonality, where the mirror of love and hate is faced 5. House of Darkness, Nothingness, the Void 6. House of Ice or Coldness, where separation from life itself is faced 7. House of Last Attachments 8. House of Dismemberment and Disintegration 9. House of Death and Final Liberation.*

The meeting and facing of the 'Houses of our Shadows,' is what is being asked of us at this time of great purification. Each 'House' is being presented in rapid succession individually and collectively as we attempt to live life as usual. We are presently in an accelerated learning course as we are being pushed to the wall to resolve these Shadow forces. If you are one who truly wants to assist in the evolution of humanity, these 'Houses' must be faced and resolved with consciousness in order to begin the journey to the Higher Worlds, working with the Higher Self. As mentioned earlier, there are guardians of the gateways to the Thirteen Upperworlds that will not let us fully pass through until we Love and integrate our separate parts. We have always been given a way to access and receive guidance from the Heavens, but this is especially true as the veil between the Worlds grows thin and it is time to evolve to the upper limbs of the Tree of Life. However, we cannot truly leave the Underworlds until we resolve and learn from the obstacles in each House. So called negative powers cannot be annihilated; they can only be faced, transformed, and assimilated.

The last House of Death is a very real presence that everyone is aware we must go through, even if you are not on a shamanic path of transformation. The World of Matter and the veils between the realms have kept death a mystery for most of the living throughout this last Era. At this time on the Planet we are going to be witness to death in ever increasing intensity, and it is important to surrender to the many little deaths in all the other Houses so we may face the 'Big Death' with consciousness and spiritual connection. As intense as the other Eight Houses may seem in the moment, the final letting go and surrender to trusting fully in Great Spirit, as we shift realities and look most deeply at ourselves, is the greatest challenge for most people. As we head towards the moment of 2012, where all roads and time and space converge, we are being asked to honestly face ourselves and the World we have created, while still in a body. As we do this our bodies and the totality of who we are, get a chance to enter the Fifth World where death does not exist in the same way. The Ego does not surrender its control easily and must evolve to make this moment a most grace filled transformation instead of our most dreaded nightmare. The Obsidian Mirror of self reflection must be cleared. It is important for the Ego to remember its original positive intent.

As all things in this third dimension have had a dualistic purpose, the Ego has also had a positive role in the individuation of our Souls, as we reside in a physical vehicle. The Ego has continued working with our Will Center throughout time, in the development of discernment to ensure our survival and the development of the variety of choices given to us in this Planet of free will. Much of what this discernment has created, has given us the ability to know and develop our Souls into individuated awareness, in the great playground of Earth reality. But it has all gotten extremely out of balance, with the Ego believing it is the central controlling force of our beings. It is time for the Ego to become integrated with the entirety of our being, as it sources back into the Light and the Love, gaining sustenance from what truly gives life. The higher Ego states can truly be sustained when there is healing of the Shadow realms and reconnection to the wholeness of one's true self.

At times the Ego can operate connected to its original gifts and abilities, to identify and discern what is needed in different situations, as well as to analyze and categorize incoming information, as was necessary in the process of individuation. The Soul needed to develop its abilities to discern without depending solely on guidance from outside of itself. But so much of this ability has turned to judgment and further separation, thus the forming of the Shadow. There is a 'High Ego' and 'Low Ego,' and we have a choice of what road to take. With love and wisdom being our guides, the Ego and humanity can come back into a state of balance. If we try to repress or make the Ego the total villain, it will just bring more negative energy into the Shadow realms.

In the changing of beliefs and behaviors inside our psyches, as well as social changes outside, it is important not to use force or judgment in the healing of our Ego and the Shadow World, which just creates further separation. It is important to also identify what our limiting negative beliefs are and to transform them into positive life sustaining thoughts and affirmations. This is a topic of immense importance, even though I touch on it briefly. Negative thoughts held deep in the unconscious of our psyches, surface when we do the work of evolving the Ego and its Shadow. If not dealt with consciously they will limit 'healing and transformation.' It is important to release them from the core of where they originated, be it from childhood, negative patterns of your ancestry, past life experiences, or at Soul levels. There are many tools available to do this work. The mind has been intricately entwined with the Ego's trance dance, and needs to come back to its higher states of functioning. When the mind functions without higher spiritual guidance, it often becomes a part of the realm of the Ego. We are being given the appropriate tools to use with discernment, to transform these powerful parts of ourselves.

Let us invoke the powerful gifts contained in the Four Directions that are there for us to work with. It is important to get assistance and support, when that which may be difficult to look at in ourselves as well as in the World, is brought to our conscious awareness. The directions of our own personal Medicine Circle and that of the Earth's, not only carry challenges to be faced, but also many tools for transformation. We call on these gifts to assist us.

We call on the East with its Powers of freedom and clarity. We call on the South with its powers of trust and regeneration. We call on the West with its powers of intuition and humility. We call on the North with its powers of knowledge and wisdom. We call on the divine guidance of the Heavens and the grounding and sustenance of the Mother Earth. We call on the balancing of all directions by the 'Spiritual Center of Love and Light' for harmony, perseverance, and patience. We call on the assistance of the guardians and allies of each direction. We encourage the parts of your being that have forgotten their original pure intent, to remember their true spiritual source and to now make better choices, having experienced greater acceptance, understanding, and love.

"Do you have the patience to wait until your mind settles and the water clears? Can you remain unmoving until the right action answers by itself?": Tao Te Chin. Let us enter more deeply into the World of the Shadows and continue from a higher view.

The Shadow has developed into an energy field within the unconscious of the psyche, becoming the embodiment of all the impulses and qualities that the Ego has found unacceptable throughout time. The Shadow became the composite of all the dissociated and un-integrated energies, 'positive' as well as 'negative.' Positive aspects (such as positive intent, intuitive guidance, and other parts of the True Self), got mixed in with the negative aspects (such as doubt, shame, and low self-esteem), and became forgotten or discounted resources and talents. Quite often the positive aspects became entangled with the negative voices, created from limited beliefs, lower emotions, and traumas. This has made it difficult to manifest one's gifts without the negative voices being right along-side. These energies are held in a space somewhere between the Subconscious and the Ego, and often block our connection to the energies and gifts of the Unconscious. Much of our energy is held here. We need this energy to move ahead into the Fifth World.

The lower Ego wants to govern the human psyche and will go out of its way to keep the mind (not intellect) busy, keeping external dramas and inner negative stories going in order to keep feeding negative emotions to the Shadow Box. Pay attention by being mindful of its narcissistic behaviors of self-centeredness, control, the need to impress, possessiveness, power over others, and fear based behaviors and intent. Pay attention so that more will not be stored in the Shadow box. Pay special attention to negative self judgment and judgment of others. This affects all levels of our relationships. The larger powers of the collective Ego will also go so far as to create lifestyles that keep one distracted in the sustaining of an overly materialistic way of living, thus keeping spiritual connection and true inner work difficult to sustain in our busy outwardly focused daily lives, making us believe everything else is more important.

The development of most western influenced civilizations has been based on the fulfillment of the egoic process. It is not that technology and science are not wondrous advancements, taking us out of a more survivalist way of living, but developed out of balance with the Earth, our wholeness, and the gifts of all nations and all races considered, the advancements have become destructive.

At some point, all of the pent up pressure of unwanted energies that have been put into the Shadow realms, must come out in the day to day personality, often leading to negative behaviors, emotional problems, and bad health. This can happen when our wounds from the past are reactivated and our feelings are changed into negative emotional states by the awakened Shadow energies, and start to pour over, into our conscious reality. At times we re-create dramas, partly out of habit and programming and the control of the lower Ego, and partly because they surface to be seen, understood, and healed. Our beings have a God-code inside that always wants to return to spiritual health and well-being. But in the way our society is set up, when our wounds re-surface in day to day life, there is often a re-shaming that occurs and the un-lovable emotions go underground all over again. As the so called negative behaviors get acted out, they surface as sub-personality complexes. These complexes, which are comprised of archetypal negative forces, desires, aversions, and childhood wounds, will all clamor for attention with their oppositional intents, which splits and sabotages the higher purpose of the more conscious parts of our personality. These energy blocks become resistant to the Higher Self and may repress the gifts of the Inner Child, keeping it repressed and locked in the past. The pure Inner Child lives in the spontaneous moment. Denial of one's feelings keep the negative feeling states unable to surface for healing, thus trapping a vital source of our power and vitality. When the wounds held in the emotions get to transform, they add to the higher Mana enriching states, such as joy and ecstasy. These states build the energy of the Magical Divine Child, enabling us to exist in a more spiritual field of 'Oneness.' Wounds that are not healed make us slaves to our emotions and retard development of the higher centers. In the Shadow World, the traumas are held that keep one in a cycle of re-traumatization, until one gets off the wheel. When these complexes get released and reintegrated, much energy is regained.

The Shadow Self has at times been called the 'Guardian of the Threshold' and as we have stated, can block entrance to the true gifts of the Basic Self or Inner Child. Because our emotions or feeling states are so intertwined with this aspect of our beings, it can interfere with our more positive feeling states, contained here. When we do not consciously own our Shadow, it can be projected out into the World and onto others, with no real resolution of antagonistic energies. Our life becomes more of a projecting of our greatest fears than a creation of our greatest hopes. Some traditions speak of how the antagonistic energies played out in the World, are truly between the Dream Spirit and the Ego, with the unhealed Shadow often acting out in a violent manner. The wounds also block entrance to conscious dreaming and affect what is created there, as well as blocking what gets communicated back to our conscious awareness. The Ego does not want direct communication to occur with our Higher Self, because that would limit its dictatorship.

The collective Ego trance has created an archetypal and yet very real being that believes it must conquer and destroy in order to survive. It is time to come to resolution, healing, and harmony. The outer collective mirroring of this is destroying our World. Unresolved individual and collective ancestral wounds of the Ego are coming to explosive levels of amplification (like in the Middle East), and we need to believe in a more positive outcome of release and transformation as we face and heal what is right in front of us. The release and integration of the Shadow opens the door for the Higher Self to shine through, thus invoking more divinely inspired states of relating from our true Essence Self (the part of us connected to the Center of the Godhead) which remembers the true purity and sacredness of all life. The relational energies of the Venus transit are there for us to face and heal 'all of our relations.'

In many psychological circles, the part of the Ego that contains the emotional residues of trauma created by egoic behaviors is also called the Pain Body. It has an addictive quality and manifests a variety of symptoms. It keeps itself in fear of running out of negative emotion to keep it alive. It can make one believe that it is a way of life to exist in pain and suffering, and it often manifests as a strong habit that cannot do without high drama. When brought up to the surface by life experiences or by focusing on its healing, it may be experienced as a feeling of constriction, turbulence, heaviness, a sense of dread and anger, or an empty hole often located in the Solar Plexus of the energy body. When we still have strong emotional reactions to people and situations, we can be assured our Pain Body is alive and well. Another indication of its existence is the feeling of not being able to speak to anyone about painful experiences in our life, because the shame is overwhelming. I believe our positive intended Will Center (which the Solar Plexus is connected to), has been covered up by the Pain Body, blocking our ability to manifest healthy realities. The Pain Body is not our enemy, but to be witnessed and transformed and dissolved, thus giving room for the resolution of karma. When we no longer carry the shame and guilt of past grievances both from us and against us, we have a better chance to not attract the same karma creating dramas again and again.

The fears that are stuck in the Pain Body are getting more and more activated as the collective Pain Body of humanity is getting amplified. As we go through the journey of healing, remember that at times we are hooked into a greater collective extreme of emotions, like fear, because of what is occurring globally. As we individually transmute the fear, we assist in the healing for the collective as well.

"If this elephant of the mind is bound on all sides by the cord of mindfulness,
All fear disappears and complete happiness comes.
All enemies: all the tigers, lions, bears, elephants and serpents (of our emotions),
And all the keepers of hell; the demons and the horrors,
All of these are bound by the mastery of your mind,
And by the taming of that one mind, all are subdued,
Because from the mind are derived all fears and immeasurable sorrows."
- Shantideva

Fear is one of the strongest emotions that recycles negative energy into the Pain Body. We are talking about negative states of fear, not those fears which we need for survival while in a physical body, such as the positive use of fear in warning us of danger. We can use the Higher Self, the part of us that is able to look beyond the drama, to be able to give us perspective on how to work through it. We can release and learn from the fear by: *Acknowledging the fear.*Looking at what negative thoughts or states you have very recently been in.*Write down what you are afraid of. *Focus on getting as quiet as you can, while you breathe deeply.*Open your mind from this place of silence to see what choices are available to change the conditions of what is causing your fear, be it outward or inner.*Remember beyond the dread and fear, the place of great mystery where these energies do not exist.* Shift your attention to a higher state of awareness, imaging your self filled with Love and Light, while watching the fear disappear.

The Q'ero, descendants of the Inca, have healing processes to keep the Pain Body clean of its heavy energy so that the emotional body can carry lighter and more spiritual energies. Countries and most geographic locations also have a Pain Body created out of thousands of years of unhealed trauma. In the past many indigenous societies had practices and rituals that kept the Pain Body of their communities healed. We need to regain and use much of this knowledge in a new way, to recover our well-being and balance.

In the Andean tradition of the Q'ero, there were ancient teachings and practices developed for the resolving the accumulation of hucha, or heavy, dense energy. Humans are the only source of this heavy energy. Sami is light or refined energy and is what is needed to raise our level of consciousness and is much like the element Ether. The Q'ero do not judge this heavy energy, but believe that we humans create this energy through our mostly Ego based interactions with each other and the natural World, generated by the power of our more negative emotions, thoughts, and actions. If this energy is not cleansed and integrated back into our systems, it keeps us from functioning optimally and prevents us from engaging in more conscious ways of living. Sounds like the Shadow energies to me! It is our responsibility to keep our energy fields clean and refined if we wish to evolve. There are a number of practices for working with this, but the Q'ero priests are masters at working with energy and they have a simple practice that I will share with you.

Through intention, the heavy energy or hucha is drawn from throughout one's energy field to just above the navel area (Dream Center), released into the Pacha Mama or Mother Earth, while high levels of Light or energy are pulled in from above the head, filling in the space where the heavy hucha had been. When done with respect and permission, the Earth loves this energy and uses it like food or an energetic meal, composting this heavy energy, returning it to us as sami, energy that has been refined. Since I learned about this process I have added a new component to it, because the Earth is busy in its own transformation and I was shown another way. This way we work with a column of cosmic energy that we invoke before us. Call in a column of the spiritual Light and Love without a Shadow, envisioning it before you as it reaches from Earth to Heaven. Gather the heavy hucha once again to your Navel Center, offering it to the column of Light and Love to be transformed and returned to you and the Earth as sacred sami or Mana.

As important as it is to release this energy, it is also important not to continue to generate it by creating further negatively emotionally charged situations. As we clear our heavy hucha and therefore our Dream Centers of heavy energy, this will allow us to open up communications with our higher aspects. Our Dream Centers are strongly connected to our intuitive feminine aspects.

The shamans and medicine people who have worked with Plant Medicines throughout time, know that the clearing of our heavy energy is a very important part of what the Plant Medicines assist with, in order to have clear visions and to have communication with higher guidance. This clearing usually happens with the purging of the physical body which makes room for the emotional clearing; the inherent wisdom of the gifts of Mother Nature.

Remember that as we are being asked to clear and balance this heavy energy, the Mother Earth, because of the energies of dissonance created within her own energy body or field, is also balancing herself within the great polarity shift we are in. Her weather is getting extreme, as well as the typical seasons being drastically altered, as the Old World is being purified and rebalanced. The four elements that personify the four seasons are going through their own transformation, as the most spiritual element Ether, changes everything in its path, beyond the imbalances created by human interference. The Underworld energy is also opening to meet the Upperworlds and we are not only experiencing more intense emotions and natural disasters, but many more illnesses, as these forces come up through the cracks of our repressed beings. All this needs to be energetically as well as physically transformed. It is of utmost importance that we work with the Earth and her changes and not against her. We are being asked to form a conscious alliance once again with the Mother Earth, as well as with all aspects of ourselves and the World that has been in darkness.

Since our emotional bodies contain our core wounding, it is important that we become 'Spiritual Warriors,' gathering the courage and wisdom to go into the depths, to heal and regain our lost, pure energy held there. It takes much courage to take a conscious look inward and face the black obsidian mirror of our own Shadow realms.

Ohky Forest speaks of the 'Five Core Wounds' which all others relate to. The directions of the Medicine Wheel offer a map of where these wounds are to be faced in our personal Medicine Fields.

"To the East we carry the Wounds of Betrayal; to the South we carry the Wounds of Abandonment; to the West the Wounds of Humiliation; to the North the Wounds of Rejection. The nature of all Wounds comes from the emotion of deep injustice. We develop three primary emotions from these Wounds; Fear (as an illusionary form of protection), Anger (as need to express our wounds), and Sadness (the deepest held emotion, believing that we are unloved)."

Remember that we come from the ever present Love and the Light of the spiritual core of Creation and that is where the center of the true healing of all wounds will come from. As we continue on our journey, it is most important to heal these core wounds and burdens from the past and not create more from our emotionally reactive states of the present.

The subjugation, disrespect, and abuse of the more dream-like intuitive feminine energies, including Mother Earth, may have possibly been a large part of what made clear communication difficult between the various aspects of what makes up a human being. As we mentioned previously, one of the gifts of the Dream Body is its ability to reveal what the Conscious Mind is not seeing; it is a way your Shadow World can be revealed and healed. The Dream Body has been busy trying to resolve much of what has been difficult to resolve consciously. It is so busy with this that it doesn't always get to show us the higher truth of ourselves and our World. The Dream Body is connected by a silver, energetic Aka Cord, and this works much like a telephone cord to bring in the positive intent and energy of grace from the Higher Self.

Women have continued to be connected to the Underworld and the Shadow throughout time, partly through the experiencing of their monthly Moon Cycle. During this Cycle, negative energy is shed, and in ancient times was offered ceremonially to the Mother Earth, returning to her the heavy hucha in a respectful manner, as in the Peruvian healing process. Each month a woman is forced to look at aspects of herself and her life that may not be so appealing or pleasant, as her heavy emotional hucha is hormonally stirred. She must face her Obsidian Mirror image. Not only is this true for the monthly cycle, but it is also experienced in a different manner in the initiatory passage of menopause. During menopause a woman must pass through the Fire of her own creative life forces and the emotional waves of her personal Underworld and her egoic attachments to youth and fertility, as well as to her identity as a mother. Her test is to come through this passageway with more of a sense of true power, wisdom, and heartfelt presence, based on going through a very deep, inner journey. In going through nine months of gestation for the bringing forth of life, a woman has to go through layers of intense emotional states to be able to be present for birthing, teaching one how to ride through the waves. Birthing forth one's Crone is as intense and is usually a much longer process.

As Maiden, Mother, and Crone, the feminine has been asked throughout time to keep going into the depths and to come through with greater conscious knowledge and wisdom. It is not that men are not also asked to go into the depths of their Souls and psyches. But most men in the World have not been given a connection to the Cycles of Life (unless they have been part of ceremonial ways), nor to the societal norms of women, to assist and support them through this journey. Many are now taking the time to enlist assistance to do so for their inner journey, especially since the consciousness raising time of the sixties.

In many of the Myths of Descent, it is the Divine Queen or Priestess who must make the descent to the Underworlds or Shadows, and if she has the 'correct way' of presenting herself to the guardians of each level, she is able to pass and become more truly human, earthy, and humbled by the journey. The guardians truly know if she has learned the lessons of the Underworlds. I believe the sacred feminine has made such a descent in the last 5,200 years and is being asked to be reborn, carrying the wisdom and transformational energies needed to heal and transform the depths of Creation. As these Shadow realms are healed, the returned transformed energy can be united and harmonized with all that has not been in union throughout the past Ages, being assisted by the exalted and evolved Venus, present in the feminine energies of all life.

The purpose and knowing of the Great Spirit, being the source and guidance beyond masculine or feminine delineation, behind all of the pulses and energies of the various Ages may not always be clear to us. I have continued listening and observing, searching for higher guidance and asking for forgiveness for any understandings put forth that offend. In the creation of the Fourth World, it appears that the Divine Feminine, the voice of the Great Mother, was possibly meant to take a back seat for awhile. This may have been necessary so that the more masculine Soul energies could develop further, for in the Matriarchal times, it was the other way around. It appears as if the heavenly masculine Creation forces got caught in the imbalances of creating out of sync with the Divine Feminine, in the denser energy fields of the Earth plane (which we will go into further later). The resulting Shadow realms may have been why the Divine Masculine force of the Christ, the Sun of the Creator, needed to birth onto the Planet, giving a way to clear the energy (sin), created by the separation of these most primal life force powers.

The harmony of the dance of the Earth and Sky and the Sun and Moon, and the fire in the belly of the Mother Earth, has kept a presence for us of how the Light and the Dark, the masculine and the feminine, and Spirit and Matter, can exist in a state of conscious unification. This awareness is most important for the journey to the 'Thirteen Heavens' and the healing of the so called 'sins' of our Ancestors and our past misperceptions of reality.

As the energy of the more masculine Ego minded process (element of Air), became more out of balance and more controlling of what it accepted and what it did not, discernment (for survival's sake) turned into judgments, creating further separation of the feeling World into the Underworld. The sacred Waters of the higher feeling states were lowered into the more negative emotions of repression and non-acceptance. The more feminine energies that became less desirable, that appeared to weaken the will force of the Ego, were subjugated to the Underworlds. The more feminine feeling states of the senses were not comfortable for the egoic mind. But this is a Water Planet, a place to learn about the feeling states, and the sacred Waters cannot be denied. In the further creation of the Fourth World, that which was being manifested was being developed out of incomplete energies. This is not so much about men and women, but about masculine and feminine primal forces. What occurs in these most powerful creation forces is also what gets played out in the social structures and norms of the World. Our Souls are here for experience and learning, and both primal forces, masculine and feminine, are being given a chance to do so through the very different energies of each 'World.'

In the denial process of the emotions, many of the lower emotions became caught in the body and could not come into balance with the evolvement of the mental body and the development of technology. Emotions are strong feelings that have gotten out of balance with the Higher Self and states of loving acceptance. Feelings are a natural part of our watery beings. Parts of the Basic Self were caught in survival level energies and fears and now need to be released so that the more evolved feeling states such as ecstasy and joy can be experienced more often. These states are necessary for the Mana or nectar needed to feed the Hummingbird Medicine of the 'Flowering Soul' of the Fifth World. The Hummingbird has the ability to handle and bring forth great levels of Light and the immense joy that comes with it.

In the focus on Eve in the Creation stories, the first woman Lilith is put aside as an unwanted part of the feminine aspects of the Creation. She represents the feminine energies of raw sexuality, wildness, and free thinking, and was pushed aside so that the archetypal energies of Eve, a more controlled and weaker aspect of the feminine, would be accepted and exemplified. It is possible that Lilith, as a most primal energy of the Great Mother and of Mother Nature, was part of the completion of the conduit necessary to keep the spiritually rarefied energy of the 'Aka Cords' of communication open, being connected by the intuitive feeling sense. This uncontrollable wild card and yet very real power of Creation, may have been a way in which humanity would have been able to keep a connection to the higher emotions and feeling states, as well as to clearer visionary states of perception. This force may have gone underground, but has still been very present in our journey through the Underworlds.

The archetypal energy of Lilith may have turned into strong primal feminine forces such as Kali and Durga from her time in a repressed state, and is now working her way through, transforming all in her path. This primal feminine force is also going through the healing of its own repressed emotions that have at times turned to anger and rage. As she heals the feminine, forces contained in all human-beings also release and transform, allowing the presence of her gifts to be revealed. It is important to have contact with this force, so as to have the wisdom necessary to make the journey to the Underworlds. To go through the Underworlds without this contact, one can get lost. These sacred powers hold the Light in the Dark, so as to be able to look within, the place of the West and the womb cave. Once again this is not about man versus woman, but about the imbalance between the two. When born in either a male or female body, it is important to open to more traditionally known feminine sensitivities such as intuition and dreaming in order to work with the Shadow.

In the past, in many indigenous societies, there were cultural norms that kept the Ego from ruling the individual and the community. As part of the Iroquois Federation and its governing body, there was a sacred circle of Wise Women that made the final decision about whom the Chief would be. This carefully chosen circle of women also made the final decision on whether it would be for the good of the people to go to war. For the positive functioning of a Sacred Circle, the Ego must step aside. It wasn't until the takeover of the indigenous people that their communities got way out of balance, even though throughout the Planet the changes were already in the Collective Unconscious, affecting all of life. Maybe this is another teaching we need to learn from the indigenous peoples' ways.

Because of the Red Race being given the guardianship of the Earth, the societal balancing of the Ego was more of a natural way of existing, even though some imbalance was still present. The element of Earth is a slower acting energy that takes time in making changes or movement. The low Ego has more of a fiery nature, not waiting to get agreement from the other parts before taking action. The White Race is the caretaker of this element (Fire), if you remember from previous information given, and the Native American is the caretaker of the more feminine and slow moving element of Earth. Does that sound a little like the way of some male dominated governments that act before getting true agreement from the whole? Much of what makes up our so called Democracy, was taken from the Iroquois Federation's governing rules and regulations. In the development of Democracy, the overseeing of decisions made by the sacred Circle of Woman was not included, which takes away the influence of not only the Wisdom Keepers, but the ability to think before acting! More of the imbalances of the inner psyche acted out in the outside World.

The journey of healing of the Underworlds is one that is difficult for both men and women without strong guidance and assistance, for even shamans can get lost in the Underworlds and Shadows, lashing out at images and projections in the 'Great Smoking Mirror,' losing the true sight, overwhelmed by the powers held here. We can develop the gifts given to us to work with, so that each day we can grow in learning how to use our higher attributes; but at times we must ask for help in the descent and healing.

The shamanic path has always worked with the forces of the Light as well as with the forces of the Dark, and shamans have always had to face their own Shadow in order to know how to work with these energies with others. Shadow dancing within this path is a challenging process of transforming the dark self or side to become an ally in the journey, as well as learning to 'eat' or absorb one's Shadow in a ritualistic manner, transforming it into the 'food' needed for evolvement. In the development of this journey, my own Shadow has continually pursued me, asking to be brought into the light of my consciousness. As I journey through this chapter on the Shadow, there is a Full Moon Eclipse occurring, and it is also the Wesak Full Moon (day of celebration of Buddha's birthday and enlightenment). Eclipses are known as a time when the Shadow forces are brought up in the emotional body and can be then consciously worked with. As I am editing and rewriting this section, we are between another solar and lunar eclipse. I am once again between two powerful eclipses that have pushed me to transform the energies held in the deepest layers of my Shadow World. Throughout the writing of this book, I have found myself connected with Mother Nature and situations that are profoundly within the web of this process. I should remember that in the shamanic way of living and true to all transformative lifestyles or undertakings, there is no real separation from the entirety of one's life and existence.

In my work with others in the depths of their psyches, I would at times see a shadowy figure whenever it was time to work with a painful energy. This Shadow would appear especially when I would be talking to the Inner Child or Basic Self, the young, feeling sense, which lives partly in the land of the Unconscious. When I would try to communicate with this Shadow, it would attempt to get bigger and take on a scary shape, or at times to disappear and to hide. When I would bring in a spirit guide, teacher, or a power animal or ally, then it would become more open to communication; and when asked what its purpose was, it usually would say to protect the

Inner Child. I discovered that it had at one point functioned to protect the innocent energies of the Inner Child from strong emotions created by negative traumas. Because it had gone too long unacknowledged and was held to its original responsibility as protector at the doorway between the Worlds, it had gathered much negative energy and had difficulty changing to fit into present time. Because it continued to receive the negative food of the Ego, it could no longer keep its ability to transform and intuit what was needed in each moment from higher Source.

This part of us contains an abundance of repressed energy and carries the Shadow energies such as shame, anger, fear, and self-hate. Our own personal Shadow being believed its job was to protect the innocent childlike, creative, juicy life force filled energies, if one was not protected by outside (parents or other adults) from trauma. Because this force is not aware of passing time, being held out of conscious reality, it does not see that the trauma has passed and that one has grown up to be an adult who can now be free to make its own better choices. This Shadow-like misguided being tends to stop one from making positive change by over-doing its job and not knowing how to connect with higher guidance. Its inherent energy began with positive intent, and it needs to be reminded what that is, as well as be given a new job more connected to present time and positive intent. As we heal these personal Shadows, it also frees up the life force of the Inner Child who no longer needs to fear its survival. This allows for more happiness and creativity to be experienced, as each moment is treated as new, which creates more sacred Mana and joyful power which is necessary for the journey to the Upperworlds.

In a ceremonial manner, within a sacred container and with spirit helpers and guides present, the Shadow can be brought up and transformed. This clears the gateway so that the messages of the Higher Self, in symbolic and energetic form, accessed through the Basic Self, can come forth. As this doorway is cleared, the prayers and positive intent of the conscious mind can also be heard by the Higher Self. The Ego and the Shadow can be dis-membered (taken apart) and then re-membered (reunited) so that they can come back into wholeness. The Body Elemental (spoken about in the chapter on elementals) has also been deeply influenced and limited by the presence of the Shadow, thus affecting the healthy development and smooth running of the body. This aspect needs transformation as well.

The higher Ego states can be accentuated, made out of the substance of reborn energies channeled and transmuted into the positive forces of cooperation; non-aggressive, inclusive, service oriented, non-competitive, spirit-invoking states of the higher Will Center of harmony and beauty. The Shadow needs to be relieved of its duty and freed so it does not block or guard the dreaming or the gifts of the Inner Child. The saying in the

Bible, *"Be as a child if you want to enter the kingdom of Heaven,"* seems pertinent here. When the innocence of the magical child is rediscovered, there appears a myriad of joyful new solutions on how to live a life of creativity and joy, as well as the uncovering of the true self. Much of our sacred life force resides here.

The more the sub-personalities (various Ego controlled personalities developed as coping mechanisms to deal with trauma) get to come back to the center of their original pure intent and unity, and the Ego is fed a more pure energy once again, then the higher egoic self can return as part of the whole self. Every part of Creation has a purpose and the Ego needs to step down from its lead rule and join into the whole. It takes some major shapeshifting and ceremonial building of Mana juice, as well as the presence of some powerful spirit guides, to balance the will of the Ego gone wild. The Ego is based on the past and fights being in the moment. *The Power of Now* by Ekhart Tolle, speaks clearly on this. The Ego has been away from the true source of its being for so long it is in fear of what will happen if the Higher Self takes over. In truth the Ego can be lifted up to a greater experience and no longer will have to feed on fear and past traumas. The cosmic energy coming through the Center of the Mother Earth also supports this process, collectively raising the vibration and consciousness of our beings, even if we resist. The resistance only causes more pain, and it is time to move ahead with the 'Spirit of Grace.'

To face our Egos and Shadows it is important to remain impersonal so as not to get caught in its trance once again, while at the same time being in a state of great compassion and unconditional Love for self and others, keeping a higher view and witness to what is occurring at all times. As we also clear and purify the negative emotions that we have gathered and stored in our bodies, our Shadow memories, then the refined emotions can strengthen our Soul connection and help us access the Higher Self. Emotions are created by the narcissistic waves of the Ego, manifested by the negative thought process, whereas true feelings reside somewhere underneath these reactionary strong emotional states.

When we are able to integrate these separated parts of our beings and be guided by our more evolved spiritual aspects, we can begin to live by higher truths instead of being controlled by egoic states of being based on the need to conquer, misuse power, and fill the great essence-self hole inside. "As above so below, as within so without;" as our lives become more integrated in our psyches, we will mirror this in the World that we create. With the great spiritual transformation of an Ego driven and developed World, we can then enjoy the great variety of experiences that we can have with the glorious diversity of life that is still available to us, as we see the other person, group, country, and race, as a divine gift from the Creator.

Listen to the instructions of your Higher Self, as well as to the teachings of the spiritual paths that speak deeply to you; throughout time, sacred truths in which to remember the original instructions, have survived hidden inside the religions of the World. Live a life that is in tune with your true self. Inner work is very important, but the way we live in our sacred Circle of Life all around us, in all directions, is how we carry the changes through in our relationships, our communities, and our work in the World. Returning to the simple truths as given by many indigenous cultures is one way to support the work of true evolvement, including the simple truths behind most spiritual paths.

One unknown Native American author speaks of the Ten Native American Commandments of Earth:

1. *Remain close to the Great Spirit.*
2. *Show great respect for your fellow beings.*
3. *Give assistance and kindness wherever needed.*
4. *Be truthful and honest at all times.*
5. *Do what you know to be right.*
6. *Look after the well-being of mind, body, and spirit.*
7. *Treat the Earth and all that dwell thereon with respect.*
8. *Take full responsibility for your actions.*
9. *Dedicate a share of your efforts to the greater good.*
10. *Work together for the benefit of all mankind.*

The Tree of Life can now become renewed and realigned as communication with more of our totality is regained. Now we can come more often from our higher guidance, choosing the loftier emotions such as non-attachment instead of fear and jealousy, mindfulness instead of desire, trust instead of fear, Love instead of obsession and greed, wisdom instead of ignorance. This rebuilds the 'Sacred Tree' so it can emanate forth the divine vibrations of true bliss and grace into physical manifestation. It is time to dance a new Sacred Dance, where the fragmented tortured Soul can come back home to its wholeness. What an incredible chance we have to remember the presence of the God-Goddess-Source in every cell, in every Shadow, in all beings and in all of life.

So use the sacred elemental gift of Air wisely; watch your beliefs, thoughts, and words so that they may be the beautiful butterflies of Creation that can recognize, reconcile, and harmonize with the higher intent. Honor your Earth energies, as those which have given you a sense of home, nurturance, structure, and form, and do not get overly attached and stuck in ways of living that no longer serve the evolving self. Do pay close attention to the Fire in your belly so that you do not act before you think. Open to the most powerful, feminine, flowing and connecting aspects of the healing power of the sacred Waters, which are birthing you in the Womb of the Divine Mother, as we enter the Doorway to the Spirit of Grace and the healing of the Emotional Body.

10

The Healing Water of Grace

We share with you as the 'Healing Water of Grace.' We are the movement and flow of the crystalline force of healing beauty and Love, freeing humanity with the flow of pure Shakti, swirling and opening the receptive ventricles of the 'Flowering Soul,' quenching the thirst of long empty caverns. We come through the doorway of Venus pouring down from the Holy Chalice of Aquarius, filtering through the multi-colored prism of the garments of the Rainbow Goddess. This essence of our 'Waters of Grace' is the pathway in which the blessings of Love and Light, joined of Spirit in Matter, fall like a fresh spring rain on the body of the Mother and her children. It is time to heal the wounds of the World and of humanity. The emotional body has held the pain of separation for such a very long time and it longs for a return to the feeling life of joy, bliss, and Love.

Pouring from the Heavens into the Waters falling from the sky, our Waters are joined together with the Waters of Mother Earth, bringing renewal in its purist form, being akin to the Universal Energy which runs through all things and dimensions of Light and Love. Your original Souls have all been birthed from our pure and Holy Waters. The Waters of the Mother respond, thirsting to cleanse, replenish, and renew the places that have been abused and dishonored. There is great wisdom in how the Mother Earth is realigning herself and working with all the sacred elements, shifting the consciousness of all in her path. Through our sacred Waters the element Ether enters, and grace comes in to transform and join the elements and all that has existed in separation. The blessed Waters break up the inertia and rigidity of the Underworld, bringing its Shadows and emotions forth to individually and collectively be healed and cleansed.

Humanity was birthed from the Holy Waters, out of the Sacred Pools of Creation, Water being the most prevalent element in the body and on the Earth, nourishing all of life on the Planet. The memory of all history is stored within the crystalline structure of Water. The renewed 'Water of Life' is a balancing force carrying the energy of neutrality; it does not have a positive or a negative charge. It is that which ties all things together in a unified field. When one feels surrounded and protected by the pool of the 'Waters of Grace,' all parts of you can be gathered together in a state of true connection and harmony, no longer having predominate feelings of judgment and separation, but of joy, harmony, and Love.

At this time on the Planet, it is most important to work with our liquid being-ness of grace, to soothe and transform the emotional body and to bring it back into balance. Your Waters have worked hard to keep your beings in flow, in spite of the force of friction created by the state of separation. The true feeling self has been caught in strong reactionary, emotional energies of the past, keeping one separate from being in present time. Use these emotional reactionary states as guideposts and entrance ways to know what to transform in your being, so that your true essence self can flower open to a new moment, new day, with each day being full of exciting new possibilities.

Let our sacred Waters cleanse the entrance to your Dreambody, so you may more consciously navigate the oceanic World of the dreamtime, the pure place of intuition, which penetrates the essence of the Worlds beyond the reflections of the Ego. Being able to be aware and awake in the dreamtime will assist you to fulfill your spiritually aligned paths, enabling you to see with true vision and to swim in the sacred Mana fluidity of Source.

Open to us, releasing the deepest fears of your being, that we will overwhelm you if we are fully let in. The other sacred elements are to be called in to provide a container in which to hold me, and to carry you through this most powerful transformation. Fear is the great suppressor of all that needs to be released and transformed and blocks true healing. It is only as powerful as you let it be.

We feel how many of you are afraid of the overwhelming nature of the great 'Primordial Waters of the Womb' of the birth of humanity. You contain the Holy Waters and we long to be reborn anew in you. The 'Water of Grace' will help you remember the spiritual energy contained within your emotions, elevating them to higher feeling states. Do not fear releasing your emotions, for they are part of you and will not destroy you. They are movements of energy and life force. When this most sacred part of humanity got frozen through the experience of being separated from God Source, with no direct lines of communication and divine support, much of your life force was trapped. Feelings of fear arose, fear of survival and a fear of not belonging, of not truly feeling at home. When even more of the feeling sense of your being was separated out because it was dishonored through the disrespect of the feminine and the Earth, more of your totality went underground. States of fear, loneliness, anger, sadness, and shame became prevalent.

The liquid Light of unconditional Love and Beauty is here to heal the womb of this most sacred Creation, of the Mother, of the wombs of all women, and the Hearts of all of humanity. As this healing occurs, be prepared to feel more for the Earth and each other, rejoining the sacred web of life that connects everything. But remember that when you are connected in your totality, you will have the awareness and tools you need to help you cope with the overwhelming nature of the floodwaters rushing through. When the sacred Water of the womb is healed, what is created in the World will no longer be mixed with the traumas of your past.

As the various aspects of humanity developed in separation, the emotions became a conduit to carry negative as well as positive energies throughout our beings. The part of you that has forgotten to function as part of the whole cannot be allowed to keep creating out of not being fully connected to your spiritual knowing. Notice if there is resistance to letting in the assistance of Spirit and ask yourself why you do not open. Feel the walls that surround you and ask if they are serving your highest wishes and dreams. Do you want to continue living in a World that is out of balance, feelings gone wild, with emotions ruled by negative thinking and projections of unhealed places? Feelings are a beautiful conduit to what surrounds you, relaying valuable information when tuned into the intuitive self, sharing the wisdom of discernment and of what to create. Feelings are essential to activate and manifest your dreams and desires.

Notice how your unhealed emotional body may tend to be drawn to negative situations. Use our liquid grace to assist in transforming your emotional being when you find yourself in negative dramas. You do not need to struggle alone. Much learning has occurred in this manner, but now it is time for transformation and healing. When the Divine Mind and Heart are activated you will no longer need to live this way. We also can help crystallize your thinking process to a higher level of mind, cleansing the negative thinking process that no longer serves your higher good. With a rebalancing of power and unification of the various parts of your being, your emotional nature can now be infused with and hold more grace for longer periods of time.

Let yourself be cleansed and surrender to the 'Water of Grace.' We of the 'Waters of the Heavens' unified with the 'Waters of the Earth' are here to assist. We respond well to prayer and positive vibrations. Encourage the Child within you to let go of the fear that it is not safe to express itself; let it return to the embryonic fluid of cosmic rebirthing. As you bath in our Waters, your younger self will be able to gently release its fear of not being protected from past traumas in present time and will no longer be as enticed by the illusions of safety given by being emotionally frozen. Your Inner Child will be able to break out of the trance that has kept it believing it is alone, held in a trauma from the past, unable to fully access the spiritual gifts that are its birthright. The wounded being inside is crying for release. As the Child within returns to a state of open hearted innocence, trust, and joyful wonder, it will remember its original state as a Divine Magical Child, held in ecstatic communion with the 'Water of Grace.' Encourage the child within to play with the Water Beings of the Dolphins, the Turtles, and the Frogs, bringing in forgotten states of joy and ecstasy.

Invite in the healing 'Waters of Grace' when you feel overwhelmed by your emotions; name them, invoke our blessings and we will respond; but make sure not to deny your feelings and emotions, for they are how we enter into your World. Open your spiritual eyes to see the truth of the situation with your higher mind; breathe into it, go into a sacred space within yourself. You are joined with us in the 'Waters of Life.' Remember that you are truly divine and that there is nothing to fear because you will always return to the center.

There are guardians that can assist you to face your fears. Call to those you trust and embrace them as you feel yourself in darkness, for they know the way. Call on Ix Balam, the sacred Water Star Jaguar Deity, who comes forth with the blue stars of the healing Waters on his black, silky body. This deity has returned to assist in the bringing forth of this most sacred time of awakening on your beloved Water Planet.

Emotional healing and release can be even more powerful when you make contact with these most holy of overseers and guardians who will assist in restoring your most sacred vessel to its ability to contain divinity. Then you can regain the sacred energies that have been lost and bring them back home to fill up the Holy Chalice of your being. All that has been healed and brought back from darkness is transformed and connected in my flow and Love. As the tears of the Heavens fall on your outstretched Holy Chalices of embodiment, open yourselves to the magnificent healing power that is showering upon you, waking up the glorious flower of luminosity and awareness that you truly are.

The 'Waters of Grace' join together the Worlds that have been divided, as well as cleanse and heal the wounds of separation. The Tree of Life is reborn, lifting its leaves and branches high into the Heavens, while reaching its roots deeply into the crystalline core of the Mother Earth. There are many blessings from this vibrant 'Tree' of newly grown Flowers and Fruits, springing forth to nourish and bring new life to your Souls. As the Waters assist in returning a state of grace to a Planet greatly in need of honoring, the 'dream time' is restored, setting a sacred space in which to shift consciousness. The dream time is a place in which one can create with amazing fluidity and grace when consciousness has been restored. It is the play ground of the Rainbow Goddess, of innumerable variety and beauty that has now been made available in waking consciousness. Be aware of what you think, what you feel, what you put out into the 'Waters of Life.' Let the 'Waters of Grace' instruct you and reconnect you to a state of sacred being-ness, where you are held in the arms of the Great Mother. You may see her as Mother Mary or Quan Yin or as an unnamable great being of magnificent wonder. Give space for the shift of the Ages as your magnificent watery self and the Planet are healed. Invite us into your life, on your Altars, in ceremony, and throughout your being.

We of the sacred 'Waters of Grace' wish to help you remember your bliss, your ecstasy. Even if the precious jewel of your inner innocence is not quite ready to come out and play, you contain the codes for transcendental states of ecstasy, and you are being readied. In the beginning, your original emotional body was infused and glowed with the unconditional Love of your divine nature. As babies, you remember this state, as well as in moments of joy and states of oneness, while in love and in the beauty of Nature, or in the act of great creativity. Remember these states and we will be here when you forget. Within our mists, you will see the rainbows appear that will let you know you are not alone. You are of the Holy Waters, as is your beautiful, glorious Planet, and we invite you to open your petals in receptivity to the blessings that surround you. As the Emotional Body of the World is cleansed, you may find that you can now have a much different experience of yourself, of each other, and of the World. You are truly blessed.

11

Sacred Union:
The Directive to Resolve Duality

You are me... I am you... We are one in the same...You breathe, I breathe...One Heart Beat... One life!

The longing for the other, the beloved, is one of the most compelling forces in the Universe. We cry for that which seems so close to our Hearts and yet so far away and unattainable. For a moment we believe we have found it, and then it is gone. We are left believing that we will die if the feeling or person is no longer available. People will go to amazing extremes to find and be with their Soul Mate, their beloved. What is it we are truly longing for? I am speaking of that which is the deeper, spiritual union we are seeking, beyond the need for a companion and a family. I am referring to the highest level of ecstatic union that we can experience while in a human form, the union with our true Divine Self and thus with our Creator. This yearning is getting even stronger as this sacred union is being called forth for us to evolve towards, to glorify in, in the resolution of duality. The polarity of dualistic forces has created the playing field of Matter in which we have been individuating and learning.

As we have already shown, the healing and union between the feminine and masculine, the most basic and Holy Soul Essences that have birthed out of the core of Creation, are a most important component of what will bring in the needed transformation for the evolution of Mother Earth and humanity. As we clear the wounds created in a dualistic reality, we can make room for a higher level of relating inside and out. This does not take away from the wonderful journey of marriage, relationship, and family, but only assists one further in creating healthier, more life-sustaining relationships that are based more on our wholeness than on our wounds. As we transform at the most profound levels of the original archetypal forces of masculine and feminine, and reunite in the sacred waves of Love and Light coming through and onto our beloved Planet, our relationships will blossom into joyful union and harmony

Many of us function as if we were only half complete. At times this feeling of incompleteness and loneliness becomes unbearable, and we go on an endless search to find our perfected other-half out in the World. If we continue searching without healing the wounds and beliefs encoded within the masculine and feminine energies which have been developed from this time of learning from separation, we will only attract more of the reflections of the 'Black Obsidian Smoking Mirror' in our partnerships and relationships. But there is another way to fill this emptiness. If we work on our wholeness and seek healing within ourselves we can attract someone with the qualities and attributes that we long for. We can have more Soulful relationships without the baggage of the past and without having our relationships negated by our lower characteristics. Not only will we be more capable of being at peace within ourselves and in our relationships, but we will be able to change the nature of reality in the World and cosmos. As we shift the core relationships inside and out, we affect the entire social structure of society.

As we heal the places of separation between the above and below aspects of the Tree of Life that we embody, between Spirit and Matter, and Heaven and Earth, we are also being asked to heal and come together with the most elemental of separated polarities of the left and right side of the Tree, the masculine and feminine parts of our being. In each one of us, the spine of the Tree is the representation of where we have come from in union. Not only does the reunion of the masculine and feminine polarities ground the coming together of the separated parts we have been working with, but it also assists in realigning and restoring the harmony between the Three Worlds. The feminine Smoking Mirror (aspects of the Moon), reflects back that which needs to be seen and integrated, while the masculine Sword (directed by the Sun) helps one to keep the focus to penetrate and expose the untruths and illusions. Together they create discrimination (not judgment), tempered with Love, while cleansing and reuniting all that does not serve our spiritual transformation and the evolution of humanity. The Father brings the Light; the Mother brings the Love.

We call on Isis and Osirus, Goddess and God from the myths of Egypt, who wish to assist us in this journey. Many of you may know their story, but if not, search it out, because it has deep meaning for our times and depicts in epic proportions what the masculine and feminine have gone through and how these two beings' commitment to each other is profound. They have evolved, healing in the higher realms the earthly passage of separation and betrayal of the masculine and feminine that has been enacted again and again since humanity's 'Fall' into density, as we split into male and female. The story of Isis and Osiris is an in-depth playing out of the un-healed male twin and the assistance of the sisterhood for healing. You may have other divine archetypes to assist you with this sacred healing and reunion that speak to you more personally, but they are who have come forth at this time and we give thanks for their holy presence.

As we have spoken of before, in the journey through separation and duality, our Souls have continued to passionately long for wholeness in spite of the distortions and loss of much of the original teachings. As we split into dualistic forms in our descent into Matter, we moved from divine consciousness into self centered individuated consciousness and forget the divinity contained in all forms, both Male and Female, and how to be in union and harmony between the two. Much has been learned through this experience, painful as it has been at times. When we are able to access the inner beloved, the universal symbol of our ecstatic bond with our own divinity at its Soul source, this will assist us in staying in contact with our Higher Self. This becomes a state of being that is no longer dependant upon the comings and goings of marriages and important relationships. This inner marriage is ours for the keeping.

To awaken the seed of consciousness of our inherent divinity and the true union while still in the field of duality and descent through the Nine Underworlds, is quite an undertaking. We are at the doorway of awakening to the Upperworlds, but the lords of the Lowerworlds do not want to give up their reign. The remembrance of and longing for the state of sacred union, as painful as it may be at times, has assisted us to continue searching for the Light and Love, in spite of all the splits created between male and female. The human Soul is amazing in that we still choose to come back home to our divinity, regardless of how far we feel from the Center of the Godhead and how much pain or suffering we have experienced. What an incredible sign of the inherent connection we have never truly lost.

The sacred Light without a Shadow that is coming in at this time, will keep amplifying the patterns of disconnection and mistrust between the sexes and the masculine and feminine aspects of one's internal makeup, until we heal them at their core place of separation collectively and personally. This Light has no Shadow because it is in union and harmony with Divine Love. We cannot hide from this time of evolution. In order to bring it in with more grace and ease, making the times of purification easier on ourselves, we must heal and realign. The gyrations of the Earth Mother are also responding to the disharmony and inequity between the masculine and feminine aspects of life, as well as the inequality between men and women in the World. She is made from both, and is ever rebalancing these energies. We are being asked to relinquish the judgments, attitudes, and patterns incurred through this time of darkness and the roles we play because of this, with each other and in our own inner sanctums. The potential is to move towards trust, openness, and unconditional Love with all our relations.

To come up with more conscious choices during our earthly embodiment, we must elevate our masculine and feminine polarities. This then makes it possible for us to express as males and females in their more matured, spiritual roles. We can work with archetypal masculine and feminine forces in their evolved status, assisting us to grow up. Choose role models that speak deeply to you. The key word is assisting, not through forcing and controlling, which was the way of most of the Gods and Goddesses of our distant past. We are being asked to move forward in a profoundly unique manner never experienced before. The old ways of being in relationship with ourselves and others cannot exist in the elevated field of the New Earth that is forming. No one is exempt from this process, though some will resist the change much longer than others and may have to go through more pain than is necessary.

The dynamic energy of the dualistic creative forces are meant to come back into a divine dance and play, assisting in the bringing forth of the Water of Grace for the blessing of humanity in ecstatic union. The gifts of the Shiva and the Shakti (from the Hindu tradition) are to be reunited as a true partnership, with continual new experiences between the two, with full honoring and recognition that one cannot do without the other. Shiva as the male principle is known to represent pure consciousness, beyond definition and concepts; Shakti is the feminine aspects of the force and allure of manifestation, being the outer garment of Shiva. Together their Love embrace creates the World at archetypal levels.

With the influx of the showering of the essence of Venus on our Planet, along with the bigger Cycle of transformation showering upon us, we have an opportunity to align the distortions of this Fourth World of Creation. The distortions that took us out of balance so very long ago, in the fall into the World of Matter, can now come back into good relations with the masculine and feminine energies, as well as all of Creation. By living out of balance with the most basic and powerful parts of our beings, individuals, society, and the World have become severely lop-sided and it is a matter of survival to bring these aspects of our selves back into conscious awareness and integration.

As we align with Earth and Sky, North and South, East and West, our Medicine Wheel can be made complete and whole. As we clear and integrate that which divides, we can enjoy the variety of what life offers! When we elevate our relationship to the Shiva and the Shakti, within and without, we bring forward the teachings of the Lowerworld, as a child brings home what they have learned out in the World to their parents. The divine aspects of the Creation energies of the World need to be healed and returned to their holy status within us (divine means 'before division,' unified in God-consciousness). This is where it began.

There are many myths that speak of the existence of Creation parents or energies, but those of the Dogon people of the West African Republic of Mali (believed to have come originally from Egypt) have spoken to me most deeply. They tell of a most profound ancient story of the separation of the masculine and feminine energies of Creation. They speak of the Nommos as their Ancestors who come from the star system Sirius, who were created by Amma (Supreme God) as six pairs of twins (original DNA helix), who were described as being part human-like and part snake or fish; Isis is also depicted with her lower body scaled and fish-like. One of the Nommos twins named Ogo rebelled (Lucifer?), and instead of continuing to be part of the initial Creation family, connected to the core of the Godhead, left on an 'Ark' and rushed into space, landing eventually on the Earth, thus bringing disorder into the World. This being, depicted as a male deity, moved away in separation from the Godhead and its Sacred Twin. In order to re-establish order and balance in the Universe, Amma (the central Creator) sacrificed one of the other Nommos to this dimension in order to balance out the displaced twin energy of Creation; thus beginning the need for sacrifice because of the great disharmony and imbalance. This separation disavowed the sacredness of creating, because sacredness is forgotten when disconnection from the wholeness and Heart of the Creation occurs.

When I heard the Dogon story a number of years ago, I wondered what had happened to the female twin of the rebellious Nommos and why she was never mentioned, because the renegade was always referred to as male! I wonder if she was connected to the wild untamed feminine energies of Lilith, who was never mated and was rejected by the controlling male forces which came to power, possibly because of the independent actions of the rebellious Nommos. Food for thought.

I discovered from researching further that according to the Dogon myth, the main power of one of the stars of Sirius comes from the female twin of Ogo, called Yasiqui. Ogo is the rebellious male Creator God, who the myth states chased Yasiqui away from following him around the Universe until he landed on the Earth. Supposedly she had come to Earth on her own before him, because she could not find him (beginning times of the Great Mother worship?). It seems that from the beginning of time the feminine has believed it is responsible to find and heal the 'wounded' or separated male. In the journey, the feminine developed its own wounds. Once again, without the harmonious balance of feminine and masculine Creation forces, distortions were created.

When the Dogon Ancestors returned to Earth long ago, according to the myths, they were sent to benefit and help direct humanity, coming as teachers and spiritual guides to help heal the rift and incompleteness created by Ogo. They came in spaceship like vehicles and pools of water, which came out of their ships onto the Earth, out of which they then emerged, being part aquatic and part human like beings. Did they need this 'Water of Grace' to keep their higher energies intact while in the third dimension? The Dogons have kept the 'Ritual of the Ancestors' going, given to them by the Nommos, to carry out the original instructions of keeping the balance through honoring all as sacred, as many tribes throughout the World have done. These rituals were part of their original sacred instructions, so as to keep their teachings and energies available to the Dogon and the World through this time of the 'Heavenly Gates' being barely held open. It appears the Godhead always gives pathways to return to balance.

One of the many reasons this story is so profound to me and why I selected it to share of all the available myths, is that long before I ever heard of the Dogon or this myth, I saw my own separation from wholeness in a past life journey I took in the late 1980s (I also connect to Sirius more than any star system). I took this journey to get to the core of why my physical health was deteriorating. In my original descent into form during my birth in the ancient times of Egypt, I was able to see with my psychic vision how my Silver or Aka Cord was cut by a masculine, otherworldly being and only my Golden Cord (carrier of life force) was left connected. The intuitive communication between all parts of my being that were connected to my original, spiritual instructions and purpose was severed. Since that time, all of the physical manifestations of my embodiment were created disconnected from divine wholeness and I went into partial unconsciousness. That time has affected every incarnation I have had since. I have been on a journey of healing and transformation to return to consciousness, ever since

I have also seen since then that this separation goes back even further to the times of Lemuria and Atlantis. I will speak briefly on this later. I have been on a journey of recovery ever since, attempting to carry out the original instructions while in separation. In the synchronicity of what has been shown to me throughout the creating and experiencing of this book, I was given a powerful message by Mother Nature concerning my return to wholeness. In Costa Rica while I was working on a rewrite, a unique silver spider appeared, with a 'Flower of Life' like silver web concentrated around it. This web was unusual in that the intricate pattern was concentrated right around the spider like it was its personal Medicine Field, instead of just a bigger web to catch its prey in. It went right along with the healing of my silver cord and revamping of my electromagnetic field. Costa Rica, once again, contains the primal life force in its rain forests and jungles, which is very important to have present for the renewing of that which has been lost.

For the healing and bringing back to oneness of the dualistic forces of Creation, the original energies and beliefs held deep inside from our archetypal ancient Sons and Daughters as well as from the Creation Mother and Father Gods, need to be healed and transformed. How can we come into union and harmony without this? The third aspect of the son or daughter that had been created from a split in the harmony and union of the original Male and Female Creation Gods and Goddesses, needs to be resolved so that we can have a rebirth of humanity at its core. This healing and rebirth will affect us profoundly at global and personal levels. This is where the true power lies, in the creating of new life and the birthing of our own Divine Child within. As we heal at the source of our wounding and search deeply into the archetypal reserves of our psyche for the truth behind Creation, we release the stories that have formed us and kept us controlled by the misinformation passed down by our Ancestors.

For there to be a Holy Trinity of Creation, it is necessary that there be the 'correct balance' between the Divine Masculine and the Divine Feminine, the union of Spirit and Matter, in order to create in wholeness rather than in fragmentation and separation. If this Trinity is not aligned with the higher energies (instead of the unhealed versions of each part), and in correct divine proportion, that which is created is lacking the full complement of Light and sacred Love of the core of the Godhead. These divine proportions (sacred geometry), are necessary to make a whole, integrated person. So much of what we spend our time healing from, is the effect of our so called damaged parents, of personal and cosmic proportions. This affects us not only in the absence of healthy role models, but also in what is held in our Inner Child.

The core wounds we have stated before are of betrayal, abandonment, humiliation, and rejection. Even though the woundings that are typically carried by the masculine are humiliation and rejection, and the wounds carried by the feminine are betrayal and abandonment, we all contain both, held in the universally carried Basic Self. When the Inner Child or Basic Self is healed and re-parented in our psyches, we can truly ground the changes of integrating the Shadows of the Underworld. A healthier mothered and fathered Divine Child, held safely by the divine energies, brings forth an atmosphere in our beings where the energies of the Basic Self are truly liberated to inspire a much more playfully and joyfully created reality. It is so very important to re-parent oneself with the higher archetypes, so that sacred union can take place, which will not occur if we keep creating male and female relationships out of the wounds held in us around past relationships. Healing the wounds of the Inner Child that hold the holographic pictures of mistrust and disharmony between the sexes, allows our most sacred of divine essences to remember true union. Out of the sacred inner Marriage of the healed archetypal energies, the Divine and Magical Child can be birthed.

There is also the trinity aspect of Creation that was established by the Creation Mother, known as Spider Woman in many native traditions, who sang the Triple Goddesses into life, so they would hold balance during the time of the dualistic forces. The Mother, Maiden, and Crone, in both human and Goddess form, are to be honored and connected to in sacredness, so that the womb and birth place of the original divine blueprint is still present for humanity to birth through to the next level, as it was for the rebirth of the Christed Jesus.

I must also make mention the great importance of taking the essence of healing to the core time of your own first embodiment on the Planet. For some this may go back as far as to the time of Atlantis and Lemuria. Be open to see and experience that which has been long hidden. In my own healing I remember before my descent into form in ancient Egypt, being a Lemurian, being more connected to the Divine Feminine forces of Creation, even though I was not fully differentiated into either male of female physical form, being of the more watery dream states of etheric reality. I remember being forced into containment against my will by Atlantean scientists who had lost their way in endless experiments, having disconnected from their Heart Centers. In this containment I was split into masculine and feminine essences that carried the pain of separation and the breaking of the divine contract of free will. I am still healing the anger and shut down in my Heart from this experience long ago and the lifetimes of holding this. I am still releasing in forgiveness of myself and others, the many karmic lifetimes created from the individual and collective pain of being both oppressed and oppressor, victim and victimizer, both male and female. To be a true Rainbow Warrior, one can no longer carry anger in one's Heart towards the opposite sex, or to any who have lost their way and separated from the Godhead. Great compassion for self and others is needed to heal this and we give thanks for the presence of the Goddess of compassion Quan Yin, for her returned presence on the Planet. If anger exists, bring it all the way through to clear and integrate on the healing path. Do not keep perpetuating the drama.

Is it possible that these scientists from Atlantis were affected on a mythic scale, as the rest of humanity's evolution has been since, by the dishonoring and separation from the twin of the Ogo (from the Dogon myth)? That the sacred union so craved and coveted, was deeply altered by the so called warp in the field of this Creation that occurred so long ago? The feminine still appears to want to heal the masculine and it has turned from a wish to come back into wholeness, from the beginning of Creation, to a struggle between the sexes. The free will directive has affected all of Creation, from the most powerful to the most humble of creatures. We are being given a chance to 'choose' to come home to the purity of our original pure blueprints, where we can experience 'Divine Union.'

In order to understand the healing journey that we are required to do at this time, it is helpful to have a greater understanding and awareness of what has come before, as painful as this may be at times. To come 'full circle in transformation and healing' we must understand our past so we learn from it and know the nature of the metamorphosis we must go through so we no longer continue to create out of the same imbalances of the past. Without this understanding we may hold back in fear and mistrust, waiting for someone to do it for us, when understanding is available for all. How can we create a new paradigm if we are still caught in outmoded ways of creating and living that are not in tune with the Light and Love pouring into our Planet? Without attempting to see the bigger picture, we may also blame our earthly parents for that which has been occurring for thousands of years.

When the mythic story of our original earthly parents, of Adam and Eve, got told in a way that shamed the Mother of all of our Ancestors, we have carried deep within us the mistrust of our own feminine beings. Blaming Eve for bringing the masculine into the lower emotional realm of desire has created a judgment of our earth-body senses and the joy that can be experienced there. This shame has profoundly affected the birthing of children, as the body responded in pain and suffering. This imbalance has affected the Creation of everything touched by humans. The sacred doorways of Creation, the vagina or yoni (Sanskrit word) and the vessel, the womb, carried these misconceptions which have been imprinting the sons and daughters of humanity with this burden. If the most sacred of vessels, the womb contained within a woman, was not sanctified, and a woman's pain in birthing was looked at as a curse, then maybe deep healing is being called for. Much has changed in the World with this, but not everywhere and it will also take time to change at cellular and collective levels. The word sacrifice truly means to make sacred. If the women who carried life were no longer looked at as sacred, then the creations of the World were no longer seen as sacred. The living of life might then seem more like a great travail than a wondrous adventure.

It is of utmost importance when in a female body, that one heals the wounds of shame and disempowerment held deep within in order to merge with the Divine Feminine, and to not hold anger and resentments towards the male. It is time that women reclaim their medicine in a new way and heal the unloved places in themselves, so they can truly give birth to a healed child within and without, and thus help awaken others. It is also just as important that men birth their Divine Child within, and as they heal the emotional feminine side of their being they too will be able to be in a different relationship with themselves, the women they love, and the

World. As the feminine is healed this will usher in the transformation of the masculine energies.

The Vesica Pisces, which is two perfected circles joined in balance together, is a profound sacred geometrical form that represents the joining of a God and Goddess to create an offspring; a symbol for Jesus Christ; part of the symbol for the astrological sign of Pisces; the vagina of the Goddess; the center motif in the sacred geometry of the 'Flower of Life;' and a source of immense power and energy in terms of being a doorway for birthing Light. In the ancient past in the British Isles, the symbol of the Vesica Pisces would be placed above the wells to draw water up to the surface. The sacredness and codes that lie within the corridors of this blessed gateway of Creation must be awakened, healed, and honored in order to create without the burden of sacrifice and past trauma. The Divine Feminine must come back to its rightful place alongside the Divine Masculine, inside and out, integrated with the Inner Child. As the deeply held wounds and emotions get to be transformed, we get to be re-parented by a more highly developed part of the collective psyche, and we can then change the course of what we manifest on a daily basis. This symbol can be invoked to carry this forth.

In order that the feminine energies be exalted and honored by the masculine as well as reconnected to the Divine Masculine archetypes, the earthly male energies must truly be healed, as we have already shared. We have spoken of the need for humanity to heal at higher and deeper layers then ever before. Held in the deepest recesses of the male psyche and connected to the most primal of human survival mechanisms are the codes of warrior-ship, misuse of the 'Ray of Power,' and the fear of annihilation and / or rejection by the Mother and the feminine as a whole. The healing of the shut down Heart and the bringing in of the higher feeling states is of profound importance for those who have been warriors in this life or in other lifetimes. It does not matter much if you are born in a male or female body, for you will most likely be carrying these codes in the collective male psyche, at the least. But the wounds do get more amplified by the societal norms of relationships and roles of both the masculine and feminine, as well as by biological influence.

Both men and woman need to remember that not only have we been both male and female in our many lifetimes, and that we contain both masculine and feminine energies, but that we both are struggling to come back and clear the veils of separation. Neither truly wants to own or destroy the other, except for the misguided few. We have been living and learning in the misguided creations of the egoic process, and true union between the dualities has not been experienced by the majority of humanity for a very long time. It looks as if the Ego driven behaviors began long ago, when the Ogo rebelled, believing it could create separate from the Heart of the Creation.

The general male population throughout the Ages has for the most part not been given the space to make contact with their own inherently divine selves, being kept busy with their role as warriors of violence, enslaved by the misdirected and disconnected rulers. We are in very different times when a much greater percentage of the male population is no longer having to be slaves of the war mongers, and can now take the time to learn to become true Spiritual Warriors, ready to give all to gain true knowledge in order to take the nest steps to evolve. With the return of love and wisdom as the true energies behind the forces of true power, much change can occur on the Planet.

When women release the deeply held anger and mistrust of the masculine (which is easier to do when the masculine is able to look deep within and face their own Smoking Obsidian Mirror), this not only affects their own true empowerment, but the opening into compassion for the masculine personified inside and out. When the masculine starts to be in touch with its emotions, this stimulates the healing of the deep layers of being judged and controlled by the feminine. This emotional release leaves room for the forgiveness of self and of all of the behaviors acted out while in separation from our true feelings. Then the feminine voice can be heard once again. This goes for our inner Animus and Anima, as well as what can be healed in relationships.

As the warrior part of humanity evolves its role and its personal connection to the Divine, and as women wake up from the deep sleep of oppression and shaming, the two can come together to be in alignment with each other. The dream of the Sacred Marriage held lovingly in the Heart of Mother Earth can then be realized. As we heal the misled parenting in our personal lives and in the sacred energies held in our Creation myths, we can unite and wake up to the greater true beings we must become to be part of the rebirthing of humanity and beautiful Mother Earth. It just might be that the need for sacrifice and bloodshed will no longer be necessary if we see and honor ourselves, each other, and all parts of Creation as being sacred, connected to the rays of the rainbow, emanating from the Godhead. We are all joined at the source of the rainbow with our multitudes of characteristics and flavors.

The sacrifice of Jesus and the other Holy Ones, such as Quetzalcoatl (all of whom birthed the Christ energies onto the Planet so very long ago) was the carrying out of a most sacred ceremony. We spoke much earlier that the lack of the presence of the honoring of the sacred partnership of the Divine Christed Masculine with the Divine Feminine because of the patriarchal take over of the development of the Christian Church, was possibly a profoundly limiting factor as to the true resolution of sin (karma) on the Planet. It appears that we were not ready yet. The time of the 'Underworlds' was to have its reign. The true sacredness of this sacrifice was not fully honored, as Jesus knew would occur. Is it possible that Jesus came from the lineage of earthly yet divine Kings, and was the last earthly but Godly male meant to be part of what had always been a ritual enactment of the sacrificing of the King (being from the highest level of Kingdoms, the Kingdom of Heaven)? The King was always anointed by the High Priestess (the Magdalene) and sacrificed within a most holy of ceremonies to ensure that the crops would grow and that the Earth would be returned to its fertile state. Because of existing in a World that was no longer fully connected to the Heavens, this was necessary. Can we now truly live the message of Love, compassion, and non-judgment that the Christ Light returned to humanity? Maybe it is time that we truly take responsibility for our own actions, remembering the original teachings of awakening the Christ within, and not wait to be saved by more sacrifice.

The ritual enactment of the sacrifice of the King, to ensure the fertility of the land, was part of many ancient cultures, and there was usually first a joining of the chosen Priestess with the King, in sacred sexuality and union, before the sacrifice. This ritual has evolved to various forms in many indigenous cultures that are still intact. The Corn Dances of the Pueblos in New Mexico are dances to ensure the fertility of the lands, especially around the bringing of the rains. Both women and men dance together, as well as the children, sacrificing themselves most of the day in the hot Sun. Santa Domingo Pueblo, south of Santa Fe, has a yearly Corn Dance ceremony where around one hundred singers and three hundred dancers swirl together in great beauty and power, with their feet lovingly touching the Earth of the Mother, as the sound and vibration of the one big drum and the synchronized dancing of the community thunder up and down the central plaza.

Many tribes have continued to ritually enact within the path of sacrifice and respect, to return the World to sacredness, working within the beliefs and structures of their individual traditions. The Sundance of the Native American Plains People is still being held today to ensure the harmony and balance between all living things. At the end of the ceremony, the pipes that have been prayed with throughout are brought together at the sacred Tree, renewing the Tree of Life at the center of the ceremony. The sacred pipe (given by White Buffalo Calf Woman) is used for this ceremony, representing both masculine and feminine. The bowl is the feminine and the stem is the masculine. The Sundance is also held to give thanks to Father Sun, so that the negative energy surrounding the Earth, given off by the human brain, can be reduced. It is most important to have ways to move the negative energy that humans create so as to not imbalance the World with this heavy hucha.

Ceremonies were developed in our ancient past in so called pagan rituals so that the men could sacrifice and offer the sweat of their bodies in the alchemy of transformation in ceremony, because they did not sacrifice monthly like womankind (rebalancing the original wounding?). Because the sacredness of the bleeding has been taken from women and from daily life, many women also have a need to ceremonially connect to these energies of sacred sacrificing and take part in the Sundance, even though it was at first created for the men. The Sundance Ritual is also for the building of the power of connection to the Creator here on Earth, for the purpose of the healing of a relative or friend who is in great need, more than for the self. It is another way to shed the isolated, egoic, individual personality, restoring the consciousness of the connection to all life through the deep caring of others, and to re-harmonize with the Universe.

As I was beginning to write this section, I was told a story by a male friend, of the powerful connection to the elements and the forces of Great Spirit working through the Earth that he had recently experienced in a Sundance in North Dakota. I too have had such profound experiences. When I had the honor of being a supporter at one of these ceremonials, I bore witness to the necessity for the honoring of the Divine Feminine (as brought in with White Buffalo Calf Woman's gift of the pipe) and the Holy Ones for the success of these most sacred practices. I also witnessed the tree that was planted in the center of the Ceremonial Circle as a symbol of the Tree of Life, being hit by lightning at the end of the four day ceremony of dance and sacrifice when the medicine man of the ceremony brought his pipe to the tree. These ceremonies keep humanity connected to the Great Spirit in Mother Nature, where her elements respond according to the pure intentions of the participants and the success of the prayers offered.

Each person has to know at what level they still need to sacrifice in order to reconnect with the web of life. The Sundance is a powerful, honoring ritual of giving of one's body and Soul to Creator so that others may live healthy and whole, and I feel great respect for those who choose that path. I also hope that humanity will be able to soon shift into the non-dualistic energies of the Fifth World, as we enter into more of the Beauty Way of learning and growing and truly unify with the new Tree of Life in our own Medicine Fields.

Before the takeover of the patriarchy, most indigenous native communities held a deep respect for women in their roles as life givers and as the primary force of the Universe. Much of the contact between the dualistic pairs of male and female was carefully guided so as to keep an honoring and respectful interplay between the sexes. The roles of men and women were meant to guide and guard that which was not evolved at the highest levels as of yet. Every part of the ethics of right and wrong, and the interaction between oppositional energies, was a matter of keeping the balance. They believed humans would destroy the balance if they were not in right relationship to all things. In the 1990s, I was blessed with witnessing a dance at Tesuque Pueblo in New Mexico, where the men were in the roles that the women usually took and the women were in the male dancers' roles. There was a lot of good humor with it and a chance to witness a moment in time, in the other's moccasins.

Many native Wisdom Keepers are coming forth with previously hidden sacred knowledge that is to be respectfully integrated and used wisely by the people of the World to assist us in the Grand Awakening. Many of these teachings are also about the reunification of the higher feminine and masculine forces. We can learn much from listening to what they have to share.

According to the ancient cultures of South America and most exemplified by the teachings held still today by the medicine people of Peru, everything in Mother Nature contains both male and female energies; the rocks, the mountains, the plants, the humans, even though some of the Soul energies carry more of a feminine or masculine signature or character. The Incan prophecies speak of the appearance and rejoining of the Priestesses and Priests, in actual re-embodiment at this time, at sacred Power Centers and Temples in Peru, as being the sign that we are ready for the rejoining of the polarities. In the ancient past they went through training and initiation separately; the young women together, the young men together, developing the gifts of each polarity individually. After their initiation rites, when they were deemed ready to teach and guide the people, the Sacred Marriage was performed so that the two would guide in union and harmony. It is said that they might come back embodying various races and nations, not solely in Peruvian individuals.

Previously mentioned is the ceremony of the sacrifice of the King, which also contained the ritual enactment of the 'Sacred Marriage' in our very ancient history. In the past, the Sacred Marriage was one of the most important rites that evolved out of the Goddess culture, enacting the union between the God and Goddess, the King and Queen, and between Heaven and Earth. These rites were enacted to regenerate the fertility and abundance of the Earth, such as during Beltane, an ancient Celtic Ritual. Gradually the ritual of the Sacred Marriage took on a new dimension of meaning and became internalized as pagan spirituality was oppressed and mostly destroyed. Instead of acting out the Divine Masculine and Feminine externally, the union was brought within and was believed to reside within each person. Within the yogic traditions, there were practices developed to unite these most sacred of energies within, in spiritual union.

The Sacred Marriage was taken to a new step of internalization and conceptualization of the psychological inner process of this union, by white shamans like Carl Jung. He named the inner feminine the Anima and the inner masculine the Animus and he called the sacred union between the two, Mysterium Conjuntionis, meaning the Mysterious Union. By healing the wounded aspects of these most sacred polarities, we will be more unlikely to project our unhealed places out onto our most intimate partners, and therefore come into a relationship more able to personify the inner Sacred Union.

The most sophisticated symbol that became associated with this cosmic (but yet quite personal) process of integration and the Sacred Marriage, was the image of a pair of snakes intertwined in union around the Tree of Life. Today this symbol is known as the Caduceus, universally representing the idea of healing. Once again we come back to the need to transform the snake into the powerful 'Feathered Serpent' which brings the unified healing and regenerative energies of the life force needed for our evolution at this time. The feminine energy associated with the Moon ascends the spine and unites with the masculine energy in the head in ecstatic union; while the male energy, represented by the Sun, descends the spine creating a recycling of renewable energy in the body. Kundalini is a Sanskrit word for the creative life force energies that rise from the base of the spine, where the Earth Goddess is believed to reside.

The return of the awareness of the sacredness of our sexuality is at the core of much of the healing between the sexes and in the Heart. This most mysterious aspect of the journey of healing could take up an entire book, but let it be acknowledged that enacting 'Sacred Sexuality' is one of the most profound ways to come into a state of ecstatic union and awaken the bliss of our Joy Bodies. These ecstatic states greatly assist us in creating the Mana necessary to sustain our energy fields in the Upperworlds. Tantra was developed in ancient spiritual societies as a tool used for weaving the threads of life into an integrated whole, working with the sacred sexual energies with great respect and co-empowerment. This honoring of the sexuality of our Inner Self, as well as in our outer relationships, is having a comeback in our culture today. Many of us are relearning that the act of sexual intercourse is not only a mysterious act of bringing new life into the World, but a sacred ritual which allows grace and the creative power of the Divine to manifest more abundantly in one's life, as well as in the World.

The sacred teachings of Yogic and Tantric practices are a powerful pathway to the union of which we speak. But most of us come from a psychologically complex western culture where much of the healing needs to work within the framework of our belief systems and social structures. Our consciousness has had to play itself out in our social interactions and norms and it is time to bring the higher states home in our daily lives and relationships. Psychotherapy and other healing modalities that work with the higher archetypal energies to clear negative childhood patterns, as well as past life work, can be very helpful for those from the western culture. As mentioned before, this awakening is not only for the spiritual adept, but for as much of humanity as possible.

Some believe that when we descended into the third dimension and our Souls split into dualistic parts or halves, one aspect remained in higher frequency, while the other existed in the third dimension. If you are female, your partner in the higher realms is male and vice versa. This spiritual essence partner draws us into the higher realms as our creational source, keeping us from fully falling from consciousness. It is curious that you rarely hear that someone has found their Twin Flame or Soul Mate. Maybe it can only exist internally in this dimension and is waiting for us in the next World? As the Fifth World is born, the re-meeting of these sacred aspects may become more possible. This reunion would be of two whole beings celebrating coming back as empowered beams of Light and Love.

As mentioned before, we are in the time of the activation and re-balancing of the left and right hemispheres of our brains, in terms of the breakdown of masculine and feminine attributes which they embody, as well as the social roles of men and women. The more feminine characterized right brain is being more strongly activated in order to bring humanity back into balance. It is a time of great transition. Many people are complaining that they barely have a brain remaining to function in the World with, as the detail oriented, left brain takes a back seat, and the more intuitively creative right brain becomes the driver, more and more often. We have created a World based mostly on the left, more masculine aspect of the brain and the transition can be confusing. One side of the brain is not better than the other, as one sex is not more important than the other. The high brain of the masculine provides the power to master your energies. The high brain of the feminine side receives the intuitive guidance from the Higher Self that we spoke of before. Once we learn how to embody the right brain, it will be time for reunion. In the union of the rational, analytical brain with the more intuitive, spatial brain, which is the balancing of the left hand of Creation with the right hand, we gain access to the information encoded in this union. Within the initiation rites of many spiritual paths, the higher knowledge was not to be awakened or shared until one was able to unify one's energy bodies and pass the tests of the Underworlds, or the knowledge and wisdom might be misused.

The healing energies of Venus are also available to help us align and heal during this great transition, in order for humanity to experience more of a balanced state with all our relations; with ourselves, each other, animals, religions, nations, Mother Earth, and Great Spirit. When in a healthier relation to all life, we can live the path of the Beauty Way, where we are drawn into relationships and situations that bring us greater joy and harmony. These shifts may make it more difficult to stay in unhealthy relationships of any kind.

The Maya had a special relationship with Venus for many reasons, but of utmost pertinence was the ability of Venus to transform itself from the Morning Star to the Evening Star, exhibiting a 'unified polarity' greeting both the Light and the Dark. I believe the first Venus transit we have already passed through, is about the healing and bringing in of the Divine Feminine energies, leading us towards the second transit in 2012, which may be the bringing in and healing of the Divine Masculine and the return of Quetzalcoatl (Christ). As each individual does their inner work, we provide an energetic shift that provides a place where these sacred energies can embody here on Earth as we experience a state of 'Oneness.'

This may all seem out of your reach to truly live and be, but it is not. Because of the healing journey you have been on, you will have a greater chance of recognizing the pitfalls created by the disconnected Ego states within ourselves and in our relationships. Because of the Healing Waters and work with the other sacred elements, we will not be as emotionally reactionary, basing our thoughts and actions on past wounding. The presence of our more integrated beings will enable us to be more humble and accepting without as much fear of loss of the true self within the dance of relationship. With higher, true self-esteem and the right use of will, we will want to see our partners and relations around us flourish in co-empowerment. This will bring joy, instead of competition and resentment. We will be able to discern what is truly needed for our highest potential while being guided by our Higher Self. It may be possible to have healthier relationships where the embodiment of grace, trust, respect, good communication, true intimacy, sacred sexuality and Love, shared creativity, and spiritual connection can balance out the moments that we may still have of egoic display.

Do not fear that we will no longer be magnetically drawn into the beautiful dance between men and women as you integrate these energies inside, for it is not the time for us to become asexual, celibate, or without attraction. There is so much more to live out and experience within the beauty of being male or female in embodiment. We now have the chance for it to be a more gracious dance, and it may now be more possible to meet and reunify with our Sacred Twins, our Twin Flames, and higher level Soul Mates, either on the inner or outer planes. Our Twin Flames are thought of as the 'other half' that we split into when we entered physical density. Soul Mates are beings that we have been with before that we have a very deep Soul connection to, with similar resonant vibrations. There may still be tests for us to go through with some of our Soul Mates because of unfinished business from the past, but the recognition of deep-connection is unmistakable.

It is beautiful to unify inside our psyches, but we are made to be social creatures and it is important now that couples help demonstrate the way back into a unified awareness. At times it may feel like we are being squeezed through an opening, like through the eye of a needle that we cannot easily pass through, as we experience birthing into a new way of being in our bodies and our emotions, with each other and the World. It is a real blessing during this great transition, to have supportive higher level relationships that are understanding of the immense changes that we are experiencing. It is important to have support while we are in the eye of the great storm of purification and transformation.

When the internalized dualities are acknowledged and healed, they are more than willing and desirous of coming back together; therefore affecting positively the outer relationship between male and female, and the wellness of the psyche. When we have healed our core wounds and are able to love ourselves unconditionally, we can offer this to those around us. As we sanctify the Sacred Marriage of our own inner sanctum and become more healed individuals who live out less conflicted and higher levels of relationships, then we can have a closer connection to the Creator, and Heaven on Earth can then be experienced. We will find that what is manifested in our role as co-creators can be birthed from a place of more wholeness and harmony.

Take a moment to tune in deep inside, becoming aware of the most personal archetypes of your masculine and feminine parts. Invite the joining together of the most primal aspects of your Soul to take place in Sacred Union, creating a most consecrated space in time to join together the sacred feminine and the sacred masculine in Holy Matrimony. You carry both of these essences in the most intimate recesses of your Soul, where they have been waiting to join in beauty and grace. The 'Flowering of your Soul' inspires this most precious moment. The Divine Magical Child within is birthed through this harmonious coming together, knowing it is held in the loving embrace of its true parents, bursting forth with great joy and creativity. Feel the fullness of the experiencing of earthly human Love, joining with the ecstatic expression of Divine Union. Envision the two lovingly embracing each other, merging in the spiraling spiritual forces of Love and Light, opening a great doorway, unlocking the Mystery of the Ages, and releasing back to you that which is inherently yours and yearns to return home again.

12

Reclaiming Our Sacred Energy

I command from the highest forces of Light and Love that all parts of me I have left behind in unconsciousness, in fear, in longing, in forgetfulness, in attachment to the past, will now return to me healed by the Waters of Grace; for it is time, it is time, it is time. So be it and so it is!

In order to evolve to the Fifth World, it is important to reclaim our sacred energy that has been held in the past. This occurs as we transform the Shadow realms, but it is important to reclaim even more of ourselves from the larger spectrum of where we have been fragmented from our wholeness. As the trance of the Ego is broken and the feeling states healed, all parts are in closer communication and harmony with each other, the Higher Self is returned as the guiding force of one's being, and the Sacred Marriage is enacted; the effect of this transformation will ripple back throughout time, as the 'Waters of Grace' bring together our personal and global Tree of Life.

Even though there may still be further healing to take place in the identification and release of individual traumatic events and experiences both from this lifetime and past, it is now possible to bring together fragmented parts of your being that were lost in time and that have been waiting to come back to wholeness. Past life work, Soul retrieval, healing of Ancestral wounds as well as childhood traumas, may still show up to be healed, but enough of your essence self blueprint has been activated to hold the space for more of you to return, and for us to continue on the 'Journey to the Fifth World.' The healing can occur more quickly than ever because of the energies now available as the World passes through this doorway of rapid transformation. In our journey of separation, much energy has been held through the constraints and in the restrictive places of disconnect and judgment. As we release these energies to their inherent wholeness the gifts contained within can be gathered and returned, along with the primal life force held in the unconsciousness. It is now time, as part of the healing journey, to reclaim the holy power, Love, and Creator given talents held in the past that are now ready to come home to your Soul.

As the traumatic experiences are understood and the lessons and teachings are gathered from this life and from many others, the essential energies that are inherently yours can be released and returned as the necessary Mana required in order to evolve at this time. As we individually heal, release, and transform, the cultures and landmasses where we have experienced our journey through the Underworlds of the Era of the Kali Yuga, also get a chance to further transform the negative patterns and trauma held there. As more and more of the collective of humanity does its individual release and re-configuration, the locations of ancient battles, discord, and violence, as well as the wounds held deeply in the cultural lineages, will be given energetic room to be released. So much of present time negativity that occurs is created because of the past traumas still being regenerated in present time. Yes! There is definitely an energy crisis going on, beyond the misuse of Mother Nature's resources. So much of humanity's life force is tied up in past traumas that we have been working with quite a deficit of true spiritual energy, for a very long time.

Time and space are but a boundary for defining in the school of learning of the third dimension. Vibrational energies, both positive and negative, radiate out from places and experiences we have had long ago. They make us who we are today, but in a much bigger sense than many of us have ever imagined. As we move into a very different energy field of wholeness and conscious re-connection to our Higher Self, it is very important to 'clean up' our past lives, which are the source of unresolved issues that keep recycling again and again, appearing in your present life as recurring lessons and challenges. We can go to the core of where certain restrictive beliefs and behaviors began and unbind them at their source in this lifetime and way beyond. No longer do we need to go through endless past life scenarios for resolution, but can go to one that contains the core wounding where the negative patterns as well as unlearned lessons and patterns originate. When we go to the core of where trauma has occurred, it unravels the threads of our energy field that lead back through time allowing not only for more of our sacred energy to return but also for a new more positive story line to be woven.

Bound in these experiences are not only the wounds but also our inherent energies and talents that when freed to their inherent, pure spiritual intent, can be positively used for the evolutionary leap we are being asked to take. When you do the work of seeing the immensity of your Soul's journey, life after life, you gain perspective not only about the core lessons of your Soul's journey, but about the absurdity of taking your personality self too seriously. When delving into the otherworldly journey to past lives, it truly does not matter how accurate the memories are of who you were as a character during that particular life. What is important are the patterns and energy to be released and the lessons learned in order to truly move ahead with consciousness. Just like in the dream time, in the past life review the psyche is very creative with what it uses to give us the messages necessary for our growth. It is important to not get hooked into the egoic over-identification of any character you have been, but instead see it as 'grist for the mill.'

Soul retrieval is an ancient practice that is currently experiencing a revival as part of the great healing journey that is taking place on the Planet. As we experience the many painful traumas of this World of separation, parts or fragments of our Soul may split off and go to what that part believes is a better place in another dimension or hover confused at the scene of the painful experience. Fragments of our beings may even be taken (usually unconsciously) by loved ones who have gone from us and are still attached to staying connected by keeping a part of us with them. These fragmented aspects of our beings usually need assistance to return, and if enough of our Soul energy is not present, we may have many illnesses, and what we do to heal may not be effective for long, and there may be a general feeling of dissociation and not feeling grounded and present that will dominate. It is important to bring all these fragmented parts back together so one can exist in a state of more totality. When one goes deeper into this work, it is important to look at the spiritual learning that was put into place with these experiences, as well as changing the habits created out of not having all of oneself intact.

Part of the great evolution taking place on the Planet, is the sensitivity and skill to better rebuild and manage our energy bodies. An awareness of this used to be the norm in indigenous societies through the practice of many healing ceremonies and rituals such as Soul retrievals, and in the social norms of conduct with each other. In the past it was normal for shamans to steal power and energy from others, which was part of a challenge and a test. In spite of the often times negative results of this, there was more of a conscious awareness by the people that this occurred with shamans and with others. In our present World there is much unconscious taking of others' energy that needs to come to awareness to change. It is now time to reclaim a greater understanding of how this occurs in order to refine our energy fields with greater spiritual awareness and to reach higher levels. As we transform back into a greater state of 'Oneness' there is less chance of this even occurring, because we will be in a state of connection to the Source of all life and will not feel a lack.

It is also important to heal and realign the wounds and patterns (our family issues partly come from these patterns) contained in the Ancestral lineage you are connected to in this lifetime. We weave in and out of various lineages throughout our time here on the Planet, all containing lessons that our Soul needs. Our Ancestry as well as our parents are often more difficult to truly release in our emotional bodies and psyches because they are held so close to us in present physical time. The collective of all our relations from the spiritual realms are there to assist us, to help us resolve the core wounding of our Ancestors. This is for the sake of us individually, for our children's children, and for humanity, during this time of 'Great Change' and evolution.

As we heal from the Shadow complexes of our psyche and the ensuing Soul and essence loss, we regain the needed cleared energy of our most sacred beings; the Tree of Life will then have the Mana it needs to grow more strong and whole, being readied to support the framework of the Fifth World. This energy is gathered from the many places and experiences we have journeyed to and through in the 'Land of Separation.' Imagine the energy that is needed for a space rocket to take off and break through the Earth's atmosphere.

In the gathering of your most holy of personal essence powers, it is also important to regain energetic contact with the restored energy vortexes and sacred sites of the Planet. Even though this is most powerful when you are there in person, since we are working with physical transfiguration during these times, you can also visit them in your Dream Body while awake, to experience what your Soul needs to claim. There may be many sacred centers you feel a personal connection with from the past, as well as powerful vortexes you are attracted to, because there is a force there necessary for your next step of transformation. These pulls may even be a call to you to assist in the shifting and activation of spiritual forces that require the particular special being you are to be present. You are in the gathering and realigning of powers that are not only part of your personal energy bodies, but are also the powers available from the vibrations being activated all across the World at these ancient sites for humanity's great transformation.

Take this journey, allowing in the guides and guardians that wish to assist you, especially working with those you know and trust. On the journey of healing, always bring a trusted ally on board to work with that will help keep you on a good path. Lion, Tiger, and Horse have all shown up to assist with this great adventure, but trust your own inner knowing on who is right for your own personal passage.

The power of the Sun and the transformative alchemy of gold are carried by Lion Medicine as it assists one to absorb this most radiant force, transforming it into the physical plane of your being. The Great Spirit of Tiger invokes the power of passion and a new sense of adventure as you reclaim that which is your birthright. The great freedom of movement and the physical power that goes with Horse Medicine lifts you to the heights of the embodiment of your greatest capabilities to take this journey with renewed confidence.

These sacred helpers all work strongly with the forces of power and are not about the misuse of power but about returning to you your valuable life force and vitality as well as the precious gifts that are now present at many sacred sites throughout the World. According to many tribal traditions, true power is known as the invisible force that emits the brightest Light (Ether?).

I will now speak from the overseeing spiritual force that wants to see you whole and complete. So we begin ...

We are your Higher Self that is connected to the collective of your Oversoul, and we are here to assist you in gathering the energy you need to move ahead into the next World. We join with the animal spirits that will empower and ensure a safe journey. We see you and want you to remember the moments throughout time when you felt the power and Love force of the Creator coming through, so that you may gather together the most sacred of experiences that have been part of your many lifetimes. Your Oversoul is connected to your Soul group that has embodied for this Great Cycle, which is also regaining its connection to sacred sites and vortexes throughout the World.

When you start to rebuild the energy body that is connected to the web of life that still remembers the original teachings, you will have the resources needed to work further and deeper with the parts that still need to come home in order to evolve to the next World. The higher guides that you have made contact with, will help navigate you to where you need to go. Much personal energy has been tied up in the hundreds of oppositional energies and inner conflicts that are now being resolved.

As we strengthen and renew the newly growing Tree of Life, all else that has existed in separation will fall away. By reclaiming and transforming the energies of the Shadow, evolving the Inner Child, clearing it of past traumas, the primal energies are made available so as to manifest more spiritually evolved creations and experiences. The healing 'Waters of Grace' have cleansed and transformed the emotional body, giving you greater clarity, more vitality, and the increased positive feeling states that are necessary to reclaim the true essence self.

Call on your Ancestors and invite those who want to see the evolution of your lineage take place. They are offering to you the wisdom and the support that is needed in order to make a quantum leap into a more spiritually alive reality. As you cleanse yourself of places of un-love and separation, this radiates out as a gift to those who have come before who are connected to you through bloodlines and genetic coding. They bring to you through both the male and female lineages, the power of the collective, knowing deeply the great work that you have done. In the great Fire of the Ancestors we awaken the connection that has kept an awareness of your Soul's journey and is a thread of the continuance of your life. This energy of power infuses you with great waves of energy throughout your body. Give thanks for the Ancestors' blessings and ask for healing for those who are not yet ready to evolve.

Connect closely with your helping spirits as they take you to the recent and ancient past where sacred energy of yours is waiting to come home. Reclaim your gifts as they were given, bringing them back to wholeness so that they can be used in a manner in which they are truly exalted and used for the highest good in the great turning of the Ages. Invoke the cleansing of the lifetimes where healing may still need to take place, asking for the blessing of the healing 'Waters of Grace.' You may invoke these most holy forces of healing to break through the inertia whenever you feel unable to move forward in your process.

Breathe back into yourself the ecstasy of being rejoined with the energies that you have been missing. Remember the great teachings, the knowledge and wisdom gained in many lifetimes, bringing them forth to connect with in present time in a great celebration and homecoming.

Open up to the part of you that knows how to experience life from the perspective of the cosmic overview. You may have physically been present at these sites some time in your past on the Planet, or you may be connected through the cosmic inter-weaving of those you have been close to through Soul contracts or ancestry. Or you may feel more of a pull to one sacred site or another because they hold the vibration of what you require for your healing journey at this time. There are many sacred sites that are not mentioned here, and we encourage you to go where you are guided.

These Temples of great majesty, being earthly mirrors and doorways to the Cosmos and the Heavens while on the Earth, are being re-activated to be conduits for the transformational process. Their alignment with the magnetic ley lines, grid-like forces of the Earth, as well as with particular grids of the star systems, makes them powerful places for initiation and empowerment. It is a very important component of not only reclaiming your sacred energies, but of realigning and reconfiguring your personal Tree of Life to a higher vibration, to work with the joining of Heaven and Earth during the great initiation you are participating in.

Until the present time of awakening beginning with the Harmonic Convergence in 1987, many of these sacred places, temples, and shrines were left mostly unused in this dimension, except by the higher initiates, because it was necessary to close these vortexes to those who would misuse their powerful forces. Many were closed as far back as the times of Atlantis. We have been able to hear the ancients' voices and feel the spiritual power present at these most holy of holy centers because of the many ceremonies and rituals that went on for eons of time, in spite of the many gates being closed. These centers are participating in the Grand

Awakening. We ask that only the purest forms of energy be available for you to experience and to come home to, as the 'Watchers of the Gates' make ready to release the magnetic powers of Light, Love, and Wisdom.

For many years now ceremonies have been held at these Power Centers by increasing numbers of groups and individuals who hold the highest good for the Planet and humanity in their Hearts and minds. Spirals of Light have begun spinning to match the harmonics of the evolvement of the telluric and cosmic energies of Earth and Heaven. You may have been to many of these sacred sites and 'Wonders of the World' in person or only traveling in your dreams, but either way you can connect into the invisible web and set your intention to gather what is needed to help in your transformation at this time.

Be aware of how the Earth is harmonizing with the evolutionary energies that are now coming through her in most powerful ways. This is occurring in important places where the underground current of Water can be most affected, circulating in the underbelly, caverns, and underworld of the planetary grid. Most sacred sites are built over powerful underground water ways. Know that what you call Crop Circles are sacred geometric creative forces that are being brought here to assist during these great times of awakening of humanity, encoding the Earth's Higher Self. These geomantic generators are manifested by the joining of the evolving elemental forces of the Earth with our Star Ancestors. As the Earth's vibration is raised, the Higher Self of humanity can be accessed while in physical embodiment. The various forms of Sacred Geometry created, stimulate and complete the encodement needed for further activation of humanity's DNA. This will awaken humanity to its innate ability to conceive and create a profound experience, greater than ever lived before on the Earth.

Let us move ahead on our journey to the deep Soulful places that carry an alignment to the Will of the Creator's intent in the dreaming of the Fifth World of unity. Continue working with your trusted guide or a new one may appear. A high level teacher may also appear to assist you when you enter the restored sacred sites. Jump on the back of the animal spirit of Lion, Tiger, or Horse, as they take you on a journey of great power and wisdom. In these places open your senses to the wholeness of the Worlds that greet you here. Ask permission to enter into the deeper sacred space of these places of great spiritual connection. These holy places were built for the people to have a place to remember the original instructions and states of being that are fundamental in assisting humanity to remember how to stay connected to the Wisdom of the Ages. Before we begin, remember that giving back in reciprocity is one of the most sacred of ways to keep renewing the energy bodies of these blessed Earth and celestially connected sites. Take the time to make an offering of flowers, incense, tobacco or whatever your own guidance tells you to give, as a humble gesture of thanks and honoring.

We begin calling in the dreaming of your pure embodiment in the blessed places of emergence of great civilizations and cultures. Put forth a spiritual intention to gather and reclaim the power of these magnificent places, from the sacred energy that creates vortexes of illumination. Gather and reclaim the knowledge and wisdom of the ceremonies of Love and Light. Put out a request to receive a symbolic and energetic gift in each sacred center that will enliven and inspire you to remember your true self before the separation from God Source. We are transforming at new levels of consciousness, but it is necessary to come 'full circle,' uniting the healed past with the conscious present, so we can truly move into a New World.

We take you to the Four Corners of the Southwest of North America that are holding the pillars of access to the unity of the Tree of Life for your rebirth, for this area is known as the emergence place of the Fourth World. Allow yourself to ground into the source of new life coming deep from the core of the Earth at this Sipapu, where all the sacred elements are brought together in balance. . . As you re-emerge out of the Grand Canyon with the innocence of a new born, awakening to a brand new day after visiting the womb of the Mother and the Light without a Shadow. . . Feel yourself being reborn in the Waters of Lake Titicaca in South America with the purity of self and memory of your divine origins intact. . . Come to the doorway of the sacred rising of the Sun at the Temple of Giza in Egypt where you go through powerful initiation as you are given passage in a Soul flight to the Heart of Creation, watching your spirit choose to return from this blissful Center to be even more present for the great transformation, returning with renewed energy and wisdom, knowing deeply your connection to Source, where there is no loss of inner wholeness. . .Continuing on to the Temple of the Oracle of Delphi in Greece, getting your instructions from the Priestess Seers on your divine mission this time around the Wheel of Life, while your Aka Dream Cord is re-established and you once again communicate directly with your Higher Self. . . Come to the Temple of Basika in Bali where your emotional self receives support for its release and return to its true feeling self. . . Purify your body and Soul in the Ganges River of India. . . Listen closely to the sounds of chanting in the sacred Temples of Tibet, awakening the spinning Wheels of Light that open you to great radiance. . . Gather the wisdom of the ancients, aligning your being to 'Oneness' on the stairways of Chichen Itzi in Mexico, joining with the Rainbow Serpent of pure energy that re-centers on the Planet during Summer Solstice. . . Inspire your being with the creation fire energies of the power of Pele in Hawaii... Nourish yourself in the vital watery lands of Lemuria in Kauai, renewing your pure

*connection to the Earth and all her children in a place of great 'Oneness'.
. . Bathe in the healing glow of the Waters of Lourdes in France, returning
your body to its original perfection and health. . . Dream your World
awake at the great rock of Uluru in Australia. . . . Align with the balanced
holy reflection of the Divine, sanctified at the Temple of the Sun and Moon
at Teotihuacán in Mexico. . .Come into love and harmony, empowered and
reunited with the sacred Priest and Priestess energies at Machu Picchu, as
you regain the balance of the masculine and feminine. . . Remember the
joy of what it is to live in sacred community, in Mesa Verde in Colorado. . .
Fill your mind and Soul with the wisdom of the Ages, inside the Sphinx
in Egypt. . . Open to the ritual wisdom of how to keep conscious of
spiritual truths offered by the Star Ancestors of the Dogon in Africa at
their sacred shrines. . . Join in the dance of the spheres as you align with
your multi-dimensional self around the stone beings of Stone Henge in
England. . . Connect with your Star Ancestors who return to you
knowledge of ways to manifest and create in alignment with Spirit in the
Kivas of Chaco Canyon in New Mexico. . . Be awakened into the energies
of the Fifth World by the appearance of the Blue Star Katsina in the
ceremonial plaza in Hopi. . . Be truly reborn with the Christos into your
true essence self at the Dome of the Rock. . .*

*Let yourself continue to travel to other sacred sites that may be
drawing you in. Give thanks at the completion of your adventure for all
that has been given. Give thanks to the spirit guides and teachers that have
assisted you. Be aware in humble thankfulness for all those who have
continued their ceremonies and ritual for thousands of years against all
odds. Give thanks deeply for the Mother Earth who has responded to the
re-opening of these many sacred centers, opening her arms to welcome
those who wish to respect the gifts she has given. Return to the sacred
temple of your own being, fully renewed, remembered, and restored in the
deepest part of your being. Acknowledge and pay close attention to what
you were given, taking the time needed to honor the profound nature of
this passageway.*

As we live more in the moment without having to take the negative
experiences of the past forward with us, a new level of grace will be part
of our every movement. As aliveness and fertility is restored to our Souls,
as well as to the Lands, we will be carried into the next Era of the Fifth
Sun and the Land of the Flowers. The joy and ecstasy of the reunion of our
sacred forces and energies brings forth a blossoming of such magnificence
that we are humbled by such beauty. The 'Flower of Life' will be restored
and renewed and the pain of separation will be a thing of the past. The
original pure spiritual blueprint of the divine human will be able to
manifest here on Earth and we may enter through the sacred doorway of
the Heart where all are truly loved.

III

The Healing of the Heart of the World

13

Gateway to the Door of Heaven

Mother of Darkness, Mother of Light; Earth beneath us, Souls in flight! Songs of Love and love of Light; Take us to our Hearts! Take us to our Hearts!

Deep within you exists the deepest, most blissful and ecstatic connection to the Heart of the Mother and to the Heart of the Heavens, that has always been and will always be. Reawakening this place within you is the key to gaining full entry into the gifts of the Upperworld and to the integration of all that has been in separation. Feeling the fullness of Love is the way to unite the Tree of Life. I am your Divine Heart, waiting to be revealed and to release healing to all. The personal Heart that is the Love you feel for your children, your parents, your partners, your friends, and your passions, has kept the doorway to the Heart of the Mother open so as to comfort you through the times of being in duality and separation. With the help of the Sacred Waters you have cleared the painful emotions of trauma held in the child within your emotional flow, freeing yourself to go deeper into unconditional Love. You are now practicing not taking in more negative emotions, letting challenging situations run through you without as much of a charge. With all the transformation that has occurred, perhaps you will be able to begin to feel the deep Love for yourself that the Creator of all of life has always felt. If you continue to not Love yourself, you will continue to feel separate from the Creator and all of Creation. The Light is grounded in your bodies and on the Earth through the healing and opening of your dear Heart. Let me help you, for I am Love itself. You have always been loved. Let your Heart fill up with the truth, leaving no room for the lies of un-love that have come from this time of separation. What do you have to lose, by truly loving yourself?

In the very beginning, your original energy body was infused with and radiated the unconditional Love of your divine nature. Over time, as you sank deeper and deeper into the density of lower consciousness, the vibration of conditional forms of loving was created, as the feeling of being separate from the Creator was experienced. Within the density of the vibrational field of the World, the connection to Source and to the Heart of the Mother was difficult to remember. The absence of experiencing the pure Love of the Heart of the Heavens is the source of all negative and painful emotions with which you have been living and creating. I wish to share the presence of pure Love, which will both sustain you and connect you to the spiritually infused realms of the Heavens.

As you now have less restriction in your Heart, you may be able to remember the times that you have felt the ecstasy of feeling in contact with the greatness of your Soul, Mother Earth, and the Creator of all life. You may feel the tears welling up, your Sacred Waters overflowing with the glory of the Heart flowering open. For this will help bring you home. Let the joy and ecstasy of Royal Hummingbird Medicine bring you home to the place where you will once again be able to feel your connection to the Creator of all life. The Andean keepers of the prophecies are reminding humanity that the Hummingbird is a most important messenger at this time, in that it has direct access to the Heart of the Hanaq Pacha, 'Land of the Flowers' or Fifth World. These beautiful beings assist in handling and calling in higher states of joy, ecstasy, and Love. Their vibration awakens the Medicine of the Flowers. Ask them to come to you and to open your Heart, if just for a moment. Let Hummingbird teach you how to vibrate at a higher level of Love and Light where there is no fear and the divinity of your being can be expressed in all of your energy bodies; physical, emotional, mental, and spiritual, awakening your rainbow Light.

Being able to feel the divinity in all aspects of your being will inspire new levels of creativity, giving you the ability to birth the Divine Child and Christ consciousness through the Heart, within and without. This enlightened energy is available for you to embody, not in waiting for the next coming, but rather in the aligning back to 'Oneness' through the very center of your being. Your Joy Body longs for expression. The healing of the Heart will release a powerful healing force, opening up the boundaries of the dream state. Now you truly can manifest a World based on Love. The distortions of the World are being healed as Love and Light return to humanity, awakening the 'I am' consciousness of unity and oneness.

My presence of Divine Love will unify in your Heart, the three-fold brilliant flames of blue, pink, and gold, in perfect manifestation of the Holy Trinity of Creation. Together once again will be the heavenly Father's creative Power (Light), the Divine Mother's Love, and the Christed Divine Child's infinite Wisdom. You have learned much on your journey far from home and it is time to bring all together as you open to the Heart of the Heavens. Heaven and Earth will be reunited.

The Violet Flame is now available for you to work with because of the reunification that has taken place, to raise the frequency of all distortions and discordant energy into the higher healing vibrations. The Violet Flame is the joined spiritual forces of the Pink Ray of the Divine Love and respect for all life of the Mother-Goddess, and the Blue Ray of our Father-God's divine Light and Will. This gift from the Heavens is to help transform all places of un-love created during the time of separation. This gift gains in power when you empower this force with feelings of forgiveness for yourself and others. Then miracles can occur.

Do not fear that the immensity of the spiritual healing forces of Love will be too much for you to surrender to. We are aware of how much you can handle and wish you no more pain. You are now much more connected to your Higher Self and the Earth, which will assist you to maintain more balance and harmony. The old ways of learning are transforming. Your time of feeling separate is ending. The Doorway of the Heart is your entryway to a place where your connection to all can be experienced without fear, without restriction, without losing your sense of connection to your divine self. Your individuated Soul has an imprint unlike any other, and it is the right moment to understand how to experience both unity and differentiated awareness.

I feel your pain and restriction. I know that to reopen fully to that which you feel in the sacred center of your being, feels overwhelming in light of the pain and suffering you have experienced under the veil and illusions of separation. I understand how difficult it has been to survive and not feel caught in the pain of your bodies at times, and to deal with a World severely out of balance. I see how your Heart has felt the necessity to shut down, since you have felt alone in the World, as if you have been abandoned by Great Spirit to suffer. I understand that at times you will still have protective patterning that believes if you open too far, you will be injured and traumatized once again! The truth of the matter is that once you have learned to connect to the part of you that is connected to the Center of the Godhead, all else is a temporal experience and does not have to be held in pain and suffering any longer.

The Gateway of Venus is here to provide a gracious yet powerful passage in your healing journey, where your places of great hurt and suffering held in relationship to others and the World now have a chance to come back into harmony, beauty, and remembrance. It is the kiss of Divine Love upon the Hearts of humanity, which is the beautiful jewel from which the 'Flowering of your Soul' can take place. This is the doorway to the Rainbow Bridge that will take you from one World to another. The opening in your Heart through unconditional Love and compassion for all beings will catapult you into the Fifth World. You have worked so very hard and for what may seem like forever through the passage of healing, and we wish for you to experience the great blessing of such dedication to be closer to the Creator of All Life.

Allow the seed of Love to grow daily in your being as you choose to express acceptance and Love of all experiences and all beings. Forgive yourself and forgive others, for you have all been through the depths of the journey of the Underworlds. The state of true forgiveness will allow the process of healing to continue until it has completed its purpose. The state of loving grace embodied will enable the most unloved aspects of yourself and others to dissolve in the great sea of remembrance of your divinity and inter-connectedness. This is your true essence. Let the loving voice of your Heart speak gently in the forefront of all other emotions. This does not mean that you are to give away your self, your destiny path, or true empowerment. The voice of the Heart enables you to tune in, making the most loving choices for yourself from a place where there is no room to feel lesser or greater than. The Lotus Blossom of your Soul is in full expression and knows the return path to the way of living a life of beauty. Let it bring you back into loving awareness whenever you feel you have returned to a state of separation. Once you have touched in on its purity, it is always there to return to.

Love yourself, each other, the World, the Universe, and all of Creation, as you breathe in every thought, every emotion, every movement, through the holy caverns of your Heart Center. The journey of healing you have been through will enable you to open to the part of you that knows how to experience in joy, beauty, and harmony. You are not alone. The Heart of the Earth and the Heart of the Heavens are surrounding and filling you with Love from all directions and dimensions, when you are ready to flower open. It is now the moment to move up the stairway to Heaven, gaining access through the grace of finding your true home in the Heart. Let yourself feel deeply. . . from that place in you that remembers and has always known home. This is the entrance way to the Fifth World and the awakening to Heaven on Earth! You are already there.

IV

The Door of Heaven

14

Journey to the Thirteen Heavens

I have come into a place of wonder, where a stream of dancing rainbows are interwoven throughout, a dreamlike landscape of great brilliance. I must still be dreaming; it is forming, it is flowering. I have awakened from a deep slumber into a New World of awe-inspiring beauty. It is breathtaking. I experience a wish to bring others here so they too will share in the magnificence of what is being experienced. We have been readied. Join with me as we trust in what is being offered by Spirit to bring us closer to our authentic self and the heavenly realms.

In this most special part of the journey it would be particularly helpful to let the story and its effects just flow through and work within your own creative response. It is difficult to put words to an experience that we are just opening to. Many of us have memories of long ago times when the connection to other spiritual dimensions was much more available. But these doorways have been closed down to much of humanity for the last 5,200 years. The Cosmic Door to the Heavenly Gates is opening once again. It is time to invite our 'Flowering Soul' to reach for the Heavens, to open more fully to the spirit realms, and to bring these realms into our experience here on the Planet. Our personal Tree of Life has strengthened its Roots and Trunk, as the vital nutrients of Mana have been renewed and returned and we take what we have learned with us in the healing journey through the Door of Earth. The sacred 'Cosmic Tree' of the New World is strengthening as we individually heal. We are now ready to reach for the Heavens as the Heavens reach for us.

So much information is out in the World at this time on multi-dimensional realities and other so called New Age information. What to trust and open to? When your opened Heart and connection to your Higher Self become a natural way of being for you, your intuitive self will intuit what 'feels right' and is congruent with your own knowing. When you have cleared the heavy hucha of your emotional body, you will feel much more connected to your intuitive self and to the Earth. All you have transformed by passing through the Door of Earth will allow you to be able to handle more easily the next steps. There are also guardians of the gateway between the Door of Earth and the Door of Heaven that will keep you in check as you pass, so that you do not lose your consciousness and forget all you have learned from the past!

Not only is there much information from outside sources to check in with, stimulating us to remember, but many of us are also awakening to our own cosmic Lightbrary (Superconcious Library), and becoming increasingly aware of our celestial origins as multi-dimensional beings. The veils between the Worlds are becoming thinner, and dream time and awake time are uniting in the great return to unity. Sometimes we may experience these spiritual realms as more real than the 3D reality of daily life that we have existed in for so long. Then at other times we feel the demands of this World bringing us flat down to the ground, back into a limited reality. We invoke the clear intent right here and now that we wish to integrate the Worlds in a way in which we can navigate back and forth, and in and out as needed, without creating disharmony or ill-ease, but rather more blessed states of grace. Continuing to surrender to the 'Water of Grace' will assist you to be more comfortable in the fluidity of the shifting dream-like dimensions.

According to the Maya, as shared by Geraldo Barrios Kaanek, a Mayan Medicine Man and Time Keeper, a new Great Cycle of the Thirteen Heavens, actually began in 1991. It has a duration of thirteen times fifty years, totaling 676 years. This does not start immediately, but begins gradually as it shifts and purifies the energies of the Lowerworlds, so the two can unify in the renewed Tree of Life. We will now embark on the journey to the Thirteen Heavens. Humanity has already been transforming with the energies emanating from these realms, opening us up to be readied for the evolutionary leap of 2012, as we enter into a very different, more spiritually infused reality.

According to Carl Johan Calleman, a researcher on the Mayan Calendar, on November 24th, 2006, we are entering the beginning of the Fifth Day of the Galactic Cycle of Creation. The vibrations of this Day give humanity further support from the cosmos to move beyond dualistic thinking to the balancing of the right and left brains and of the energies of East and West; another surge of vibrational energies to assist us as we near the doorway to the Thirteen Heavens. We will be going through many more.

Working with the accelerated evolutionary process along with the new vibrational energies, can be quite challenging at times. If you are someone who is very sensitive to shifts in energy and consciousness and have been living a spiritually connected lifestyle, you may have been feeling the intensity of shifting forces since the Harmonic Convergence in 1987. Since the turn of the century, there has been an even more greatly intensified activation emanating from the Core of the Galactic Center to help us resolve our personal and global places of polarity and separation. The Light coming in and the many other phenomena we have spoken of previously, are shapeshifting the World and all its inhabitants, even though some may be resisting the shift even more. There are those whose Ego trance states have taken over more fully, who are holding on to hierarchical control and misuse of power more tightly than ever before.

As our Ego flails in its loss of central control and our more spatial right brain is activated, we may feel as if we are losing focus and direction. At times we may feel very disoriented by the activation into higher ground as all our Worlds collide, making it necessary to harmonize and align all past lessons and experiences for this monumental shift of consciousness. It is important to reframe the doubts and confusion that may be experienced while passing through this doorway into more of a state of surrender of the 'old' to the 'new' as we trust our higher guidance. There are doorways and spiral entrances that are appearing right in front of us to transform through and it is important to have some understanding of what is occurring.

Because of the misuse of power during the demise of Atlantis, a small group of more highly evolved Atlanteans and Lemurians shut down the high level vortexes of the Earth so that these omnipotent forces would not be further abused. Only the 'Seven Rays of Power' that are more connected to personal embodiment and empowerment and less to the highest vibrations were left open. These Seven Rays are connected through our Chakras, which we will focus on later in the journey. These energies and 'Powers' that were still present brought us into the evolutionary process we have been in since then. The closing down of the higher centers put a stop to the continued manipulation of the most powerful Earth Grids, thus not allowing total destruction of the Earth, thus humanity. This also slowed down our evolutionary process so we might have a chance to go through more of the 'earthly' school of life. The closing of these higher vibrations may have also been part of the 'Fall from Grace,' bringing humanity into a denser vibration for the purpose of learning and being humbled through the journey of the Underworlds, as we experienced the pain of our creations, in the Smoking Obsidian Mirror of karma. This is of course in total divine order as all things are, so that there would be an evolutionary process of becoming more matured Souls, able to take more conscious steps towards the handling of higher powers.

Rays of Power stem from the Universal White Light and represent different aspects of the Divine as it manifests out into Creation. For a time after the closing, there were still present on Earth evolved Souls dedicated to the evolution of humanity who built the Great Pyramids and many other Great Temples and structures in order to keep the cosmic energy present on the Earth. After years in the increased density, many of these Souls fell into the misuse of power or left to dimensions of a higher vibration. Most of the knowledge on how to build such magnificent sacred sites disappeared into higher dimensions as the veil between the Worlds increased.

In the last ten years, all Twelve Rays of these powerful vortexes of cosmic energies have been opened for the first time since Atlantis, with the Thirteenth Ray, which wraps around the other Twelve, being the most holy of holy Christ force. Supposedly we came into this realm with one ray being the main learning energy we were to evolve and learn through, as you can see when you review the patterns of past lives. We now have the chance to work with all Thirteen of the 'Divine Aspects' of Creation (the Thirteen Heavens). It may seem as if the majority of humanity has not evolved enough to work consciously with these Powers, but it is time for our evolvement and there is spiritual assistance available to help us do so. It is said that if at least 144,000 Souls awaken (the original number of Souls birthed onto the Earth) to the new consciousness, at least a portion of humanity can embody the vibration of the New Earth, and there will be much less destruction in the changing of the Ages as more Light and Love are anchored in.

It is important to bring the immensity of these spiritual forces into the awareness of our personal lives in order to work with them. There are effects from these Powers that are occurring, that might be helpful to identify. Note these symptoms (listed below) and see if you recognize them in your own experience. You are not alone. You are being pulled, led, stimulated, showered through and through with the radiance of enlightenment, so that we can make it through this particularly powerful evolutionary gateway with our consciousness intact and with more ease and grace. We have listed some of the symptoms at the beginning of our sojourn, but these are even more connected to the entrance of more Light, as our vibration quickens. Many have reported all kinds of disorienting states of being and experiences that are becoming more and more commonplace. Some of the shifts are enjoyable, as we feel more Love and grace in our lives, while other symptoms may make us feel downright crazy.

By going through the healing journey of the Doorway of Earth, we will now be more able to stay grounded in this time of great transitions. By coming into more of a unified field from transforming our energies of separation, the strength of the rooted-ness of our new Tree of Life will not allow our Tree to be so easily blown over by the intensity of the Light and Love which are coming from both Heaven and Earth. Being grounded is very important as we free float through the 'in between' Worlds; no longer comfortable here in the 3D World we have been living in, nor arrived fully yet into the Fifth World. Hopefully some of us may already be through the hardest part of the transformation of the Ego and most of the uncomfortable shifts and are now cleared enough to handle more Light and Love without being as amplified with intense lessons needing to be completed. You have been called to evolve and you are needed to assist in the creation of a new paradigm. Be kind to yourself wherever you are on the journey, because most of us go in and out of graceful states of being all the time. At least now you have more awareness and spiritual guidance to help when you forget your way.

The road of great revelation and healing is a long road, but it is the path we must take. But wherever you are on the healing road, do your best to not compare yourself to others but be thankful and at peace and acceptance with where you are in present time. Please also allow space for others to be where they are, while being clear with what you see and the help you may offer if asked, for it is all a journey, not a destination. Focus on your own growth and healing as the greatest help you can give, and that will radiate out to all through whatever service is your calling.

The symptoms created from the heightened spiritual forces radiating transformation onto the Earth and humanity, will come and go as the waves of energy pour through our lovely Planet. There will be various vibrations to be downloaded and adjusted to. If the uncomfortable symptoms persist, they may be a catalyst, prodding you on to make more changes in yourself and in your life. Pay attention to ways of living and being that no longer serve you, be it a location, a job, or a relationship. Make the needed changes. Use the following list for understanding and for motivation to participate in group activations and ceremonies, as well as giving more attention to your own spiritual path. The guardians of the 'Gates of Heaven' and the guides who reside in the Upperworlds, want us to bring Heaven to Earth for this is humanity's destiny. Powerful animal allies will continue to take us through this healing journey, traveling with us into the Upperworlds, for they will assist in the embodying of higher energies as well as assisting us in navigating through the more dream-like and ethereal dimensions. Higher archetypal teachers, Ascended Masters, and angelic forces may also appear.

Listen closely to what is true for yourself, as you feel recognition of the changes you are going through:

1. *A strong urge to return back home to God Source.*
2. *Synchronistic and meaningful experiences occurring on almost a daily basis; being in the right place at the right time.*
3. *As you think about something or about someone, it happens or they show up.*
4. *Feeling like you are less grounded in the density of your body than you have been in the past.*

5. *Difficulty getting your daily tasks done, with the movements of your body in the World being much more sluggish and difficult.*
6. *One minute you are going in one direction in your life then you are going in another.*
7. *Sudden urge to move or to make a big change, even though it does not seem very practical.*
8. *Many sudden changes in relationships and in other places of attachment and old patterns.*
9. *Resistance to doing anything that does not bring you joy and fulfillment.*
10. *Feeling like you must be going crazy, because you feel so much intense energy and shifting, that you are not stable in your concept of yourself and your surroundings.*
11. *So many tests and difficult situations coming at once that you believe you can handle no more.*
12. *Dreams being more intense and vivid than usual.*
13. *Short term memory loss and difficulty focusing.*
14. *Being in the present moment is the only state of mind that makes sense.*
15. *Feelings that come from nowhere identifiable, such as great joy and bliss, not connected to an outside cause.*
16. *Feelings of great fatigue, as well as a greater need to live a simpler life with more nurturing and restfulness.*
17. *Seeing and hearing things that are not in your so called 'normal states' of experiencing reality.*
18. *Extremes between sleeping all the time and not being able to sleep at all.*
19. *Seeing yourself and others in a strange new Light.*
20. *Feeling immense compression, as if you are being squeezed through a very small opening.*
21. *New illnesses and aches and pains in your body, as well as weight change not based on what you eat.*
22. *Feeling disoriented and out of place and out of time.*
23. *Buzzing and tingling at the top of your head or Crown Chakra.*
24. *An increase in your psychic abilities.*
25. *An ability to share more Love and non-judgment.*
26. *Feelings of instability, as if you have one foot in one World and one in another.*

Is this the creation of a New World, while the old one is on its way to disintegration?

Now take a deep breath and understand that we are in a great passage of rebirth, in the tunnel of the birth canal, with the Light and Love guiding us through. Be kind to yourself and to others. Know you may have been chosen to be a wayshower or lightworker for this awakening so that you may assist others in navigating through the passage. Do not let this awareness hook into any delusions of grandeur and back into an Ego trance. It is truly just a wake-up call to be all you can be. With the intensity of the shift, at times you may be overwhelmed, so much so, that you can barely be with yourself, and at other times you may feel quite strong and can be a helpful and loving presence for others. It is our individual path to take responsibility for our personal evolution. But we also need to remember more than ever, that we are part of the great web of life that is connected to everything and everybody. We cannot do it alone.

I am a seeker like you, and I am discovering my path as I go. I may speak at times like an authority because the information comes through so loud and clear. But in true humility, I am always on a path of learning and hope to inspire you to explore your own knowing in every moment. On the journey to the Upperworlds, I will share with you some of the information that I have gathered in my own awakening, as well as information from others, to help give you some sense of what is occurring. Of course, you will have your own personal experience in this gateway that will teach you as you go.

I often speak of indigenous wisdom because it comes from ancient times and cultures and offers grounding for what is coming through at this time. Remember that the Red Nation was also given the guardianship of Earth, the most grounding element. I have mentioned knowledge and wisdom throughout, because knowledge turns to wisdom when it is carried out and matured through right action. Knowledge on its own can be misused and misunderstood.

As mentioned before, the doorway of the Rainbow Goddess we are passing through, offers so many creative energies at once, that humanity can get lost in the ungrounded state of having too many choices. Much of this ancient wisdom was to be kept secret until now. Often what comes through the spiritual Ethers, the higher information being offered directly from the Heavens and the Higher Self, matches that which has been passed down for eons of time through the Wisdom Keepers on Earth. This ancient wisdom offers a grounding and longevity to an experience many of us are just discovering. New Age and indigenous wisdom can come together in a respectful manner. I have shared some of this indigenous knowledge when appropriate. It is also stated in many indigenous prophecies that it is the ones that embody the Rainbow Beings who will learn from the indigenous Wisdom Keepers and bring together all the teachings. They will integrate and share the unified teachings of many cultures as the various nations come back together from the Four Directions. It has been said that those who embody the teachings of the Four Directions and Four Races will fulfill the prophecies. They will assist in bringing humanity to the place of honoring the many ways and paths, unifying our Medicine Fields and Hearts and minds once again. Always check in with your own intuitive knowing, for that will be your discernment through this passage of becoming more aware and trusting of the Upperworlds, which is at times a most intangible experience.

We are evolving as a species and it is a rare person who does not see that we need to think and experience outside of our normal sense of reality, in order to come up with solutions for how to navigate and create in a World that has become greatly out of balance. To do this, it is important that we remember and reconnect to our multi-dimensional beings. Long ago humanity was able to access many more dimensions before the 'Fall from Grace,' and even for a time after. We are talking of states of greater spiritual awareness and Light. The Tree of Life is a focal point of perception once again, for the concept of multi-dimensionality. Imagine how we can go up and down this Cosmic Axis into different fields of reality, as if each rung of the ladder we use to climb is a dimension that moves us closer to the Godhead. But dimensions are really spirals of energy and we are over-simplifying the concept for the clarity of this journey, as we re-open doorways and channels for awareness and spiritual growth.

Once we are connected to our core self, where both our Gold and Silver Aka Cords are connected, we can feel a solid connection to the trunk and roots of the Tree of Life. Then we can expand to greater spiritual heights without losing contact with the Earth and all we have learned. It is important to know that contained in the Core Self are the true higher feeling states that are so necessary to keep our connection clear. We have gotten to experience the transformation of our emotionally reactive parts that had been stuck in the traumas of the past in passing through the Door of Earth and have learned tools to transform each time we forget.

I would like to continue to keep this experience simple and heart centered, being as powerful as it can be, and to keep you on a feeling level experience while you stay in your bodies, which is very important to do while on the journey to the Thirteen Heavens. Another reason it is so important to stay grounded, is to not forget what you have learned on your sojourn through the Door of Earth. This is what we were not able to do on previous attempts to evolve to the next World to bring forward in consciousness that which we had gained through experience before.

Do not stop here because you believe you are not complete with your healing. We will be shifting back and forth, in and out of consciousness, and falling back at times into old habits and patterns. Be kind to yourself on the road, for we are reaching for the stars, as the stars are reaching out to us, and we have traveled for a long time in forgetfulness. Every moment we get to choose again and to begin anew. Do not give up, for we are in the shift of Ages, getting closer all the time to a life where grace and Love are the norm.

The journey into the Upperworlds or Heavens had been attainable for just a small number of individuals or only in rare moments, during this last Great Cycle of learning through separation. The information was held tight by secret societies and by the elite, be it part of a greater religious system or a spiritual sect. There were always the few, who when they reached an enlightened place and ascended through the Thirteen Heavens, came back to assist in the evolvement of humanity. But these are different times. In order to shift the paradigm of the past, there is a necessity to awaken as much of humanity as possible. This path is no longer only open for the chosen few. The times of hierarchical ways of existence are coming to an end in all ways. The spiritually enlightened few will not be able to hold the doorway open for long, and much larger Soul groups are needed for the full bursting forth into a New World.

When we come through the Doorway of the Heart after healing our places of separation, we will be more prepared to open to higher dimensions of Light and Love. As I have gone through my own process of awakening, I would find that my Shadow and Ego would often go into full rage and resistance in my life and within my psyche when the Light was being activated. I would like to see others have a more graceful experience and walk ahead in the Beauty Way of less pain and more grace.

The wisdom and higher knowledge contained in the Thirteen Heavens have guardians at the heavenly gates that will not allow full passage through until the higher Heart, mind, feeling and physical states are reached. It may appear that the so called Fallen Angels are able to misuse higher knowledge and have access to these spiritual realms, but there is a limit to that. These beings are also being given a chance to move into a state of evolvement at this time. As we enlighten ourselves and others, this elevates the energy field on the Earth, giving the separated beings a greater chance of coming home to the Light and the Love. Remember we have all been a part of the 'Fall.'

It is said that only through the reconnection of the Silver Aka Cord that joins our Physical Body to our Dream Body and our Dream Body to the Cosmic Dream of the Universe, can we receive the greater spiritual teachings and find our true purpose and embody our most sacred self. By staying connected to our Heart Centers and to higher feeling states, we can continue to keep the cosmic lines of communication open. To travel up the ladder to the Upperworlds, it is important that we stay rooted or the Tree of Life will fall over. Having access to the higher truths and frequencies of the Upperworlds as a way of daily living, not just in other Worlds, is what is needed for the transformation of humanity. While we have been in the

'School of the Underworld,' we have had access to these gifts at times. But with the opening of our Heart Chamber and the healing of our places of separation, we will be able to have more consistent access in a unified field.

The Silver Aka Cord connects our Physical Body to the Dream Body; the Dream Body in turn connects us to the greater spiritual Universe. Each Medicine Center or Chakra can be connected by this energy cord once we can navigate within the Dream Body, so that there is communication and inter-connectedness through all centers. We have cleared the blocking of the Shadow from the umbilical cord of our Inner Child, opening us to this most divine channel of communication. The messages from the dreaming space of the Cosmic Mother and Father can once again be heard, as well as the positive intentions and prayers of our 'True Self.' When the Tree of Life is brought back into wholeness and the Worlds are no longer separated, we will be fully joined in the dreaming of our reality. The spiritually infused umbilical cord of our original birthing has kept us connected to the Cosmic Dream of the Great Mother and will also connect us with the Grandmothers.

The Teachings of the Thirteen Grandmothers is coming back into consciousness on the Planet at this time, as a way to stay connected to the Earth reality as we travel to the Heavens. Being grounded and experienced in more evolved ways of living on the Mother Earth, is what the Thirteen Grandmothers are here to assist us with at this time. They offer a teaching of a lifeway in which to embody the powers of the Upperworlds. They have brought the cosmic wisdom of the stars and of the higher dimensions through the Divine Feminine, grounding through the Earth and the Moon, having kept watch in the great ancient standing stones. The sacred Grandmothers have quietly and humbly been waiting for their time to come forth once again, to ground the energies of the Star Nations through you and your children's children. They not only shower blessings from above but from deep inside the ancient Earth. They have continued to tell their stories through the indigenous grandmothers of many nations.

Call on the Thirteen Grandmothers to surround and guide you through this journey, as well as staying connected to the gifts of Turtle Medicine. The Turtle (North America is called Turtle Island by many Native Americans), will keep your energy field grounded and intact while you embody the many dimensions, reminding you that you can be taken back home to Earth whenever you journey too far. Turtle Medicine helps one stay connected to the Earth while journeying to the stars, and more deeply to oneself. The Turtle, with its thirteen sections and its ability to carry its home on its back, is a mediator between the Earth plane and the Thirteen Heavens. As we feel the security of our connection to God-Source and our true home, this allows us to become less attached to earthly concepts of what home is; concepts that are just holding us back in the comfort zones of our past.

Give an offering of corn meal, the most precious food of the people, to the sacred Grandmothers, who at times appear as the sacred Corn Mothers, requesting us to get to know them. They are here to remind you of the gifts that are to be experienced and lived here on Earth while on the journey of the Thirteen Heavens. They are a sacred extension of Mother Earth's divine aspects, as well as being the embodiment of our Star Sisters from above; these energies have been waiting to assist in the Earth's and humanity's evolution in this 'Great time of Awakening!'

The Thirteen Grandmothers have re-emerged to rebalance with Sister Moon and her cycles, to ground sacredness in the World once again and to shift the role of the feminine so it can be in balance once again with the Sun and the masculine forces. They are intrinsically connected to the Thirteen Cycles of the Moon and have been dreaming the vision of the Fifth Sun deep inside, until the time was right to come forth; a vision of a time where all would be brought forth in wholeness. Each gift they carry is to work in harmony with all other gifts, and is to be integrated into the human experience by staying in touch with the higher feeling states. The Cycles of the Moon continue to amplify that which is out of balance in our Waters, as well as assisting with the full expression of the higher feelings states, when the Moon is honored and respected. The Grandmothers offer a sacred vessel, a Sacred Circle in which to go within and tune into our higher feeling states where we know nothing but the truth. They ask us to walk the 'Beauty Way Rainbow Trail' so that our new journey can be lived here on the New Earth as she changes.

As I was working with the teachings of the Grandmothers, I became aware of a gathering of the Thirteen Grandmothers right here on Earth. These prophecies were to be embodied by those who have chosen to walk the good road, listening to a calling from Mother Earth, Sister Moon, and Great Spirit, to come forth at this time. I was able to gather sacred coals from the fires ritualistically used at a ceremony of the Thirteen Indigenous Grandmothers at Star Dreaming Temples south of Santa Fe, New Mexico in 2005. The Grandmothers are actually gathering in this 3D reality to fulfill the prophecies and to come together for teachings and ceremonies. The first actual gathering was on October 11th, 2004, in Phoenicia, New York when Thirteen Grandmothers from around the World met. They met in the area of this country where the Grandmothers of the Iroquois Federation met so very long ago. These Grandmothers who are trained, initiated shamans and medicine women, met to discuss the fate of humanity on the Earth and how to revive the traditions, rituals and medicines that can save it.

There are twelve stone labyrinth temples built by James Jereb, a dear friend of mine, who is a visionary artist and temple builder extraordinaire at Star Dreaming, a multidimensional sacred site in which to experience the spiritual forces coming in during these great times of change and evolution. After the twelfth labyrinth was finished, (the Temple of Magic) and the standing stones were raised, the thirteen grandmothers appeared as if by magic and asked to be at the Temple for the closing ceremony of the 2005 gathering. These twelve temples very much embody the powers of the Twelve Rays, creating a field of unification in which to bring in the thirteenth sacred energy of the completed Sacred Hoop of the Wisdom and Love of the Grandmothers, birthing our evolved 'I am that I Am' presence. The twelve temples and labyrinths are: *the Temple of the Sun, the Moon, the Stars, the Milky Way, Lightning, the Heart, Dreams, New Atlantis, Rainbow Serpent, Avalon, Violet Flame and the Temple of Magic.* I am thankful there are those who have the great vision and power to bring to Earth such holy places, where we can more easily have access to the spiritual realms.

Jamie Sams has brought forth from her traditional teachings, the attributes that each Grandmother carries and writes of them in the book *The Thirteen Original Clan Mothers*. These attributes or gifts, are not very different from those that one of my teachers, Ohky Simine Forest, has shared with me as the spiritual powers that are available for us on the journey of the Thirteen Heavens. These gifts are available to us to connect more fully to, after we move through the lessons of the Lowerworlds, inherent in the human condition in this last Era. These energies are what access to the Higher Self offers for our evolvement. These powers are connected to the Thirteen Chakras, which we will touch on later; thirteen being the number of enlightenment and Christ consciousness, as well as the Thirteen Moons or Lunar Cycles. The year 2013 is also when the Fifth World is to be made fully manifest. Numbers and lists are a way to assist humanity to chart that which is beyond definition in the spiral dance of the unseen Worlds. Numbers also carry specific energetic encoding. Each of the thirteen levels of the Upperworlds, has a correlating guardian of both male and female creation beings or Gods and Goddesses of our Universe, as a representation of the embodiment of these powers. They are Mayan Deities according to Ohky's teachings, but may appear to you according to your personal spiritual tradition. The Creator Gods and Goddesses had left these abilities in the ethers, until the right Cycle for humanity occurred to pick up these gifts. I will not go into detail on them, because it is a teaching to be given by those who are deeply connected to that tradition. These powers also reside in our energy fields and as we expand our consciousness, we expand out to connect with them.

The spiritual gifts of the Upperworlds are being made more available to us at this time, as it is of profound importance that we make an evolutionary leap. We are becoming more aware of the necessity of our evolution as conscious co-creators of the 'Fifth Sun.' The Holy Ones can assist us, but we must grow up from children or adolescents into spiritually adept adults, in order to make it through the passageway and graduate into a World imbued with spiritual consciousness. We must learn to embody the higher traits and energies, surrendering to the mysteries of a new frontier, therefore gaining greater access to what is needed for the World's and humanity's evolution.

We begin with naming the powers from the more mysterious perspective of the ancient Mayan Codexes, as researched and brought forth by Ohky Simine Forest, before we ground back to Earth with the teachings of the Grandmothers. As we expand and develop these gifts, the new Tree of Life can flower and bear fruit. We start with the first branch of the 'Tree' as it reaches to the Heavens and moves upward:

Birthing through the naval where the Dream Body is attached to the unified field of the higher realms of the Earth, becoming the dreaming* *Life Knowledge offered through the Ancestors of Oracles and Divination* *Higher Intuition* *Spiritual Will* *Use of Discernment without Judgment* *Wisdom through the Heart* *True Empowerment* *Connection to the Sacred Silence within the Void* *Higher Mind Center of all Imagination* *Trust and Faith in the Spiritual Self* *Higher Consciousness access with the Spiritual Music and the Sound of the Divine* *Divine Order and the State of Pure Feelings* *Cosmic Totality; the Thirteenth and highest seat of the Upperworld, where the Divine Plumed Serpent of the Morning Star Venus greets us and showers us with life sustaining Love, in the rebirth of the consciousness of Kulkucan, Quetzalcoatl and Christ. *

What great gifts we have to look forward to on our journey to the Thirteen Heavens..

The attributes that Jamie Sams speaks of are lessons and gifts that were made into shields held by the sacred Grandmothers. These gifts become manifest as talents, strengths and abilities that move us ahead in our personal and spiritual growth. These ancient Grandmother spirits have been able to humbly hold these powers through this time of the dishonoring of the feminine forces of Creation. You were able to hear their voices if you listened very closely to the standing stone circles of ancient times and to the crystals used in sacred rituals. They have now been awakened by Mother Earth's stirrings. Through being encircled in a humble way by these ancient Wisdom Keepers, by those who share with Heart and true power, we may be inspired to live in a very different reality where we use our spiritual gifts for the good of 'all our relations,' as a lifeway. These sacred gifts cannot be solely used for personal gain or selfish attachment to heightened states of awareness. These powers are shared naturally with others, as their inherent qualities tend to birth altruism in its highest form.

Within the Sacred Circle, as exemplified by the Thirteen Grandmothers, each individual is equal in importance, none elevated above the other, all concerned about the well-being of the community, embodying the collective wisdom of its members. Each individual is connected to each other through their connection to the center of the circle, the seventh direction in the Medicine Wheel, and to the spiritual center within, each having a place on the Sacred Hoop of Life. This Sacred Hoop was dishonored long ago by the hierarchal view and rule of humanity and its people, and is now mending to make the people whole. The Thirteen Grandmothers stand together, united in the Circle, ensuring the non-egoic use of these most sacred energies from the Creator.

Many of us are remembering our stories from the past, of a time long ago in Atlantis, when our Creator given powers were misused to manipulate Mother Earth and each other. We are up against a very similar story once again, but this time the manipulation is becoming World wide and the stakes are much higher. Not only are the possible negative effects more profound at this time, but so is the potential for humanity to heal the wounds of separation at core levels, which then create a wave of profound, positive change throughout our entire Universe. But we must make a conscious choice. We are being given the chance to take the Rainbow Trail, where the gifts of the multi-colored cultures of many nations are joined together in service to all life. When we join in humble Sacred Circle, there is less chance to misuse Creators gifts unwisely and selfishly.

Because it is time for us to embody and be the wise ones, and not give our power over to others, we are being given choices and information that were held secret before now. We are being given a great opportunity by those who have developed these abilities for humanity while being deep in the dreaming. While in the dreamtime, the Grandmothers have been able to grow within their own knowing and integrate what they have learned in the deep passage and patience of a very long Cycle of Time. We give thanks for these Wise Women, as well as to many other sacred helpers. We must not waste this most profound time, but work instead to integrate and remember our lessons of the past so that we will birth a very different spiritual reality during this passage from the Fourth to the Fifth World; thus the possibility of creating Heaven on Earth.

These thirteen attributes are to help us remember, as we connect with our Higher Self, the teachings that were given from the beginning of time. The original teachings are coming back through the Thirteen Grandmothers, as was arranged by Spirit, to bring back the wisdom of the

Divine Feminine in its matured form, developed from its passage in the Underworlds. The wisdom of the Grandmothers was dishonored when they were not included in the development of the new government of the United States. Their very sacred role in the Iroquois Federation was taken out of what was copied by our founding fathers, from their native tradition form of government. The thirteen aspects of the Upperworld are traits that we can all seek to embody and are carried deep within our cellular memories, waiting to be awakened. The Thirteen Grandmothers teach us how to take these gifts back out to the community, for that is how the higher Worlds can be embodied on the Planet. These higher energies are also being rekindled in every living thing.

Call in the presence of that which has held safe the ancient stone circles and that reaches out far into the future. Honor each Grandmother as a part of you that is coming alive. I honor Jamie Sams once again, as the one who has come forth with the following sacred information and for those who are bringing this into manifestation at this time. These are the gifts, as gathered and shared by Jamie Sams:

Gifts of the 'Thirteen Original Clan Mothers'

1. *Talks with Relations* the understanding of Mother Nature's rhythms and guardian of all her relations
2. *Wisdom Keeper* the protectress of sacred wisdom and ancient memory in honoring of all traditions
3. *Weighs the Truth* the guardian of divine truth and justice, self-determination and responsibility
4. *Looks Far Woman* the seer, keeper of the dream time, and interpreter of our vision
5. *Listening Woman* guardian of introspection and inner knowing
6. *Storyteller* guardian of the wisdom stories, teaching with the balance of sacredness and irreverence
7. *Loves all Things* the mother of unconditional Love and all acts of pleasure
8. *She who Heals* keeper of the healing arts
9. *Setting Sun Woman* Keeper and preserver of Mother Earths resources so that with right use of will we fulfill tomorrows dreams for our children's children
10. *Weaves the Web* the bringer of creativity and manifester of dreams
11. *Walks Tall Woman* the keeper of leadership and beauty and grace in all things
12. *Gives Praise* the guardian of ceremony and ritual, thanksgiving and abundance
13. *Becomes Her Vision* the keeper of transformation and transmutation, emerging Spirit into physical form

From the Book *The Thirteen Original Clan Mothers* by Jamie Sams

Jamie Sams has done an amazing job of bringing together these sacred gifts, in making a journey of discovery within her native tradition. They are here for us to aspire and awaken to, not to make us feel less than because we fall short. Remember your personal 'Medicine Wheel' and honor where you are on the journey, also accepting that others are also wherever they need to be in the moment, on the pathway of evolution. It is only in total acceptance of where you are that the journey can truly continue. May the Medicine of Turtle help you accept the pace at which you grow and move, even if it may seem slower than others.

Long ago, when it was time for the energies of the Thirteen Grandmothers to leave the realm of the human and return to the Heart of the Earth Mother, the Thirteen Crystal Skulls were created. These Skulls contain the Love, Wisdom and Power of the Thirteen Heavens. Many of these Sacred Skulls have surfaced to teach humanity, as have the Grandmothers. The center of each Crystal Skull contains the reflection of the Great Smoking Mirror and reflects any intention back to its point of origin, therefore not allowing any misuse of its powers.

All parts of this journey are equally important for both men and women and for all our relations. Of course there are many male elders who have been passing on their spiritual message. But the Circle of Grandmothers are doing their part, and their message is for both men and women. The higher attributes are for all who take the sacred path and are not part of the dualistic World. As we further resolve our duality and go through the journey of healing in the Door of Earth, we rebalance so that our Tree of Life can truly reach the Heavens. Much of humanity has had the experience of having grandmothers who have provided them with some insight and knowledge when they are being honored and treasured for what they know.

Imagine the Thirteen Grandmothers surrounding you, assisting you to ground here on Earth, as well as opening doorways to the Heavens. Remember that all the gifts they have to offer are already deep inside of you, and they are here to remind you of what they are. We are being asked to use wisely the creativity of the Door of the Rainbow Goddess, aligning with both ancient and cosmic knowledge and wisdom, so that we do not spin out of control with all the choices that we have as young co-creators of the next World. Each one of us can do our part, not leaving it up to the few to bring us back into balance, to turn us from the road of destruction we are on. Many more creative solutions will be available to use as we raise our consciousness. When all aspects of the Creation, including the Great Mother, are honored once again, the full spiraling vortex of our twelve-strand DNA can be reactivated and the 'Flowering of our Souls' may be made real in a World desperately in need of the teachings and gifts of the Thirteen Heavens and the Thirteen Grandmothers. Many ask, 'What will this New World look like?' I ask, 'What do we want this New World to look like?' What will it be like when we recognize the God Light and Love in ourselves and each and every part of Creation?

The Twelve Sacred Powers, before they reach the Thirteenth Level of enlightenment, are also connected to the Twelve Signs of the Zodiac, for we are deeply connected inside our consciousness fields to the constellations above. When the thirteenth level is reached, we become the Ascended Masters, returning to assist others in the journey from a place of enlightenment and true guidance. This realm sustains the entire Universe in a sea of perfect and pervading Love. This is where we unify with the Christ force of perfection, unifying in great Light and Love. May the Wheels of Light guide and inspire your way.

15

Doors to the Cosmos, the Chakras: Inspiration of the Rainbow Serpent

L et the Rainbow Serpent be your guide, as you explore the 'Wheels of Light' that are your energy gateways to the Thirteen Heavens. The energies of the primal serpent have been healed and brought to its exalted state as the guardian and guide of the Fifth World. The prophecies and visions of many indigenous cultures have spoken of this occurring since this ancient power got caught in the split of duality, embodying both Shadow and Light. Before this archetypal Snake Medicine transformed into the full spectrum of the rainbow, through the doorway of the Thirteen Heavens, it has greatly assisted humanity to keep us in touch with the Earth's rhythms and movements. It is an integral part of the primal life force and its realignment with the new energies can help recalibrate the electromagnetic energy fields of the human, as it is already doing with the Earth.

The electromagnetic field is Spider Woman's energy web that surrounds all of life. This immense essence force organically aligns with the shifts and changes in the cosmic vibrations, entering into our dimension, as well as keeping connected to the changes in the electromagnetic field that are occurring on the Earth. The electromagnetic field on the surface of the Earth is in alignment with its crystalline Center.

It is said that the Mother Earth has taken her protective energy away from us and that it is very important to be aware of the need to care for and sustain our energy bodies, our personal sacred vessels. As she changes her seasons and her rhythms from the four seasons that we have grown to count on, she is making way for the element Ether or Spirit in Matter, to be present as the primary element, making Spirit more tangible for our evolution to continue. Mother Earth seems to be pushing us on to our next evolutionary steps, as well as going full throttle through her own, even if all humanity cannot join. It is an individual choice. As the Mother Earth's elements are moving in profound ways with volcanic activity, earthquakes, hurricanes, tsunamis, drought, tornadoes, floods, global warming and so much more, we are being asked to tune in to her, each other, and ourselves, in a much more energy sensitive manner so that we can move with the energy shifts and not against them.

It is important at this time and for the initiatory journey of awakening, to have at least a very basic understanding of consciousness and the electromagnetic Universe. Electromagnetism is the energy that comes through the Sun that generates life here on Earth. Everything in our known Universe is energy and there is a grid or electromagnetic plane that weaves everything in Creation together, making us all part of the same tapestry. The Aka Cords are part of this web. When we speak of Spider Woman creating the World, we are speaking of the web that she spins using the cosmic and solar energy of the life force of Creation, creating a blueprint or story-line, from which life is birthed. She is a Native American archetypal symbol that represents powerful Creation energies that are truly beyond most of our perceptions. In the journey of healing the threads that surround you and connect you to all life, are being cleansed and revamped so that a new story can be written and lived.

Throughout time, there have been special beings that have been able to read the bioelectrical emanations that exist in the human energy field and on the Planet. Many of these beings such as mystics, shamans, and medicine people, were able to access their abilities through various spiritual practices, working with otherworldly allies and with powerful 'Plant Spirit Medicines'. Mother Earth contains all that we need to know within her sacred web. This knowledge and wisdom is being imparted to many more of Earth's children during these transformational times. This relay of cosmic energy comes not only from the Creation sustaining web of Mother Earth and her children, but from the energetic emanations of numerous other dimensions we will speak of in the next chapter.

I want to briefly mention that we have four basic energy bodies that make up a human, as part of the web; the physical, emotional, mental and spiritual. We have been in the journey of the Lowerworlds, and it is now time to evolve to the higher states of these energy bodies as the emanation of the heavenly realms shower upon and through us. It is not always easy to know when we have moved successfully through the embodiment of these forces, but one way to know is to look at the types of people we attract, the way we respond to them, and what else we create in our lives. Our ability to sustain higher emotional states much longer, like peace and joy, whatever is occurring outside of our inner world, will also let us know where we are on the journey. While we are in the door of purification and on a strong journey of healing, it may seem as if our lives are falling apart more than others, because we are clearing karmic patterns at ever increasing speeds. Do not give up. Even as we relive and heal old karmic situations one after another, it is important to make a strong effort to respond to the World with more detachment, instead of reacting from our arising emotions. By doing this we will collect less and less karma and eventually create a very different reality. We must continue to face the often painful truth of what yet needs to transform within us. As we get clearer in our emotional bodies, this allows us to keep our mental state more positive as we vibrate within the higher feeling states. As we realign our emotional and mental states, our physical bodies can be attuned to the higher energies as our DNA spirals into further activation. As we make greater contact with our Higher Self and evolved Will Center, we are directed more by the higher spiritual realms, instead of by the trance states of the Ego.

Many of us are being asked to simultaneously bring all our 'bodies' into a higher state of conscious functioning, for we are in the quickening. Doing this at an accelerated speed can be rather challenging at times. It is important to know about the energy bodies, so we can consciously work with the various shifts we are going through and attune to the higher frequencies. There is an etheric sheath that extends just inches from the physical form that serves as a transmitter and receiver of the various bodies, emanating into the greater field of the aura, which is where our Rainbow Body manifests to form a bridge to the higher dimensions. Our Rainbow Body is the unification and working together collectively of all of our energy bodies.

The energy byways of the etheric are comprised of Nadis or primary energy roads; and where these energy streams meet, there are energetic Wheels of Light or Chakras. A Chakra literally translates as a 'radiating spinning Wheel of Light'. These sacred centers can be accessed within our personal energy fields to fine tune the emanations of spiritual energy within and without. These concentrated centers receive divine life force energy (Chi, Prana, Mana) from the Universe and transform this refined power so that it can be assimilated and distributed to the various energy bodies of the human.

There are two primary currents of energy which flow in and around the spinal column. The current on the left is the Ida or feminine force; the current on the right is the Pingala or masculine force. The seven primary Chakras are attached along the spine from the base to the top of the head, being held in place by these currents of our life force. The endocrine system, autonomic nervous system, and the spinal cord, are connected through the Chakras to the subtle Medicine Field or Aura that surrounds us.

To work with and to align to the cosmic energies coming in, it is important to take a journey through the 'Wheels of Light' of our energy bodies to gain greater understanding and further transformation. *Each Chakra may have a different spirit animal as its guardian, connected to you personal Medicine Field, but to simplify for the purpose of full integration at this part of the healing journey, we turn to the Rainbow Serpent to guide us.*

The main system that has classified and described in detail these spinning energy centers, comes from the Hindu spiritual system and can be thought of as a map laid out on the vertical axis running down the front and back of the body in the etheric field. The Q'ero, descendants of the Inca from Peru view the energy centers in a different way. They see the Wheels more like bands or rings of energy that surround the body. Often the more Earth connected indigenous people work with energy from both a horizontal and circular perspective, not focusing solely on the Axis of Heaven and Earth.

There has been some correlation drawn between the Chakra System and the Native American Medicine Wheel. Instead of being mapped solely between the vertical axis of Earth and Sky, the energy bodies of the human are mapped out horizontally on the Medicine Wheel as various powers or attributes, and can be worked with on an Earth centered directional grid in which to align with in a sacred healing walk. Being on the horizontal grid of the dimension of Earth, this system supports the realignment of our energy fields that are directly related to life on the Planet Earth. This orientation is exemplified by the manner in which the Thirteen Grandmothers bring the higher teachings down to Earth.

There is much information available today on the Chakra System, and it is necessary to take this most important part of the journey to gain further access to the Thirteen Heavens. I will share information that is primarily based on the Vedic system because it is the most known; but I also incorporate information gathered through years of modern day energy workers use of this system, including my own. It is not necessary to get caught in the different versions, but rather to focus on the information more as a metaphorical map for the purpose of integration and harmonization of personal and cosmic energy.

Before we begin on this journey there is additional information I would like to share. Most people are aware of the Seven Chakra System but we are going to work instead with the Twelve. We spoke earlier on how the doorways to the higher dimensions have been re-opened and made available for the true seeker, so that we may be able to open to these higher level vortexes. We are being given a great opportunity as we are given a chance to take on more responsibility for our evolution.. We are moving out of the harmonics of Seven and into the galactic harmonics of the Twelve; the Thirteenth level being the realization of the Christed Self, which includes all other Chakras or levels. Chakras are the energy Centers that when fully opened to, balanced and embodied, bring us to the entrance way of the Thirteen Heavens

The Seven main Chakras relate more specifically to the body and to embodiment, starting at the base of your spine and moving upward. There are at least five more that we are aware of that are outside of the body. These Twelve energy vortex Centers correlate to your twelve-strand DNA, and once consciously worked with, are a doorway to higher consciousness. Activation of these Centers can occur in numerous ways, such as through the breath, working with Light and sound, as well as conscious intent and visualization. These Centers are meant to work together in harmony and affect not only our alignment with the intense shifts of these times, but also our ability to experience more joy and contentment. It is important to bring the physical Chakra System into balance as you access the ever-increasing strength and power of the higher vibrations, or their opening expansion can be overwhelming. Anchoring into the Earth with the assistance of Turtle Medicine and working with the Grandmothers is very important so that our physical, emotional, and mental bodies can withstand the magnified influx of cosmic energy and our 'Flowers of Light' may open gracefully.

The *Seven Rays*, which are the virtues and attributes of the Creator for our solar system, are the higher source of the energy of these 'Wheels of Light' and are expanding to make available to humanity the *Twelve Rays* and Chakras. The *Seven Rays* humanity have had available to aspire to, are: *1.) The Ray of Power, Will or Purpose 2.) The Ray of Love 3.) The Ray of Active Creative Intelligence 4.) The Ray of Harmony and Beauty 5.) The Ray of Concrete Science of Knowledge 6.) The Ray of Idealism or Devotion 7.) The Ray of Order or Ceremonial Magic.* We are just learning what the higher level Rays that are now entering our dimension, are offering for our transformation, as we experience the re-opening of the doorways to the higher realms, in order to assist us through the evolutionary gateway we are in. We suspect that they are connected to the energies of the higher Chakras outside of the body system.

The Chakras of the body are the energetic counterpart of our endocrine system, while the higher Centers are more closely connected to the non-physical spiritual realms of our beings. The lower Centers are denser and are thought to be the points where cosmic energy manifests on the material plane. The first three Chakras have been the foundation and entry point for where most of humanity has collected its emotional trauma and reactive emotional responses. We are now collectively in the process of shifting our emotional center of response to the Fourth or Heart Chakra, as we heal from past wounding and the old pattern of reacting from a place of trauma. When we center ourselves in the Heart Chakra, we can create each moment anew with more joy and Love and can be more open to integrate with the energies from the higher Centers. When we learn to come from a place of less reaction and more loving acceptance, our physical bodies can also enjoy more vibrancy and health as well.

In the Door of Earth journey of healing, much has moved and integrated to make way for the energies of the Fifth World or Sun, but it is important to reactivate, tune up and harmonize that which has been shifted in profound and mysterious ways. The Wheels of Light are beautiful flowers that when properly watered and cared for, will help us open to the Land of the Flowers, and are the places where memory both positive and negative, can be moved and integrated with the assistance of the higher forces.

These Centers of Light are connected to star systems and dimensions and are adapted to the energy of our particular Soul imprints, calibrated and overseen by the guardians of our personal gates (like guardian angels). We are now learning to be more responsible for our subtle bodies, being made more aware of needed tune-ups, so that we truly can work with the higher energies coming through now. The loving gateway between Heaven and Earth is located in the Heart Center, where manifestation and divinity come together. This Center is the unifier of all others. When all of the Chakras are activated and cleansed and are vibrating in harmony with each other, they form a Rainbow Bridge that lights up the spiritual filament of the electromagnetic web that surrounds us. Therefore a Cosmic Bridge is created between the vibrations of the physical, third dimensional reality and that of the faster moving frequencies of Light and Love from the Fifth World and further. Let us open to the wonder of what lies ahead.

* * * * * * * * * * * *

Begin to become aware of the spiritual field around your body that penetrates to the physical, emotional, and mental bodies. Call in your Higher Self and the spirit helpers you have grown to trust. Have your feet firmly planted on the ground, as you call in Turtle Medicine and the sacred Thirteen Grandmothers to encircle you with loving wisdom and protection. Coiled deep in the Earth resides the Rainbow Serpent, guardian of the New World, one with the sacred Fire, the Light without a Shadow in the Center of the Earth. As you connect with this sacred being, feel the stirrings below your feet underneath the Earth, and let the Rainbow Light shine its healing transformational vibrations one shining flower at a time, as you are blessed with the attunement of the Ages. This being contains all the darkness of the Underworld, transformed into the full Light spectrum of the Heavens, and is duality resolved.

* * * * * * * * * * * *

Below your feet, just under the Earth, is the *Earth Star Wheel* where you where first anchored into the time and space co-ordinates of the Planet. This Chakra forms prior to birth in the geographic location and familial circumstances required by your Soul to ac- complish the lessons you are to master. Also contained in this energy vortex is that which was created in the distortions in the matrix of separation, and is now ready to be cleared and rebalanced. The white solar spiral of the masculine energies are re-united with the dark lunar spiral of the feminine, and they merge in ecstatic, harmonized union as a wave of the Light without a Shadow passes through. Let the vibration of the Rainbow Serpent move through and transform the archetypal beliefs that physical incarnation is a 'Fall' from grace and is a painful karmic cycle of birth and rebirth, full of suffering and loss, and that because of original sin all life forms are separated from the Divine. Release the belief that life on Earth is limited to the five senses and is cut off from a more ecstatic experience. Open up to the element of Ether, as the strong presence of Great Spirit opens us to a divinely expanded sense of self.

As the spiral moves through the *Earth Star* it shifts and opens you to the knowing of your Soul's highest intent for this lifetime, where self-mastery, expanded awareness and connection to more evolved life forms are made available. The Earth incarnation no longer has to be experienced in a limited fashion, restricted to 3D senses of time and space, but can now shift to a greater state of expansion and connection to other dimensions, especially to the element Ether, Spirit in Matter. The Milky Way's Silvery Star Light emanating within the field of the black night, is rising up through the core Fire of Mother Earth, grounding the Light of your Soul with that which will realign you with her newly recalibrated, electromagnetic field.

* * * * * * * * * * * *

As the energy rises it reaches the energy *vortexes* of your *Feet*, expanding your auric field so that your dance on Earth is more connected to the divine activation that is occurring at this time. This is where the grounding of your energy in connection to the Divine Feminine power is made available here on the Earth; bringing her forth in each conscious step as you give back to the Mother Earth and to humanity. The creative potential of the Yin energies are brought to Earth at your feet. This energy is newly energized by the Divine Union that is occurring in the Center of the Earth. The pads of your feet are opening as you bring in Earth renewal and grounding. This Center opens and closes as necessary. At this time it is also important to open the minor *vortexes* in your *Hands* so that the new vibration can balance out your ability to give and receive in the World in entirely new ways.

* * * * * * * * * * * *

The Rainbow Serpent coils itself in the *Root Wheel* at the base of the spine, the seat of the Kundalini. The movement in this vortex assists you in evolving core issues concerning survival fears and traumas, as well as the beliefs and energies that limit your new roles and destiny paths that are based on the stories of the past. Release what no longer serves you in the expanding deep ruby red of your Ancestors, calling what still may lay hidden from the past that is still unresolved. Take in the gifts of your tribe while opening to a greater sense of belonging to the cosmic family. Ask for your connection to your greater Soul family at this time, as you give thanks for all of your relations. Feel the inspirational Fire arising from the core of the Earth, renewing and awakening the raw power of dormant, un-manifested potential; cleansing and energizing your cherished physical body, while restoring your will to be alive with enthusiasm. You may now experience greater calm, vitality, and trust in your right to be on the Planet, living in a state of balanced abundance and a profound sense of belonging, beyond family, clan or tribe. Gather to yourself this wonderful feeling of connection in the present moment to the sacredness of all things. This state of being will be with you wherever you go, which allows your roots to reach to the Center of the Earth in a new and profound manner. You no longer feel alone. You are reconnected to the sacredness of all life.

* * * * * * * * * * * *

Spiraling up the center of your being, you feel the stirring in your *Sacral Wheel* below the navel, where the cellular memories of sexuality and creativity are being evolved to a higher level; where suffering and guilt, as well as limited experiences concerning creativity, no longer exist. Let the wounds of your womb return to the Mother Earth, as food for her soil, as this sacred container returns to its original purity. Let new inspiration glowing with the orange of the rising Sun so that your creative life force can be devoted to higher aspects and manifestations of the self. The joyful energies of the Light and Love without a Shadow can be the source of your creations. You no longer need to carry the collective fears that come from creating from a place of imbalance.

Open up to receive guidance and wisdom from all of your sacred Wheels as they flower open, for it is the integration of all parts of one's being that we can consciously join in as conscious co-creators of our World. Within this great shift and healing of the womb and creative center, humanity also more capable of birthing high Souls who know they are fully loved and carry much wisdom for our times. You can now experience much greater support within yourself, as well as improved relationships and emotional balance as this Center is cleansed and renewed. This Center has done the job of digesting the heavy, negative energies that filter down from the Solar Plexus, where we have been confused about the right use of power and will. As all Centers shift the patterns formed from the World of separation, each one will work with the other in much greater harmony and with increased spiritual power.

* * * * * * * * * * *

Be aware of the *Dream Center* that is now once again beginning to be re-acknowledged as a most important energy vortex for the dreaming of the New World and a doorway of communication to the Higher Self. Encircle this *Center located at the Navel* with the Rainbow Light, so that the Dream Body's connection to the Divine Source is renewed and cleansed being supported by the Divine Dreaming of Heaven on Earth. You are being asked to become a conscious dreamer and co-creator of the next Era. Feel the waves of dream time and waking time becoming one conscious experience, with an innumerable variety and intensity of colors, choices and beauty radiating out in all directions. Dream your World Awake!

* * * * * * * * * * *

Rising up to the energy of the *Solar Plexus*, just above the navel, we feel the power of the rising Sun and the color yellow, releasing any fear or held patterning of the misuse of Power, either as predator or as prey, victim or victimizer. Radiate the Light and Love coming through from the Earth's Core, as it joins with the Light from the higher Centers as they are opening. This radiance assists you in no longer having energetic space to take on the heavy emotional, negative projections of others or self. As a second 'Sun of Radiant Power' rises out of the phoenix transformation of the warrior codes carried in both men and women the wisdom of 'right use of will' and power is downloaded from the higher Centers. In connecting to the Will of the Divine we find here a balance between action and non-action, as well as a greater ability to utilize spiritual force in the art of moving well in the World. Remember to trust your true feelings and gut intuition to guide you, as you discern how to make your way through this one precious and beautiful life. Greater emotional and mental control in this Center can assist in focusing the new dream of the Planet.

* * * * * * * * * * *

The warm loving glow of the most *Sacred Flower of the Heart* has been waiting for the return of the Love of the Heart of the Mother on the Earth to bring you home within your Soul, within your body. The Rainbow Goddess that has entered through Venus and through the newly reopened Heart joins us here in our journey. Take a moment in this most sacred of temples to rest and feel safe in the arms of the Mother, where the vibration of the pink color ray, elevates your emotions to the feeling of Divine Love, permeating your entire being. Bask in this glow and open to receive the soft green nurturance of the Earth, bringing you back to greater compassion for self and others.

The Ego surrenders its control in this holy of holy temples where all wounds are to be healed by the Light and Love without a Shadow, where the power of the Love of the Creator shines through in tones of pink, gold and azure blue. Trust once again in the Higher Self as your true guide. You are taken to a place beyond judgment, where devotion to living a life of sharing your gifts of Love with grace and ease is remembered as your birthright. Awaken to the knowing that you are always truly loved. Feel the harmonization of your Sacred Wheels; as above so below and let your Love radiate throughout. This is the place where all roads converge and our divine contract is experienced and renewed, in remembrance of a sense of true home and connection to Source. The burdens you have carried are gone! Let yourself truly rest and be filled here for a moment in time.

* * * * * * * * * * * *

As the Rainbow Serpent is renewed and elevated within your Heart-full Center, it showers its blessings upward to the *Throat Wheel* where the Light of the brilliant blue aspect of the spectrum is amplified to clear any misgivings or oppression about speaking or living ones truth. The blessings of the Heart Center provide the self acceptance and non-judgment necessary for the evolvement of this Chakra. You are being inspired to attune to the higher mind and to join the gifts of your individual self expression with the universal spiritual truths of higher knowledge that wish to be actualized at this time. The power of the 'Word' is brought back into alignment with the magic it truly carries, expressing more of the divinity of one's being. Allow the deep sounds of your unique expression to come through in luminous harmony, joining the music of the spheres, without limits.

* * * * * * * * * * * *

We spiral to the *Third Eye Wheel* located just above the point between the brows, where the indigo flame activates your higher intuition that can see beyond the veils of the limited 3D reality and the illusions of the mind. See the dissolving of any limited concepts that may still bind you to a past way of being that no longer serves you. Trust in your ability to utilize your visionary insight to journey to places of amazing beauty and wonder that exist just a breath away. Remember that you can dream a new glorious World by picturing it with your higher vision, seeing the divine perfection in all things. Remember that we all have psychic abilities and can access the ancient memory of all times, as well as the higher dimensions. Let the way be clear to receive and envision guidance from your Higher Self through this doorway of spiritual sight, on any matter where you need deeper understanding. Ask to see the road to take towards fulfillment of your spiritual mission on Earth from the hall of records that is contained in the Chakra above your head.

* * * * * * * * * * *

As we move to the *Crown Wheel* just above the head, the Rainbow Serpent joyfully moves into a shower of the Violet Flame vibrations, receiving the blessings of the doorway of the Divine Will. This creates a stronger link with the higher aspects of awareness and 'Oneness.' As we join here with the gifts of the otherworldly Wheels, we may experience the integration of the conscious and the subconscious, and the unifying of the two hemispheres of the brain. We can now touch on the Ray of our own mastery and get a glimpse of the Mind of the Creator. Feel the sensation of tingling on the top of your head that is the connection to the otherworldly Chakras that have existed outside of the realms of embodiment. Once again we remind you that it is most important to awaken and integrate with the radiating, spinning Wheels that are more accessible within the energy field of the body, before you can aspire to the less tangible energies. Wait until you feel balanced and calm before you proceed. The Rainbow Serpent integrates and aligns the Seven Chakras through and around your body, back through the *Earth Star* before it rises out from the top of the head once again.

* * * * * * * * * * * *

In order to access and bring in the new reality, many of us are being asked to further activate the Twelve Chakra System which leads to full connection to God Source at the Thirteenth Chakra or level. The *Earth Star* and the *Dream* or *Navel Center* are part of the opening and new awareness of our higher Centers. We are just getting to know these Centers that are newly available for us to open to after thousands of years of shutdown. It is important to move ahead with the beginner's mind of discovery. In the far distant past there were a number of evolved cultures that had a very unusual, elongated skull structure that speaks to a time of access to higher Centers, as evidenced in ancient Egyptian, Peruvian and Mayan relics. It is time to move past this period of seeing the Creator as separate from the individual self, and to move closer to remembrance of our beings as Divine. Let any feelings of sadness, irritation or grief, for the releasing of attachment to old ways of being, pass through as you let them go. Be kind to yourself and others as you are asked to expand up the ladder of evolution even further. You are needed.

* * * * * * * * * * *

We journey on to the Golden Light of the *Gold Sun Wheel* which is where the Divine Masculine or Yang principal is available to us, as well as attunement to the Higher Mind of the Christos. This Center has the role of being an energy storehouse and clearinghouse, giving birth to original thought imbued with spiritual inspiration. It is vital to generate energy from here in order to provide a higher energy source to our systems that is not affected by the constraints of the 3D. The *Gold Sun Chakra* is now able to operate in balance with the Divine Feminine embodied just below your feet, the two vibrating together in harmony as the unified field radiates throughout your system.

* * * * * * * * * * * *

You now experience being lifted even further as you expand to a greater connection to other beings of Light, opening to the *Soul Star*, where the collective highest dreams and aspirations for humanity and the Planet are radiating out onto the planetary light grid and where the White Light shines fully upon us all. This Center has now been rejoined with the *Earth Star*, where the union of creating with Earth and Sky becomes manifest. This Wheel of Light joins you with the most loving essence of the cosmos, personalizing it into the domain of the human Soul.

* * * * * * * * * * * *

As we move into the *Stellar Gateway* of clear Light, we are opening to the full expression of the Higher Self that is now enabling us to be more aware of and able to recognize the presence of the ascended ones and the angelic realms of Light. You have been made readied to open your Soul to the healed connection with the part of you that is a galactic, inter-dimensional starseed. Embrace the ecstatic joy of being in touch with Divine Source and Will. Connect to the multitudes of Lightbeings of the Universe at play in the fields of the 'One.' When this Center is fully open we experience the state of the 'I am' presence of ultimate spiritual Source within all, catapulting us into the thirteenth Wheel of Light and Love. In this Center the Rainbow Serpent opens its multicolored and multi-dimensional radiance in brilliant connection to all stars and galaxies, as it returns home to source for just a moment to assist us to get a glimpse of what there are no words for; the full glory of the Love and Light of contact with the blessed Core of all Creation, in the Heart of the Heavens.

* * * * * * * * * * * *

As we slowly return to the Earth we have never truly left, we are filled with wonderment that we have returned with such blessings and give thanks for the gift of profound transformation. We know that we can never live life in the same way, ever again. Blessed be...blessed be...blessed be.

16

Star Beings Remembered

*V*ery long ago in the distant past, Mother Earth was whole and healthy. All beings lived in harmony with each other. There was an abundance of food and essentials. There were other beings who also lived on and in our Mother Earth. These beings were the Star People.

There are a multitude of other civilizations that exist out in the vast Universe. Many have come to Earth for numerous reasons in those far distant times of long ago. One thing that they were able to do besides soaring among the stars was to see into the future, similar to the visions experienced during a vision quest. Some of what they saw and shared with us was the coming of this age of ignorance that is upon us now.

Finding out that the ancient wisdom would be misused, exploited, and perverted in destructive ways, the people gathered the sacred power objects and concealed them in the womb of our Mother, in caverns and hidden places. This was done the whole World over.

The Star People withdrew for a time but only after making sure the power objects had been concealed. They appointed watchers to guard the entrances to the sacred sites. All of the secrets were to be completely protected. Now it is the time. As has happened in the past, Earth changes are occurring and will continue. Our Mother is greatly burdened. She is heavy as a woman long due with child. She will give birth and soon, too. It will be within your season; that means within our lifetime. Of course as with all deliveries, there is pain:

When Mother Earth has contractions, we will perceive it as earthquakes...
When the Waters break, we will perceive it as floods...
When the Blood gushes, we will perceive it as lava from the volcanoes...

There will also be energy changes; maybe a shifting of poles. However, when the new life comes into being, all that will be forgotten by the Mother. There must always be destruction of the old to bring forth the new. Young life feeds off old life; that is the way of the Circle of Life.

Afterwards comes a time of healing. The Mother and her new children are cleansed and cared for. All rest easy. The Earth is brought back to a green and fertile state, a 'Garden of Eden.' The young ones grow from day to day. That is when the secret places will be opened and the ancient *wisdom renewed for the benefit of all. The Star People will return to our Mother and the times will be as in the long distant past. There will be celebrations in abundance throughout the Universe. Choose not to harm, as our Mother is carrying us all. However, one day she will shake herself and lessen this load. Many will not survive the changes. Be a helper. Do what you can to ease our Mother's labor. It is fine to feel and share her pain. But you will also find ways to heal the wounds.* (Story shared by unknown Native American woman, passed down from her Grandfather.)

As we continue our journey through the Door of the Heaven, it is important that we open to the gifts available to us from our connection to our Star Ancestors. What an amazing experience we get to have as we look above and have the stars shine down upon us, reminding us of the grandness that is ours and the immense vastness of the Universe. As we come to a greater place of wholeness in ourselves, more comfortable with the energies of otherworldly beings as guides and allies, excited by the Wheels of Light being rekindled, we may be able to return to trusting in our divine origins. As we re-connect to ourselves as multi-dimensional beings, we may remember how to evolve further, as we reach for the stars.

Native Americans, as well as many indigenous people throughout the World, have kept sacred the wisdom that has been passed down from ancient times of their star origins and contact, as well as of prophecies of what would occur in the future (as spoken of in previous chapters). I would like to share some of this knowledge to ground the 'journey to the stars,' not only as coming from New Age information but as wisdom that comes from messages past and present, passed down by respected Wisdom Keepers. I encourage you once again to open your mind and Heart to that which can assist humanity in taking its next steps so that we can join the 'Shining Ones' in assisting with the birth of a New Earth and a much more spiritually inspired reality for humanity.

These following messages are a shortened version of much more evolved information that comes from a people who have never truly forgotten their special connection to Spirit and Mother Earth.

We begin with the prophecies of the Hopi Elders that speak of the Star Beings. These prophecies have been passed from generation to generation through oral traditions and ancient rock pictographs and sacred tablets, as are many of the sacred native traditions. The ancient prophecy states, *'When the Blue Star Katsina makes its appearance in the Heavens, the Fifth World will emerge.'* Many speak of how this Holy One comes from the star system Sirius, Sirius being the Blue Star that shines most brightly in the sky. It is said that all Hopi ceremonies will cease when the Saquasohuh (Blue Star) Katsina dances in the plaza and removes its mask. This will mark the time of the ending of the Fourth World we have known and the full entrance into the Fifth World. The ceremonies that have been carried out by the Hopi, according to the original instructions given to keep spiritual consciousness here on Earth during the time of the Underworlds, will be no more. More specifically this holy messenger is spoken of as being a unified twin Katsina of both white and blue, bluish white being the color of Sirius A, which has a twin, Sirius B.

Katsinas (Kachinas) are sacred supernatural spirit beings who are the Ancestors of the Hopi who came from the stars, intermingling with humans in the ancient past, then leaving to be in the more spiritually infused, less dense realms. They are honored and danced back into the realm of the human in carefully chosen natural and Cosmic Cycles, continuing to guide and enlighten the Hopi, as well as raising the vibration on Earth. They are at the center of Hopi spiritual life. The Katsinas stay with the Hopi for seven months every year until July, when they return to the Upperworlds. The Katsina dances restore and maintain harmony in the spirits of all living things. They embody in male Katsina initiated dancers, ceremonially reconnecting the people to their star origins and teachings. The Kachina dolls are to teach the children about these Holy Ones. There is also a petroglyph that shows a maiden riding in a wingless, dome-shaped craft. The petroglyph signifies the day when the true Hopi will fly to other planets in a ship without wings. The Hopi also believe that they originally descended from the Pleiades.

I would like to mention before going any further, that the Dogon Tribe from Mali in West Africa that we have spoken of before, has passed down astounding information on the star system Sirius. I mention them particularly because of how their ancient knowledge from the past has been confirmed by the present day scientific community. They have known about Sirius A and it's Twin (invisible to the naked eye, star Sirius B), for the past 5,000 years, long before the technological Age. They also claim that a third star Emme-Ya-Sorgum Female exists in the Sirius system. How interesting that this star system, which is looked upon by the Egyptians as the true home of the Goddess Isis and the place Souls return to in order to get re-geometrically created before coming back to Earth, may have a third major star. They state that all three affect the movements of the others. The triangle and the energy of three and the Triple Goddess are required for creating true beings, as we spoke of in the Chapter on Sacred Union. What amazing correlations!

How did they know these things? The Dogon say that this information and much more was given long ago by their Star Ancestors. Isn't it interesting that the Hopi speak of a holy being coming from Sirius, this place of new cosmic birth? Not only was the Egyptian calendar based on the rising of Sirius and its effects on the rising of the Nile, but the Sun is conjunct Sirius (according to astrologists) every year on the 4th of July, the birthday of the United States. Some Mayan groups have kept their New Year to July 26th, when Sirius rises in that part of the World, showing their deep connection to this particular star.

The Dogon believe that approximately 5,000 years ago Amphibious Gods called Nommo came to Earth in three legged space ships from the Sirius star system, as sacred teachers for their tribe as well as for other communities, and would return again to help in the evolution of humanity. They have described perfectly the DNA pattern made by this elliptical orbit created by the two stars as they rotate around each other. They believe Sirius to be the Cosmic Axis and Navel of this Universe, and from it all Matter and all Souls are produced in a great spiral motion. The majority of Heavenly Bodies represent the 'external' star system whose influence on terrestrial life according to the Dogon is relatively small. There also exists an 'internal' star system which participates directly in the life and development of humanity. This includes Orion, Sirius, the Pleiades, and a few other star systems. These Celestial Bodies form the support as the cosmic board of our World, with Sirius occupying the main seat. Celestial influence and its effect on the Planet Earth is widely accepted by the modern World, especially since there have been technological advances that can measure some of these effects, such as from solar flares. But most of the so called civilized World does not acknowledge the effect that these forces have on the human psyche. Ancient cultures were much more aware of otherworldly influences in the time when the veils between the other dimensions and realities beyond Earth were much thinner.

Some tribes honor the Thunder Beings as messengers of the Star People. If a Thunder Being pays you a special visit you may become a Heyoka spirit, who is the human counterpart of these Holy Ones. We spoke earlier of how the shamans and healers are often these Heyokas, who think and act 'out of the box' of so called normal consciousness. Many Heyokas of every color and race are being contacted by these messengers from the sky. They are being charged with the great honor of being midwives of the Fifth World and can call to the Thunder Beings to help transmute the negativity and separation that still exists. In Peru, I met two 'Lightning' female shamans who were Lightning Healers. The highest level of female healers in Peru, are hit by lightning at some time in their lives. One of the healers I met was hit twice by lightning and I witnessed her perform an amazing healing on a close friend. The other had a harelip scar that looked like lightning; her mother had been hit by lightning when the healer to be was in her womb. These are not just made up stories.

The constellation of Orion is in the area of the sky known by some as the Heart of the White Buffalo Constellation. In the prophecy section we have spoken of White Buffalo Calf Woman. I want to also mention that her return to the Planet once again also signifies the return of the Star Nations. Some say that she originates from the Constellation of the Seven Sisters in the Pleiades. Regardless of the different information given, it shows the deep connection that native tribes have had to their celestial roots and origins.

It is said that the Seven Sisters of the Pleiades offer gifts or roles that humanity can aspire towards, to assist in bringing Star Woman's great knowledge and wisdom to humanity. These roles are: *Spirit Keeper* as shamans and medicine people, *Mind Keeper* as observers and storytellers, *Wisdom Keeper* Sages and Teachers, *Fire Keeper* World servers and givers of compassion from the Heart, *Time Keeper* like the Maya and Hopi, *Vision Keeper* to bring in the bigger spiritual picture, *Life Force Maker* leaders and chiefs. Which one are you embodying?

There are Native American Elders who have taken seriously the prophecies that have instructed native Wisdom Keepers to reveal Indian spirituality to those with a 'Red Heart' who may be a different skin color but have the Heart of a native person, when the time was right. We are now in those times. They are also revealing the truths about their contact with the Star Nations that were kept secret until now, except within sacred and Elder Councils.

In the Winter of 1995, during a four day praying fast (Hambleca), Standing Elk (whom I have received teachings from), a Ihanktowan Dakota spiritual advisor and Sundance Chief, began receiving instructions from sacred Star Beings on many things, including a vision showing that it was time to share Native American teachings about the Star Nations, with the World. He organized the first Star Knowledge Conference in the Yankton Sioux reservation in South Dakota in June of 1996. This conference also fulfilled ancient Hopi and Lakota prophecies and since then there have been yearly gatherings which speakers from many tribes have attended. Among the many tribes attending were: Plains Tribes- Lakota, Ogallala, Dakota, Nakota, Blackfoot, and Miniconjou; Eastern tribes - Iroquois, Oneida, Seneca, Choctaw, and Cherokee; Southwestern Tribes - Hopi, Yucka, Aztec, Apache, and Maya. Even a Maori Shaman Chief came from New Zealand and a Sammi (Traditional Laplander) came from Scandinavia, because they also had seen that it was time to share openly about their star origins, the influence of Star Being visitors on their culture, and the imminent return of these Star Nations.

Standing Elk states that the Star Beings are here to teach, to foster spiritual growth, and to prepare us for the upcoming Earth Changes. These extraterrestrials are communicating telepathically with many native Wisdom Keepers as well as with many others. The original language of the Sioux is designed to stimulate other worldly communication. Standing Elk believes there are a few negative renegade ETs that have collaborated with the Shadow Government, but that the majority are here to help and are of a higher order.

Once again, if we clear and integrate our own inner World of the Shadow and negative energies and come to greater wholeness and guidance from our spiritually reconnected Higher Self, we will be much less likely to have any contact or to be influenced by the few negative ETs. Be aware, ultimately trusting in your own deeper knowing on these things.

Following are excepts from various speakers at the conferences: Wolfheart spoke of a white man called Wakea, who came from the Planet Venus, who taught them how to pray and conduct ceremonies, who walked on water, talked to the elements, healed the sick and the dead, and said he would be back some day (similar to stories of Quetzalcoatl and Christ). He also speaks of the head beings of the elemental realms who will be in charge of the great purification, naming these beings the Thunder Beings.

Looks for Buffalo of the Ogallala tribe, spoke of how each Native Tribe has its extraterrestrial race of origination counterpart and that to bring in the higher vibration of the Star Beings, we must have a purity of heart and good intention. There are seven galaxies represented here on Earth.

Steve Red Buffalo, Lakota, states that the Seven Sisters (Pleiades) are connected to the 'Chunupa,' the Sacred Pipe.

Holly Bull, a Lakota Medicine Man, states that there are sacred rituals carried out in native sacred sites, where knowledge from the Star Beings is kept and honored. The Star Nation Altars that are honored send a Blue laser Light into the Heavens, which the Star Nations see as beacons. Interesting how the 'Blue Lights' show up again connected to higher realms and star dimensions.

Rod Shenandoah, Blackfoot-Oneida Medicine Man, states Native people consider themselves privileged to have regular visits from Star Beings during ceremonies and consider these events as 'sacred.'

Rod Skenandore, Blackfoot and former NASA contract engineer, states, "We are getting word of the ETs coming now!" He has been taken aboard UFOs several times, including once during a 'hanblechia' (vision quest).

Wobleza, a Dakota, was visited during an Inipi (sweat lodge) ceremony by a large silvery spaceship from the Buffalo Nation, and states that little elders will come in the children being born now, who will suddenly talk early.

Pathfinder and Silver Star, both Cherokee, said we are responsible for the vibration we are living in, so bring in the Light. The Star Nations are making the Crop Circles and will land soon. All the self-destructive karma from Atlantis and Lemuria is being healed. The Diamondback Rattlesnake Deity or Feathered Serpent (Quetzalcoatl and Kulkukan) says to invite him in to transmute the false DNA. Everyone can become the Christ, Quetzalcoatl. Be in balance with the elemental beings of Earth, Air, Water, Fire, Ether, and Mana.

Grandmother Windrider, a Mayan Elder, previous to this time not allowed to speak to white persons of the Mayan tradition kept by the women, shares: "Extreme changes are taking place. Karma cleansing is over. Things are speeding up. Do not hold on to old victim attachments. The Maya, Toltecs and Olmecs have a tradition of contact with ETs. The gateways are being positioned to allow in the celestial avatars. Your bodies are going through a great mutation to prepare for the Millennium. In the upcoming Earth Changes, some who are not ready to make the transition to the Fifth World will reincarnate elsewhere, on a Planet at a more primitive evolutionary stage, similar to the one Earth has been in. Some will reincarnate to clean up the debris here and make the transition to the higher-consciousness World-society, into which Earth is transitioning. Some will be taken off by the Star Nations to voluntarily live with them. Changes are coming. Raise your consciousness so as not to miss the wave when it comes through. Learn outdoor survival skills. This society is sick and it is time for the women to gather together and heal each other, then they will go heal the men..."

Singing Bear, Cheyenne, states, "All of Nature is showing signs. The World has to spiritualize together, or there won't be a World. The World and the entire Universe is shifting right now. People have to raise their harmonics and the only way is to raise spirituality through the Heart Chakra. We have to attune ourselves to all of our parallel and inter-dimensional beings consciously. The Space People are already here. My people, we have communicated with other beings forever, it's nothing new for us…Once we raise our vibrations and are willing to accept them as part of us, then people will start seeing more of them. We have much to teach the Universe and the rest of the Universe is waiting for us."

We are fortunate to have such ancient knowledge so deeply rooted in tradition coming forth at this time. Remember that most of you have also already been in touch with spirit beings that come from dimensions other than the third dimension in the form of animal spirits, guides and teachers, as well as elementals, deceased relatives, and Angelic or other Holy Beings such as Ascended Masters. Some of these may not be as far from this dimension as others but they are otherworldly. Take a deep breath and tune in to what you are feeling… Are these ancient messages familiar to you? Do they bring up fear? It is important to release the fear (not the wisdom and discernment). When we have healed our places of separation and fear, we can return to trusting in our celestial origins.

Many ancient traditions from Native American to Egyptian, to Peruvian, to Mayan and African, speak of teachers and Holy Ones coming from the stars, who have not only come here to advance and inform humanity but have in ancient times interbred or star seeded the Planet for various reasons. The more positive intent was to raise the consciousness of the human being so that the evolutionary process would be accelerated. There are also stories of some of the Star Beings losing their integrity as they descended into the denser realms of the Earth, in the misuse of power over Earth Beings, and that many are being given the chance to heal that karma by helping humanity at this time. There are some who believe that many of the star-seeded Souls were meant to go through many lifetimes of Earth reality, to go through the school of Earth, in order to better know how to be of service during these great evolutionary times. Some believe that you cannot evolve as quickly on any other planet beyond this solar system, as you can through the Earth experience, because of its distance and separation from the Godhead. What an amazing leap in the evolutionary journey, to remember one's divinity in the midst of the field of suffering and separation.

When you begin to connect more to the star-seeded part of your being you may experience a number of changes not unlike the ones named before, as symptoms of evolvement into the higher realms. You may become much more sensitive, not interested in connecting to mainstream society, look for others more like you who are interested in joining together in the 'great work' of these times. You may be more attracted to creative and esoteric fields, as well as healing, searching for the bigger truths and one's true Soul mission.

Even if you do not fully connect to yourself as a Star Child, the doorways are open for the intuitive, inner sensing parts of your being to be more fully developed. Every human is a divine seed that has the right to grow in all directions, moving closer to the Center of Creation, reaching for the stars. There are gifts awaiting us that must be accessed, so that we can truly transform into the Fifth Sun and no longer have to exist in a World of pain and suffering.

The awareness and activation of your Chakra System, of the spinning Wheels of Light, have readied you so that you may gain passage through the various stellar doorways. They are connected one to another, and as we learn more about our dimensionality we will see how the various dimensions are also connected to these personal yet cosmic energy vortexes. As spoken of previously, the first Seven Chakras are more connected to our personal energy bodies. The other Six are much more connected to the more cosmic and universal dimensional fields that exist in the various Stellar Worlds we are now bringing to consciousness in our Earth experience. The concept gets easier as you go through each doorway.

Since ancient times, Astrology has been a way for humanity to connect with the blueprint and inclinations of their personality self and greater Soul. This speaks to the effect that the planets and the stars have on the formation of our individuated beings. As we evolve and work with the higher aspects of our charts and learn the lessons of our unconscious material, we can travel further out of our solar system to the higher celestial Heavens. To be ready to receive the activation of the Star Gates of 2012 and to pass through the doorway to the Fifth World successfully, it is important we have some practice in navigating in the spiritual realms and working with our subtle bodies. Our survival may depend on this as we must learn to create from these celestial realms and use energy in a way that does not deplete or destroy the Earth's resources and balance. Our survival as a species may depend on our ability to be guided by our Higher Self in all of our human and other species relations.

We can create a higher vibration in our Etheric Body to intentionally hasten our evolutionary process by consciously and energetically visiting advanced star systems. Our Etheric Body, which is composed of fine interlocking strands of material upon which the denser, physical forms are constructed, will be able to filter down to our 3D reality what we have gathered there. This will assist humanity to come up with solutions and experiences that are way beyond the limits of what we have known, as these celestial energies are downloaded into our personal electromagnetic fields.

The stellar field is the star field in which your Higher Self operates. The greater the connection and knowledge you have of these Worlds, the greater the embodiment of these energies here on Earth can be. Do not be afraid to open to these Worlds. You have journeyed far, and to navigate well in the dimensional fields it is important to be connected to at least one of your primary star origins or affiliations that can guide you. You will only travel as far as what is in alignment with your divine self, so it is important to connect in here first. Attuning to the spirit animals, in the way you have connected to your power animals and higher level guides and teachers who reside in the Upperworlds, will assist you in experiencing the higher consciousness of your personality. Look to make contact with these Holy Ones before you begin.

Let your being shapeshift into the Star Jaguar, so that you can safely navigate to the unknown places of the stars in a sacred vehicle that offers itself to you as the powerful guardian of many star systems and dimensions. This Sacred One radiates the dark of the sky at night as well as reflecting the blue healing star light of its elevated essence.

Star Jaguar is pure divine and cosmic intuition. It vibrates blue white energy lines that radiate from its star spots, connecting to all of the stars. It also reflects star energy back to Earth, helping us to embody these higher energies. It is raw, primal courage and power that has become enlightened while in the midst of the darkness in the journey through the Underworlds. The Jaguar has transformed from the deep black of the night into the yellow of the Sun, spotted with the black in remembrance of its journey, finally returning to the celestial realm where its black has expanded into blue stars. It has been able to stay connected to its star origins even while moving into unconsciousness while on the journey through separation. It has gone through humanity's initiation. Jaguar, therefore, is the keeper of the Mystery and the gatekeeper to the unknowable. Get to know this Holy One, as it will greatly assist you to stay conscious while on a most amazing and spiritual journey.

You may feel yourself wanting to linger at one planet, star system, or galaxy longer than another. Let yourself go more deeply into wherever you are guided. If you get confused or too uncomfortable, go back to the safe keeping of the grounded Turtle energy and the Thirteen Grandmothers for further clearing and guidance. We are not going to journey through every star system but to those that seem to speak the loudest during these transformational times. You may be tempted to go into past lives and previous connections that you have had before. This is fine, but you are encouraged to also be in present time for what you are to hear, activate, or gather for this moment in your incarnation. You may meet Star Beings in each part of the journey or at times it will be your future self that is returning to greet you, or a Soul Pod family of Star Beings to assist you in moving ahead in your evolvement. Always check in with the trusted guides you have brought with you, making sure what comes to you is for your highest good. Open to this and ask them if they are willing to be guides for you when you return to Earth, to be of better assistance for the advancement of humanity.

Let yourself ground in your body on the Planet Earth, standing in your Jaguar body on top of the great sacred Turtle, surrounded by the Thirteen Grandmothers. Let the Jaguar Beings' physical beauty and sustaining life force fill you up for the journey ahead. You will find yourself pulled through the Center of the Earth, where you are now in alignment with the Light without a Shadow. Your sacred vessel is now ready to journey afar because you are now realigned with your Tree of Life and grounded into the Earth Star in a new way.

Moving out to the Moon, we renew and connect with our deep feeling self and our ability to self-reflect and be receptive, attuning to the higher rhythms of life* * * We open ourselves to higher levels of communication through Mercury* * * Going through the very important doorway of Venus, on the Beauty Way Road, we reconnect to Venus and the Rainbow Goddess who will help us keep our Hearts pure on our journey, which is truly where our safety lies, inspiring us to new levels of creativity* *

Joining with the strong, active nature of Mars assists us in manifesting and focusing the creative musings of Venus in a more balanced way, where the masculine force no longer acts out separate from the feminine * * Expanding our beings through the vortex of the planet Jupiter, we free ourselves to grow and expand more fully* * * Swirling outward we get pulled into the rings of Saturn that help us feel the boundaries and discernment needed for a safe journey* * * Coming to the asteroid Chiron, we feel the places where our Soul has been healed from its time of separation on the Planet Earth, knowing as we heal we can heal and teach others* * * Being pulled through to the erratic Nature of Uranus, shocking and awakening any part of us that is still in trance* * * Dreaming the new dream awake with what Neptune has to offer, moving with the deep oceanic Celestial Waters, uniting the Unconscious with the Superconscious* * * Rebirthing through the depths of the Underworld with Pluto, regaining the power lost in the dark recesses of our psyche.

We complete our journey of our solar system, being pulled back through the Center Solar doorway of the Sun that shines on us daily as a beacon of Light, connecting us to the life force of the Central Sun of the Creator. We are reborn out of the depths of our Soul, being taken to a new level of Light and vitality as we integrate the higher teachings of the Planets we have known since childhood.

We continue to navigate with Star Jaguar, while the Rainbow Goddess remains at the gate to our solar system, so she can assist in keeping us connected when it is time to come home. She sends us forward on the Rainbow Bridge, where we take a visit to Sedna, the newly named Planet that is in a solar system close to ours. This is the first Native American named Planet, which speaks to respect returning for the Wisdom Keepers and the deep feminine that hold the care of the Earth so dear. Listen to her story, as this Goddess heals any remaining places in your energy field of past victimization that you have experienced while on the Planet. She connects you to the aspect of the Divine Feminine which protects one from victimization of any kind and offers her gifts freely as she transforms us.

As we move out through the dimensional gateways of the star systems that deeply affect humanity, we leave much of the guidance of this experience up to your own deep intuition and knowing, for we are in the rediscovering of these Worlds. Use what you hear to guide but not limit you. Connect closely into your Navel or Dream Center with the Silver Aka Cord that you will follow all the way to the Galactic Center of the Milky Way, where the sacred milk or life force there will provide you with the real Mana and true intuitive guidance that is necessary for your Soul travel into deep space.

We soon come to the dimension of the Pleiades, where we join within the immensity of the Love that knows no bounds, enlightening our Heart

Centers even further. It is here, to the doorway of the East of the Medicine Wheel, that Rainbow Woman leads us, giving us insights into creative solutions for the bigger picture of our personal and global lives. The Rainbow Goddess is waiting patiently to help us bring back to our solar system what we gather from the Seven Sisters of Creation. It is here where we may be able to truly help heal the rift created by the separation from the Heart of the Mother of Creation, by unifying ourselves with the Holy Beings that have been holding the space for humanity to expand into the Celestial Realm of the Heavens; our next step as co-creators of Heaven on Earth.

As our Hearts are filled, this radiates out to Orion where the distortions of the masculine archetypal energy as victimizer and of the warrior codes disconnected from God-source, are elevated into the Divine Masculine who protects and reveres the Divine Feminine and all life. Your Will Center is joined with the Higher Will at this place of intense power. The Cosmic Galactic order is re-established in your DNA codes, where honoring, truth, and respect for all are upheld. This Center overlooks and guards the next Star Gate, making it safe for the sacred birthing process to occur without interference.

We are guided next to the Divine Feminine Womb of Creation to the Sirius Star system, where we are geometrically re-created and our original divine blueprint is re-encoded. The Triple Goddesses make a doorway in which to rebirth, being directly seeded from the highest spiritual intent of the Godhead. Here we also receive the wisdom and unity of those from the Sirian High Council, who carry the highest good for humanity, who have been like parents to us. They glow with the royal blue and white glow of divine wisdom and power. It is necessary to give these omnipotent beings permission to share the gifts they have to offer, permission which is required in these most enlightened spiritual realms because of the respect for the rule of free will. It is important here to reconnect with the process of High Ritual and Initiation in even more of an enlightened manner than before, attuned to the energies of these times.

As we are reborn through this most sacred Womb, we journey on highways of Light to the Andromeda Galaxy, where the presence of high levels of electromagnetic wave reunite the frequency of our dualistic masculine and feminine energies. We feel waves of bliss in the remembrance of joining with our Twin Flame, where we no longer experience the separation of duality. Our DNA is activated in wholeness and we return to the Milky Waters of Creation.

We return to the Milky Way where we float in the amniotic fluid of the Galactic Center, from where the evolution of humanity is being inspired and directed as it enters into the Planet through the core of the Heart of the Earth. We are synchronized with cosmic time, as we get a concentrated dose of what is being activated within the crystalline core of the Earth, as we are being changed to a silica based, no longer carbon based creature. This will assist us in handling and embodying the higher frequencies. For a moment in time we join with the radiance of total bliss of Love and Light in 'Oneness.' We are now made more ready for the Shift of the Ages. We are connected to all the stars of the Milky Way and no longer need to feel separate or alone.

Take in a deep breath. Close your eyes and ride the Milky Wave back home, with the Star Jaguar carrying you to the doorway of our solar system, where the Rainbow Goddess aligns and recalibrates your Rainbow Body so you may return into the field of Earth with grace and ease. Gently returning to your body, giving thanks to the many magical places you have been, more swiftly than the speed of Light, returned in the still point of 'Oneness' in the here and now. Rejoin with the Circle of Grandmothers who are awaiting you with open arms, to ground and to bring to Earth the gifts and awareness you have gathered. They remind you that you were given a great dispensation in being allowed access to places that only initiates of the Mystery Schools were allowed to take flight to in the past. The Grandmothers remind you that it will take much responsibility and a pure Heart to bring these experiences to Earth and to daily life in a sustaining manner. They offer to continue to give you guidance and assist you in creating a ceremony to honor your Star Ancestors and all you have received. Your vehicle of movement, the sacred Star Jaguar and all other helpers who have assisted you in embracing the great unknown, are part of this ceremony as you shower all with loving appreciation.

You can remember your journey by setting up a Star Altar, as well as in meditation, dream time, while chanting, making love, at times of New and Full Moons, Solstices and Equinoxes, and other powerful astrological configurations, and by visiting sacred sites and in ceremony. You will see your World and your life shift right before your eyes, as the wonders and miracles of Spirit become who you are. There still may be challenges ahead, but you have gone to places you could never have dreamed of before and your entire being will assist you to be in a state of knowing the Spirit in all things, in all beings, wherever you are. It is time to be ready to be more conscious of our roles as co-creators of the New World. It is important to direct our intentions for manifesting from a higher field that is beyond conscious or unconscious trauma and the effects of the time of the rule of the Underworlds. We are now more capable of creating and being with the spiral energy and highways of Light and Love, for we have taken a journey through the realms of many dimensions.

17

Dimensional Shape-Shifting

I am in a state of deep remembering, as I feel a strong pull to break out of the normal boundaries of my being.
Spiraling outward to a sense of greater expansion like the rays of the Sun, I reach out to greet the parts of me that have always been.
I open to meet the Holy Ones that have been waiting to take me to Worlds of profound wonder and grace!

In order to come up with solutions and answers from a higher part of our beings, for the survival and powerful movement forward of humanity, we must remember how to consciously move in and out of and reach to higher dimensions, while embodied. As we have stated before, our ability to access multi-dimensional consciousness may be a basic survival skill of the times, as we are put through an accelerated, evolutionary initiation course on the way to 2012. We are being asked to become larger than life as we reach out to the stars and to the deepest parts of the Soul, coming into fuller awareness of ourselves as multidimensional beings. As we align fully with the newly reconnected Tree of Life, we can stay connected to all parts of our wholeness, enabling us to travel without losing consciousness.

You have been brave and have taken an amazing voyage into your Higher Self through the Wheels of Light that are not far from home, and through the Star Centers that have seemed so very far away. Any traumatic memories or fears that may have surfaced from the deeper recesses of your cellular memory on the journey to the stars, now have the potential to be healed instantaneously because of the contact and integration with your Higher Self and the entirety of your being and the higher archetypal helpers and guides. Now you may open to the shifting that is occurring, trusting the depths of your new abilities.

Beyond getting to know the multi-dimensionality of the Universe, it is also important to recover and connect with the parts of your energy that may have been stuck in dimensions that are no longer useful for your embodiment on the Earth. This is something that one should do with an expert spirit guide, as to ascertain what is for your highest good. At times it is important to be in other dimensions as you are embodied on Earth, and at times it is important to have more of your total self gathered consciously here in the electromagnetic field of Earth. As you learn to be more sensitive to the ebb and flow of your energy body and receptive to higher guidance, you will become more aware of how to navigate and make shifts in your personal Medicine Field.

Before we get into the descriptions of the dimensions, while your Star Odyssey is fresh in your mind, we want to address the many benefits and possible experiences you may be having as a result of spending more time in the higher realms. You may be surprised at your ability to stay longer in states of higher functioning. By having more divinely connected experiences, we can also help elevate collectively the consciousness of the human species, for one's personal evolvement affects the whole.

Take a deep look at yourself while going through the list below. Become aware of the positive changes which have occurred for you after going through profound transformation in your passage through the Door of Earth and in experiencing the beginning stages of shapeshifting through the divinely spiritual realms of the Thirteen Heavens. As you find yourself relating to the changes, may you be inspired to continue to keep focusing on your spiritual growth and on new ways of living on the Planet. You may also use this information as a springboard for states of being you may want to aspire to, as well as where to focus your conscious intent:

1. *Contact with spiritual energy on a more consistent basis, with an increased ability to access and align with these divine fields.*
2. *A greater feeling of grace and ease.*
3. *Lack of limitations, with improvements on manifestation abilities and the fulfillment of one's dreams.*
4. *A greater sense of renewed vitality and health, joy, excitement, and bliss, as well as an increased love and compassion for all living things.*
5. *The relationships that continue in your life are much healthier.*
6. *You reunite with people who are like minded and find spiritually connected affinity Soul groups.*
7. *You attract a relationship where there is much more bliss, harmony, compassion, and understanding than you have ever experienced, as well as a feeling of total trust in your wholeness as a unique being.*
8. *You discover your destiny path and know the steps to fulfill it.*
9. *You move to a better job that supports the true expression of who you are.*
10. *You experience greater abundance in all areas of your life.*
11. *You have total trust that all you need will be provided.*

12. *You move more quickly and gracefully through drama and karmic contracts.*

13. *You make decisions based much more on your higher 'feeling' intuitive states.*

14. *You allow life to happen instead of having to fix or force the flow.*

15. *Your intentions are in alignment with the Higher Self and there is more of a sense that you are where you are meant to be, at the right place at the right time.*

16. *As you are able to focus your emotions into higher feeling states, you are able to create your world without doubt or fear.*

17. *You see the inter-connectedness of all things and that everything that occurs is in divine order.*

18. *All stress is gone as you live in the moment, trusting in everyday as a 'new day never been used.'*

19. *Your Basic Self, or emotionally reactive self, no longer carries the wounds of the past and is integrated into your wholeness so that life becomes much more fun, enjoyable, and filled with laughter.*

20. *Your thirst for knowledge and creative expression is increased as you find great fulfillment in your artistic endeavors.*

21. *You come to the place where you no longer judge yourself or others, but discern what you are attracted to in your life from a place of greater balance.*

22. *Your connection to Source is the place where you are directed to and impassioned from, in your every move.*

23. *Your health improves and you have all the energy and focus you need.*

24. *Your life is simplified, so that you have the time to savor and appreciate every moment.*

25. *You naturally want to give to others and to the world around you and this gives you even greater joy.*

26. *You see and bring out the higher aspects of those with whom you have contact.*

27. *You are living the 'Beauty Way' and this sacred path is filled with your brothers and sisters.*

28. *You experience great Love and Light and you share great Love and Light.*

All these gifts and so much more can be the way in which we embody, enjoy, and bring into manifestation the Fifth World. It is not as far away as it may seem. Fill yourself up with these gifts from the Heavens.

You are now joined by the Record Keepers of the Cetacean Nation, the Whales, who will be your spirit guides on the dimensional wisdom ride so that you may have greater understanding of the dimensions through which you have journeyed. They assist by working with the frequencies of divine sound as well as holding the records of the Universal Mind of Great Spirit. The beautiful sound that they make when they are embodied on Earth is made by the 'Waters of Grace' that surround their brain. Shapeshifting with these sacred beings will make it easier to bring in energy and wisdom from the multi-dimensional fields, since the Higher Mind is needed to direct the process. Whale Medicine can help one tap into Universal Mind so that we can access the records we have activated in taking the magic Star Jaguar ride to the cosmos. Once we have learned to navigate here it will become more natural.

The idea and definition of dimensions is a tool created by humans to better understand the Universe. The dimensions correlate to the Chakra System, as well as to the Rays of Power, but expand out even further from the body in an energy field the size of which is unimaginable. You may have felt the immensity of it in your odyssey to the stars. The dimensions have been put into a system of numbered levels, both scientifically and esoterically, to give some sense of definition to that which is far beyond linear thinking. They are numbered to give understanding and boundaries to their existence.

Some have even connected the various dimensions to particular star systems, as if each star system contains a gateway into another dimension. I am thankful once again for the ability of some mastermind's ability to delineate and define the intangible. I will attempt to give a synopsis here of what I have found, including what I have learned on my own journeys. There is a lot to learn in how to work with the unseen Worlds, but much is being revealed at this time as the veils between the Worlds grow thin. With the assistance of the Whale Medicine, we will take you on an educational sojourn that may help you be more comfortable with the new knowledge and energies you have gathered.

The dimensions can be defined as interpenetrating levels of consciousness which resonate to a harmonious set of frequencies and vibrations. Each dimension is less dense than the previous one, as it vibrates back towards the Godhead, carrying a more refined frequency pattern, which in turn contains vaster, more complex cosmic knowledge and universal laws. Everything that has ever been created is manifested through intent and will, composed of energy vibrations of different frequencies. The density of Matter increases in the dimensions that exist further away from the great Central Sun where our Father/Mother God resides. We are now more aligned with the true Will of the Creator and can let go even further in trusting our inner higher knowing.

The dimensions have also been likened to the Ages or Worlds we have already gone through, as well as to the ones that are yet to come, as levels of consciousness that we are to learn and evolve through. So far the human species tends to go through its shifts into the next dimension or Age with only a few survivors, having to begin again with only a very few left who contain the wisdom and knowledge gained from the past. We cannot move to the next Dimension, World, or Sun, moving along on the Earth's pathway of illumination as a quantum evolutionary leap, unless a large portion of humanity heals and gathers all that is needed for this most special of passages.

Each dimension has a guardian or keeper and it is important to work with them if you want to continue to participate consciously in the World of stellar and dimensional shapeshifting. This is similar to navigating with plant medicines, as it is very important to work with their guardian spirits in order to have a beneficial experience. These guardians are to be met in your personal journey and will reveal themselves when it is the right time. You can still travel through various dimensions, but your journey will go much deeper with connection to these guardians.

In the myth of the descent of Innana into the Underworld, it was necessary for her to connect with the guardians of each of the levels of the Underworlds by which she is given permission to pass, moving through the various gates. It seems this may also be part of the so called 'safety valve' that only allows passage to the higher gifts of the Upperworlds when one is truly ready to wisely use them. In the journey through the Thirteen Heavens, let us be reminded that we can not gain full entry until we truly learn the lessons of the Door of Earth. We may visit and have an incredible experience, a reminder; but to sustain the energy we must truly have passed the initiation of the Underworlds or we will not be allowed to stay in the higher realms but for a short moment. In initiations of the ancient past, the powers and knowledge revealed in the various levels of indoctrination could be misused if not shared with a more highly evolved individual and could also create a state of great overwhelm if one is not prepared.

Find yourself rooted into the crystalline core of the Heart of the Earth with the essence of Turtle Medicine supporting you below your feet. As you look around you at Middle Earth you are still surrounded by the Thirteen Grandmothers as they keep the rhythm of their rattles in attunement to your heart beat. The celestial teachers and guides and your Star Ancestors open you further to receive a deeper teaching on the many realms of existence. The spirit essence force of the Humpback Whale sings to you a most beautiful song, awakening in you a great wisdom and knowing much greater than you have known before in this World. Their sound also activates the opening of your own divine records where whatever you need to know will come forth. Their presence helps you go deeper, far beyond just the information that is shared with you. Trust them! Trust yourself!

The Ten Dimensions of Existence

The First Dimension: The realm of the pure crystalline structure of the Earth where primal Creation energy manifests as electromagnetic waves. The life force of the Planet is generated here as it connects into the galactic headquarters of the Milky Way. This place is very pristine and can not be accessed unless one has reached a higher state of consciousness. The Earth and all her plants and creatures must be honored before entrance is allowed here. This may be the place that native people speak of, where there is another perfect mirror World of this one, within the core iron crystal matrix at the Center of the Earth. This is where the blueprint for our divinely inspired true self is kept safely waiting for us, to be claimed as we awaken from our deep, unconscious slumber. This is where we can ground deeply with our energy fields.

The Second Dimension: The World of length and breadth without depth as well as the World of the elementals and source of our vitality. Primitive life forms begin to form here. This is where we work to help heal our body elementals as well as those of the Earth located beneath our feet deep into the Earth. They wish to return to being under the guardianship of the Heart of the Mother and to no longer be influenced by those who wish to control and enslave them. As we clear our places of separation we can assist in reconnecting the unity and health of many dimensions.

The Third Dimension: The Three Dimensions of the World that we have been living in, are of length, breadth, and height (or depth); the physical and material World, anchored in linear time and space. Much more complex combinations and varieties of Creation exist here, as well as the World of duality. It is in this realm that we experience the limitations and boundaries of time and space. Things that exist in the same time also exist in the same space here, which changes in the next dimension, especially as the Fourth Dimension bleeds into the Third.

The Fourth Dimension: Here we add a greater awareness of time to the other measurements and experience the shapeshifting of time. Many believe that this is the Middle World dimension we have been transiting through, the doorway of purification, since the time of the Harmonic Convergence. This dimension helps us move into greater mastery of emotions, thus assisting in the healing of old wounds and the releasing of past life material, as well as any part of the history in the Fourth World that keeps us from being in the moment. This is the World of the collective mind where myths and archetypes exist, as well as the memory of all that has been. We bridge here the tangible and invisible realms and tap into our higher feeling states. Here, in this space, the higher dimensions are able to transmit to us advanced knowledge and we can begin to experience the presence of Spirit in Matter, Ether. There are sciences that are helping people relate to this from the viewpoint of the mind, such as Quantum

Physics, especially as it relates to how we create our own realities. We are more aware of being in the playing fields of the Gods and Goddesses here, as we see the direct results of who we believe we are.

The Fifth Dimension: The beginning of where the manifestations of Spirit from the higher level realms can be accessed in a more consistent manner. We enter this dimension after we truly go through the healing of duality, as we move through the Door of Earth. It is here where we begin to journey further to the stars and the higher dimensions. Duality no longer exists here and neither is it necessary to any longer activate the law of karma. The element of Spirit manifest in Matter (Ether) is added here as a primary presence, beyond time and space limitations. We can fully experience this realm when we have unified in our Hearts. This is where the masculine and feminine forces remember how to harmonize together as the divinity in both is birthed through the Heart. The beings that exist here and who are ready to guide humanity are highly evolved, including but not limited to Ascended Masters, the Great White Brotherhood, Buddha Consciousness, Archangels, and Guardian Angels. These Holy Ones exist here in order to be closer dimensionally to the Planet, so that humanity can more easily access their spiritually elevated healing forces and guidance. The Christ consciousness is also more available in this dimension, to help us tap into this field of the untainted harmonics of Love and Light. You are able to connect here through your Higher Self to the Three Fold Heart Flame of Divine Wisdom, Divine Will, and Divine Love. This is what we may have ahead of us in the New World that is being created.

The Sixth Dimension: Here we add the component of deep compassion for all beings, as well as the energetic Creation fields of sacred geometry. The highest untainted blueprint for our embodiment on Earth exists here and we can heal further our earthly elemental energies from this dimension. The sacred Womb of Creation exists here, as well as the birth canal of the Divine Feminine. The Higher Council of Elders meets here often, and this is where the collective consciousness can truly be experienced. We can connect with our higher purpose from this dimension, as we experience the divine initiation rites.

The Seventh Dimension: Here we complete and become the Higher Mind of perfected Truth, receiving the galactic information on Highways of Light. We experience varying spiral patterns and have a greater knowing of the collective consciousness within the harmonics of divine sound. This is the origin of the messages that have been transmitted into the crystal Lightbrarys on Earth, so many years ago, of absolute knowing and truth. Our personal crystalline structures are vibrating with the information carried here, assisting us to remember how to move objects through space and manifest creations that bring new sources of renewable energy back to Earth as we learn to focus with sound and Higher Mind working together.

The Eighth Dimension: Cosmic order is restored here as a high intensity beam of Light is focused on whatever is needed, to enlighten those who need to be rebalanced with higher intent and will force. This rebalancing restores the right use of will, so that we may be directed by the highest order of Creation, in our intent behind giving to others. Pure essence and exaltation in the high states of altruistic Love are realized. The Divine Masculine principle of Light is formed here, giving further focus and high intent to the energies of manifestation.

The Ninth Dimension: This dimension is not influenced directly by the energy of Earth. This is the continual evolving Galactic Center of the Universe, guiding the inhabitants of the Universe towards a higher evolutionary state. Holy Ones beyond definition exist here. This Center is connected to all the stars of our Universe and exists in a total state of bliss. Many of the embodiments of the Eternal Buddha come from this place of cosmic time and Love. The highest form of Love available to humankind is that of the Ninth Dimension. As we ascend, there are even higher levels available; but to be able to access them without burning up with the intensity, we must evolve further.

The Tenth and Higher Dimensional Universe: There is no ability for an individuated self to conceive of these dimensions. In these highly spiritually infused zones, we are nearing total union and absorption into the Oneness of 'All That Is' where we know nothing of separation, where our Soul group has absorbed into the unified field. Most of us cannot even fathom these states from the point of where we are in our evolution. The Eleventh and Twelfth Dimensions expand us into the Light and Love of the Thirteenth Dimension, returning us to the consciousness of the absolute 'I Am Presence.'

We are connected with all these dimensions by a beam of Light that runs through our core being, realigning and renewing our blessed new Tree of Life so that we can become 'Flowering Souls' of the Fifth Sun. Give thanks to the being that has assisted in the relaying of this wisdom, the knowing spirit of the Whale, as well as all others. Remember to especially give thanks to any guardians of the heavenly gates that have blessed you with their presence. Ride the Highways of Light that have now appeared before you, to carry you to the place where you now embody as the...

18

Light of the World

The Great Invocation

From the point of Light within the Mind of God,
Let Light stream forth into the Minds of All,
Let Light descend on Earth.

From the point of Love within the Heart of God/Goddess
Let Love stream forth into the Hearts of All,
May Christ/ Soul consciousness return to Earth.

From the Center where the Will of God is known,
Let Purpose guide the human wills of all,
The purpose which the Masters know and serve.

From the Center which we call the Human Race,
Let the Plan of Love and Light work out;
And may it seal the Door where Evil dwells.
Let Light and Love and Power restore the Plan on Earth.

We come from the Light. We are made from the Light. We will return to the Light. The Mother Earth is in a process of attaining her Lightbody and entering into her next evolutionary state. We are being activated by the Center of Creation, through the core crystal within the Planet and the Heavenly Bodies above, to transform with the Light without a Shadow.

The Milky Way Galaxy contains a massive ring of inter-dimensional Light called the Photon Belt. Photons are subatomic particles that are the building blocks of pure Light. We have been on the outskirts of this belt since 1997 and will be moving deeper into the field as we approach the year 2012. We will at that time be catapulted through a stargate or cosmic portal that will fully shift those who are ready, into the Fifth World. An entire belt of photons has the power to 'light up' and transform human DNA and therefore affect the enlightenment of humanity. The Science of Genetics has seen by blood tests since 1992, changes in our DNA and that the mutating of our species has already begun. The opening to our full Twelve-Strand DNA correlates to the opening to the Twelve Chakras, the Twelve Dimensions, and the Thirteen Heavens.

The Lightbody is our vehicle of Ascension. As we move into higher and faster moving states of consciousness, we activate our entire Tree of Life to re-member the Source energy force within our cells where we still carry the Light and Love of Creation, as it expands through and lights up the entire 'Sacred Tree.' We have all seen the halo of Light that glows from the ascended Christ and Mother Mary. These Holy Beings of Light and Love are here to assist us to be able to hold more of this pure essence. We are now able to unify and truly evolve in a most conscious manner, now that the Heart of the Heavens is returning in all its pure Love and Glory. The gateway and loving vibrations of Venus and the Rainbow Goddess have also assisted the Light to enter, in a way where it is more possible to live the 1,000 years of Light and Love that have been prophesied. It is up to us to continue our journey. We have come far through the Door of Earth and of Heaven and it is time to join the two and complete the transformation of the Tree of Life. The process of initiation that we have transfigured through truly has to do with preparing ourselves for higher doses or infusions of the frequencies of Light ((embodied with the Love).

Call in Dolphin Medicine to assist you to embody this Light, as we have already opened our Hearts to the Love that exists between Heaven and Earth. These beings teach us how to be with our breath in a way in which to integrate the Light, entering in with balance and harmony. They truly exist in a state of joy, knowing how to be part of a pod consciousness and share their high frequencies with others. Their left and right brain act and communicate as one brain, as they exist in the deep trance of the Waters of the Cosmic and Earthly Worlds. Hummingbird Medicine has been with you throughout the journey to the Heavens and will continue to be with you as the vibrations of its wings keeps your Heart open to the Light of the Fifth Dimension and beyond.

We are truly multi-dimensional beings who are now remembering more of who we really are. The Lightbody is the part of us that takes us from lifetime to lifetime, from dimension to dimension, and carries an imprint of our Soul signature. Both the Silver Cord of our Dream Body and the Golden Cord of Spirit manifest, join together in harmony in the highest element of Light and Love. If our Hearts have not been healed and opened through the gateway between Earth and Heaven, we cannot truly activate our Lightbodies. We are now glowing in connection with our Higher Self, which is now able to shine its radiance throughout. Spirit is the undifferentiated Light that is in connection with the God-Source. Our Soul is the differentiated Light that exists within embodiment. It occurs when our Matter based Physical Body is transformed into a Light-based, Physical-Etheric Eody, vibrating at a vastly higher rate than before. Our Etheric Body has been holding the blueprint of a higher functioning system but has not been able to download into our systems. It is time now in our journey for it to do so, as we connect with this blueprint as well as to the higher vibration of the Mother Earth, where she is already manifesting a New World.

We have now come to a place on our journey where we can feel more of the benefits of all our hard work. Our four main bodies, including the subtle bodies, are part of the Lightbody system when it is fully activated; including the physical, the emotional, the mental, and the spiritual. When activated they form our Rainbow Body which then can filter the Light inward and out. Our spinning energy Wheels of Light have now been 'amped up' so that they can handle the Fifth dimensional frequencies, and they will continue to be activated as we move through the various levels of Lightbody Ascension.

Many of us have heard the message that we are ascending with the Earth this time and that when our Rainbow Bodies have been made readied, we will move into a higher functioning level never experienced before. It is possible that when we move into the Fifth Dimension we may no longer be able to fully remember what it was like to live in the Third Dimension and how we could have lived without the experience of Love and Light made manifest. We do hope that the lessons learned from the past will be remembered and fully integrated. Supposedly many of us have been operating in the Fourth Dimension since the Harmonic Convergence, as it was a major doorway of transformation into the New World.

When we can stay in a so called 'enlightened state' more often, then our consciousness will be able to thrive and create far beyond the limited matrix in which we have been living. We can only begin to imagine and continue to seek divine guidance on what we want to aspire to, so that we may truly live in the 'Land of the Flowers.' To evolve, to seek enlightenment, is truly the goal of a conscious being. The steps towards this are meant to be fully experienced and fully lived; the journey being as important and meaningful as the returning home. We all long to find home, to belong and to be loved. We seek it so passionately in our lives, then find it, only to feel it so easily slip away. This is the root of our deepest longing, the longing for the part of us that contains the Holy Seed of the Creator. Can we reawaken this divine spark and never let it go out, ever again?

If there is an aspect or common core to World religions and sacred traditions, it is that humans have the potential to become more evolved or enlightened beings. There are various names given to this sacred Body of Light that is the Vehicle of Ascension. Some of the names are:

*The Resurrection, Celestial, or Spiritual Body, in the Judeo- Christian tradition. *The Most Sacred Body, in Sufism. *The Diamond Body, in Taoism. *The Light Body, in Tibetan Buddhism. *The Vajra or Divine Body, in Tantra and some schools of Yoga. *The Body of Bliss, in Kriya Yoga. *The Superconductive Body, in Vedanta. *The Radiant Body, in Gnosticism. *The Glory of the Whole Universe and the Golden Body in the Alchemical traditions. *The Immortal Body, in Hermetic traditions. *The Luminous Body, in Ancient Egypt. *The Indwelling Divine Potential, in Old Persia.*

Is it possible that in the activation and changing of our bodies from a carbon based system to a crystalline structure that some say we are going through, that we can now truly hold the Divine Light and Love 'I am' presence in our embodiment? Is this immortal Body of Light going to be attainable by more than the few? It is said that the changes that take place affect the density of the physical as the infusions of Light activate certain cells that then in turn affect all four bodies, from the etheric blueprint inward, from the Light of the Soul outward.

The Lightbody is a grid work of Light that unifies your physical, emotional, mental, and spiritual being. This body can radiate Light throughout your electromagnetic grid, connecting your multi-dimensional self with the higher frequency energies of the Heavens. As you activate, build, and integrate your Lightbody, a stronger connection to the Light of the Creator (and your Higher Self) is formed. As your molecular structure is reorganized, the body becomes less densified, able to exist in the vibrational field of the Fifth World, with hidden talents and knowledge being more fully awakened. This transformation assists us to embody the gifts of the Thirteen Heavens, as encoded in our cells. This does not happen over night but must be integrated with the embodiment and World in which we have been living. Some believe there are Twelve levels to the Lightbody Activation. As each level is completed the new level of Light must be integrated in all four energy bodies.

Most of you know that DNA is the scientific name for the blueprint of life and is located in every cell of the body. As we vibrate in a field of higher feeling states, more of our DNA is stimulated to open. As we experience the activation of our Lightbodies, we are actually waking up more of our DNA. As we are more and more guided by the spiritual, good intentions of our Higher Self, we integrate the knowledge contained in the unused portion of our DNA. Most of humanity has been living with only two strands of our DNA chromosomes in use. In our original divine blueprint there are an additional ten strands of DNA available to each human that have been dormant since the beginning of recorded history. When all twelve become activated, we will have access to living a much more spiritually infused and grace filled reality. There has been so much suffering during the Era of the Kali Yuga that this suffering is encoded in our DNA and in the elements of the Earth and needs our conscious positive intent and embodiment of higher energies to transmute.

The ancient meaning of the number Twelve is 'Thy will be done.' Once again we see how the number Twelve correlates to so much of what the higher levels now have available to us, with the activation of the Twelve giving us access to the Thirteen, which is the awakened Christed Self. The connections are endless, from the Thirteen Grandmothers (which is about full embodiment) to the Twelve levels of Lightbody Activation, the Twelve Signs of the Zodiac, the Twelve months of the year, (awakening to the Thirteen Moons), the Twelve Chakras, the Twelve Rays of Power, the Twelve Dimensions, the Twelve Tribes of Israel, the Twelve Angels, and once again, the Twelve-Strand DNA. The number Twelve keeps showing up as of great importance for the balancing that is needed at this time, as we have spoken of earlier. Twelve, in the Tarot, is also the sacred number of the completion and union of the dualities, adding the number of the Lovers Card, six (female) + six (male). The number and energy of Thirteen is where we transcend to our divine self which is beyond polarity.

As we open to the totality of our spiritual true selves, we now have the possibility of accessing the Thirteen Heavens, a higher state of consciousness and therefore of existence. Our Vehicles of Ascension light up, aligning with the Earth's expanding Lightbody which has been shining from deep in her core, waiting for the celestial moment to put on her glowing coat of brilliance. We can now become more aware of who we really are, with our true history and our purpose for evolvement revealed. The Lightbody activation can increase states of health and emotional wellbeing, psychic awareness, and manifestation abilities beyond your grandest dreams. But mostly it will assist us to move further up the ladder of the Thirteen Upperworlds, closer to the gates of Creation, bringing Spirit into Matter, able to embody our Higher Self. In our initiation journey to consciousness it is of utmost importance that we activate as much of our twelve-strand DNA, genetic and spiritual potential, as possible, to break through with consciousness into the Fifth World.

New directives are being given to the cells and it is important for there to be a recognition of Light, as a prime energy source for us, rather than solely the energy that comes from food. The cells are learning to decode the Light. The pineal and pituitary glands are also going through great adaptation so that the brain can translate the changes in energy. Now we are able to truly live in a state of higher intuition and awareness. Synchronistic and meaningful connections occur daily, as well as many deep insights. We begin to live in the now, trusting more in the presence of

Spirit on Earth, so that we are no longer controlled by the mental body that lives in the future or by the emotional body that lives in the past, nor by the Ego that has fueled both. We are now living the magic of life in the present. Be ready to accept the change.

There is mention in various prophecies that we will go through three days of darkness that is a passageway in which we will be tested before we fully gain access to the Fifth World. It seems that it would be immensely important to be able to know and be fully connected with our inner spiritual 'Light' so that we will be able to stay conscious through the darkness, able to move through fears and negative thoughts.

The Lightbody process of activation is not a complicated process, but a simple and most profound one. It has to do with activating our various bodies with high infusions of Light. This raises up the vibration of our energy bodies to function at higher levels of consciousness. One of the reasons I felt moved to come up with a more evolved healing process was because of the intense crashing that I experienced when I had Lightbody activation. I had done much personal growth work, for many years, and what came up for me was still very intense. I wanted to provide individuals a much more graceful process of evolvement, if that was at all possible. All that has been experienced in the journey of healing will enable the process to happen more easily. There are books and manuals that give additional information on this powerful process, but I am sharing enough with you so that you may understand more about what you might experience and what is occurring. I advise you to work with a trusted guide in the process.

At the end of each level of Lightbody Activation there may be a period of experiencing a feeling of being in a deep void that can be likened to an Ego death. This may be characterized by a type of depression or a great overwhelming sense of emptiness. It is important to fill the void with joy and other higher level feeling states and a greater vision of what you want to create in your reality and in the World, by listening to the whispers of Great Spirit.

Even with the immense amount of transformation you have gone through, the steps you have taken may bring you through more intense changes, requiring of you the use of all the tools you have learned. As changes occur at cellular levels from the infusion of higher levels of Light, we may experience further and deeper release of the emotional and chemical toxins that have been built up inside. It is important to know that as much as we are able to have higher and longer states of spiritual connection and ecstatic states, right alongside we may still have to go through further states of purification and cleansing. It is important to know that not all of the movement towards awakening is blissful, so you will be prepared and not give up. The distortions created from the last Era, the

Kali Yuga, have to be dealt with as we move out of this way of learning through pain and suffering. On its way out it is holding on, kicking and screaming, and we must be prepared to be vigilant in discerning which habits and behaviors no longer serve us, using the abilities of the Higher Self to oversee from a place out of the drama, so as not to get caught. The shamanic path never denies the Dark, as well as the Light, even as we enter into the Upperworlds. We still will be going back and forth within the polarity dance until the Worlds are truly joined. This is another important reason to go on the healing journey, so that we may experience these activations with more ease and grace in a sustaining, not fleeting, manner. We may still have more unfinished karmic and past life business to complete from the cause and effect of this time of separation; but we can now move through much more quickly and with less emotional attachment to the 'Game of Life' that we have been playing.

It is important that we are not disappointed by not always feeling in a state of grace and bliss. Have great compassion for yourself and others. Many of these changes may make you feel disoriented and ill at ease. This will pass. As we move up the ladder of the Upperworld experience, the conflict of the Ego and the Light may become even greater and it may feel like we may regress. As we infuse with Light and Love with an open Heart and we switch from an Ego directed reality to a Higher Self guided life, the confusion may be overwhelming at first. Do not give up, for grace is there to assist you. At times we must revisit where we have been before, practicing our new found abilities and gifts. The core issues we are being pushed to resolve may be amplified in the mirror of Light reflected, but the transformation that will occur will also be greatly increased.

Reach out and surrender to divine guidance, for there are many blessings for you and if you fall you will not fall far. Loving hands will reach out to catch you. Use the tools you have gathered and remember to take time for moments of integration. We are still in a process of letting go of old patterns, dropping old structures and frame works. Allow yourself to surrender to your evolutionary experience, knowing the true self inside that has never really been disconnected from the Heart of the Heavens. Being in union and harmony with the Earth, as well as with our higher spiritual guidance can assist us to make it through the 'ups and downs' of the Light of transformation.

Because we are experiencing the impetus for Planetary Ascension, not solely the transformation of a small group of enlightened individuals, there may be great stress being felt by many, even if they have worked with considerable devotion to achieve a higher state of consciousness. Because we are realigning with the knowledge that we are all connected, we may have a sense we are holding back from taking the next steps for which we believed we were ready. Maybe we are giving those who have newly awakened a chance to 'catch up.' This does not mean that we are to continue to take on the dying and sufferings of the old paradigm energies, but rather to understand what is occurring and hold the Light for those who wish to join in the Grand Awakening. This may be easier to do when we are not in the full throes of the resolution of our own beings. Keep making the choice to remain conscious and awake and do not buy into the limited view of what is occurring for yourself and for humanity on the Planet, in spite of what you may be feeling.

As we enter into more daily contact with our Lightbody, we may also be able to sustain heightened states of ecstasy for much longer. Remember how, in the Door of Earth, the shaman is able to reach to the 'Other Worlds' in an ecstatic trance state in order to bring healing and messages from the Holy Ones. You are now going to be able to access more easily and hold these states of joy much longer, which can help shift you into the higher octaves of the Upperworld. The core cylinder of your inner Light that runs through the center of your body is vibrating at very high levels after all the attunements you have experienced in passing through the Door of Heaven. This core cylinder is now expanding throughout our cells, as they vibrate at faster frequencies and unite with the Light without a Shadow that is emanating from both earthly and celestial influences. Remember this state, for it will be what sustains you through the turbulent times. We are getting to experience a purer connection to the Center of the Godhead than the majority of humanity has ever experienced before.

The attainment of ecstatic states is an inherent aspect of your nervous system and cellular identity, but it has been suppressed by religions, power hungry systems, and societal ways that encourage productivity, not joy; that keep us in endless striving for survival and illusionary fulfillment. It is all about balance and we are sorely out of connection to our Joy Body. This is not about being gluttonous in the extreme with entertainment, material objects, and sexuality. It is about seeing and feeling the beauty in all things, without the lower emotions blocking out our true feelings. To truly move out of the Era of learning through suffering, we must reawaken our Joy Body so that we will create our reality from feelings of more optimism, strength, confidence, enthusiasm, and a greater sense of aliveness.

Many of you may have experienced in a ceremony the ability to go on all night in prayer, dance, and song because of the incredible, sustaining, spiritual energy created. This Soul awakening vibration is that which truly keeps us alive and which will give us solace in the eye of the storm that is gathering. When our Lightbodies are glowing we can have more access to the rarefied Ether force of Creation. We will be able to sustain ourselves with the true sources of holy Mana. This process has many stages and layers to it, but is truly available to assist us in our evolution, being a Light that has been untainted by this time of separation. This profound process can only occur and be sustained when our Hearts have been deeply healed and opened. Once again, be kind to yourself and trust the journey.

Now that we have transformed many of our fears and have activated our Light Bodies, the states of bliss can be entered into more easily. The Dolphins have been assisting us through this process and are ever so happy to share with us how to sustain our Light Bodies so that we may truly bring Heaven to Earth. The gift of the Hummingbird to sustain joy and bliss and to help us find the nectar of the essence of Spirit has been greatly appreciated. Our ability to enter these states allows us to tap into our inter-dimensional awareness, which is directly related to the awareness of our Earth as a conscious being. When we can enter into the energy body of the Mother Earth, because we resonate at her higher frequencies, we then can have access to information and guidance regarding our survival and on ways to work with intense Earth changes. If we stay in connection to her voice, then she will guide us through this intense purification in a more graceful manner. We were never truly separated from Mother Earth nor the Creator. We just thought we were, as we fell into states of unconsciousness and separation.

It is also important that we offer our joy and bliss back to the Mother Earth whenever we can, because she has been brought greatly out of balance through having been polluted, both by our chemical and emotional garbage. She has been greatly brought out of balance by our lack of ceremony and ritual for giving thanks to her and for all the gifts from Nature we take for granted. Send your gratitude down into her as you exhale deeply, giving back to her especially when you have some refined, spiritual energy (sami) to offer, when you are in a state of divine rapture.

Ecstasy is a bridge between the World of earthly embodiment and the transcendent self. Your ability to navigate in your Lightbody through the multi-dimensional changes of Earth may be what enables you to avoid catastrophe as well as what empowers you to assist others and to live out your higher calling. It also places you in a vibrational field of consciousness that is beyond the field of fear and greed that seems to be perpetuated throughout the Planet in ever increasing levels, not out of the denial of what needs to change but from a higher perspective from where true change can take place.

We are in the times of purification and transformation and the time of being in-between Worlds. Many are experiencing personal traumas and inner pain beyond what one could ever have imagined. The extremes of humanity's negative behaviors are escalating and being revealed, and the Earth is speaking loudly through the changes in her weather patterns and seasons, in the increase in droughts, floods, hurricanes, tornadoes, earthquakes, volcanic eruptions, and global warming. This is the time of transmutation because all negativity that has been buried in the Underworld will only continue to cause pain, disease, and imbalance. What else do we need to experience in the way of pain, to wake up! If you are still feeling that the pains of the World are not yours to evolve, look again. You have taken the time to embody what it is to expand to the Light and the Love. Let this sacred force be that which you return to when you forget what reality to give focus and attention to. Let the Net of Light hold you while you establish your place in it. It is the right moment to evolve to a place where we no longer need to be driven by pain to learn and grow. We can no longer live this way. It is time to create a better way of living, for our children's children, for each other, for humanity and the Earth. It is the right moment because of the deepest pure intent and wishes of the Creator. It is time to create a new Sacred Bundle...

V

A New Dawn

19

Creating a New Sacred Bundle: Walking the Rainbow Trail

You have taken the journey. You have walked the sacred road for the healing of all times, for the healing of your humanity. It is good, it is moving, you are growing, and the way is full of Light and Love... You walk in the Beauty Way on the Rainbow Trail. All that you have gathered and all of the spirit animals who have blessed you with their presence, as well as the many other Holy Ones you have met, are available to assist you in the creation of a new Sacred Bundle.

It is important to bring together and integrate all the changes you have gone through and to keep the 'Good Medicine' working itself. This is not a one time deal. It is an ongoing process of growing and flowering, becoming the beautiful blossom that has been waiting to open into its fullness of Love and Light. As all is brought together in its rightful way, you will feel how changed your personal Medicine Field and Inner Self have become, as you now experience a greater connection to the source of all life. The fragmented parts of your personal power that had been scattered to the four winds during the times of separation, have come back home. Now it is possible to have the Mana and reclaimed pure, spiritual intent that is necessary to make an evolutionary leap into the 'Land of the Flowers'.

New feelings, thoughts and inspirations, will be coming forth to guide you. It is important that you have a place to come back to that will remind you of the evolved state to which you have awakened. In case you return even for a moment to the place of forgetting your true essence self, it is important to have a place to return to that continues to exude and generate the spiritual power and energy that is needed to continue the passage into a new way of experiencing oneself and the World. It is time to ground the high level energy of Ether back to the element Earth, as carried by the Red Nations.

What is a Sacred or Medicine Bundle or Mesa (as called in the Andean tradition)? Let us discover this through the indigenous knowledge that has been passed down. I do not know when the first inspiration occurred for the creation or gifting of Sacred Bundles by the Holy Ones, for it was a very long time ago. The five fingered human beings of the Earth were given tools from the beginning of time, to assist them in keeping contact with the One Supreme Being and all of the Creators helpers and Holy Ones sent to assist us. Sacred Bundles are one such gift.

One of the primary tools used by the Andean Priest is the Mesa, which is a Sacred Bundle that contains the Paqos' (Medicine person) most sacred objects. Generally Paqos carry one Mesa or portable Altar at a time, but they may have several. Contained in these Bundles are power objects that have been infused by the most refined energy of the Paqo, from sacred sites and special teachers, from mountain Apus (spirit beings), and so much more. The objects within the Bundle are varied, but most often are stones of power, crystals, shells, healing plants, animal parts, as well as other natural objects and symbolic items such as the cross. The Mesas are recharged as they are united in the Bundle by exposing them once again to sacred places, to especially powerful healers and teachers, as well as by feeding the objects with pisco, an alcohol made from grapes which is widely used in ceremony.

These Ritual Bundles gather much spiritual energy and are used as spiritual power sources, which are connected to the Mother Earth and Great Spirit. They may be used to gather energy for initiation rites, for healings, or to carry out one's dreams. They are also used to remove heavy hucha or dense energy, and to keep one's energy field clean and in harmony. They are much like the Medicine Bundles of North American Natives.

There are stories from various Native American traditions of many different kinds of Medicine Bundles that were given to the people by otherworldly deities as gifts to stay connected to Mother Earth and her spirit helpers, and to the Thunder and Star Beings. Medicine people or individuals would create the Bundles for special needs, being guided by the Holy Ones. These Bundles would then be infused by the blessings of these otherworldly deities. There were Bundles for personal Medicine, Tribal Bundles, Warrior Bundles, Sun Dance Bundles, Giving Birth Bundles, Dreaming Bundles, Hunting Bundles, and Visions Bundles. Every Bundle had a specific purpose and most had certain instructions given on how to keep the power charged and held within, with specific guidelines of proper use. Some of the tribes especially from the plains region of North America still pass on and remember their Sacred Bundles origination stories, in spite of most of the Bundles having been taken or destroyed.

Some tribes have worked hard to regain their Sacred Bundles, many of them having sat in Museums and private collections for decades. The

Hidatsa are one such Tribe who were able to persevere and have had returned from a Museum, a most important Buffalo Skin Bundle, which contains two sacred skulls. These skulls represented two Thunderbirds, the Sky Spirits that bring rain. For years, with the absence of this Bundle there was much drought in the area that the Hidatsa called home, because this Bundle was not properly used or cared for. Once the appropriate ceremonies were completed, the rain returned and the covenants with the Spirits who help with rain were re-honored and regained. It is essential to take good care of the Medicine Bundles.

These sacred objects actually embodied great power. The synergy of the power objects uniting together within the Bundle, create a web of immense energy that was to be used for the good of the individual, family, and tribe. Bundles were made by individuals, inspired by sacred dreams and visions and infused by sacred beings. They were utilized for both personal and communal benefit. Each Bundle held different spiritual powers to be used in a variety of ways, but were all used as a primary way of connecting the physical World to the spiritual realm; of Heaven to Earth. Some of the Bundles held the name of the particular Clan or Animal Medicine with which they were associated with.

Mostly objects and gifts from the Mother Earth are contained in the Bundles, which are bound in material that is usually made from animal skins or fabric. These objects may be: herbs, rocks, crystals, feathers, bones, other animal parts, tree parts, seeds, rattles, fetishes, pottery shards, pipes, etc; similar to the contents of the Peruvian Shamans. To honor and feed the Bundle to keep it active and power infused, it is important to offer tobacco, corn meal, sage, sweat grass, and other sacred herbs or flowers to it. It also replenishes the Sacred Bundle to bring it to sacred sites, ceremonially renewed with the energy of Mother Earth and Father Sky.

A Personal Bundle may be made with objects that have helped you in your spiritual development or were given to you as gifts, from powerful teachers that carry special meaning. The Bundles that are for the people, for healing and ceremony, contain things that the nation needs to survive. The medicine people or healers who take care of these special Bundles, have been chosen by the Spirits and carry these items as gifts for the people. Your personal Bundle may also be made with the intent of being a gift for the people that by keeping the 'Good Medicine' you have gathered alive in you will assist others to go through a journey of healing through your presence. You will very soon create this Sacred Bundle to help maintain the tangibility of the profound initiation rite you have navigated through with such fervor and devotion.

A number of the Great Plains Tribes remember the ancient origins of their Sacred Bundles (in spite of years of destruction and oppression), and have interesting correlations that tie into the importance of creating personal Bundles anew at this time. The Shawnees have passed down the story of how their Sacred Bundles were created. They tell of a special deity, called 'Our Grandmother', who entrusted the care of a Sacred Bundle to each Shaman, which directed the Shawnee people on how to live a spiritual life and to take care of themselves, their tribes and Mother Earth. Are these the original instructions of which we have spoken; the gifts of the Grandmothers returning? The Grandmother Bundles were the oldest and most sacred. They carried the collective spirit of all tribal members, as well as the most potent tried and tested Medicines which were needed for the healing of all their relations. It seems that the teachings and guidance of the Grandmothers are once again needed in order for us to take an evolutionary leap as shown by the most important Bundles of the past.. We can no longer live without these teachings. Your Medicine Bundle will assist you in keeping connected to the Mother Earth and to the Grandmothers so their voices can be heard.

The Sahnish or Arika (relatives of the Pawnees), speak of how there is one Supreme Being of great power and wisdom, but that the Chief gave Mother Corn (represented by the cedar tree) authority over all things on Earth. The Mother Corn Ceremony was a ritual which centered on the theme of World renewal, linking the Universe to the keepers of the Sacred Bundles and their Relations. Each of the twelve Sahnish village bands that lived along the Missouri River had a Medicine Bundle associated with the Mother Corn Rites. Bundles, whether personal or group, provided an object-based connection with spiritual powers that though beyond the realm of daily life, were needed to exist in the everyday World. Just like the teachings of the Thirteen Grandmothers, Mother Corn instructed the people in how to live in a good way, instilling in them respect for plants and animals and 'all our relations'. She also imparted knowledge on how to hunt, grow food, and build sacred structures, as well as how to create beautiful crafts, sacred objects and ceremonies. Through this knowledge, ceremonial lodges became symbolic of the structure of the World.

I share these stories because it is important that we come 'full circle' with the original teachings that were given for the Door of Earth we have passed through, even though much has been forgotten or lost. I share this with you, because most of us have forgotten how to communicate with the forces of Nature and will need that connection more than ever to survive and evolve through these times. Nature is not here solely as a playground for our working out of karma and unconsciousness. She has her own journey to take. But Mother Earth is also connected to us and to the forces of Light and Love that are coming in from the higher celestial realms and will twist and turn in response to these energies in order to wake us up and to find her balance in a World that has become toxic and out of balance. Her forces are also being played with by those who do not want to let go of domination and Ego control, which does not bide well with her or her spirit guardians and we wish to balance this with the more positive ways of working with her forces

The Sacred Bundle which you will now create, is one for you to gather together all the good Medicine of your 'journey of initiation', so you may continue your sacred walk.

We ask for a blessing by the celestial Spider Woman who is weaving a new Creation matrix for the time upon us, reflecting the Beauty Way of Love and Light of the Rainbow Goddess. We ask for the teachings of the Thirteen Grandmothers to be gracefully shared with your new Medicine Bundle so that you may walk your talk and live your grandness in daily life with all your relations. We ask for the blessing of your Ancestors and the presence of the many great beings you have met on your journey. We ask for the parts of you that have returned home from their long passage in the many Worlds and lifetimes you have lived, to enter in. We bring in the Divine Feminine and Masculine energies that have been through the Sacred Marriage and have returned to you. We ask for all the parts that had been separated, to unify and harmonize together in wholeness with the Light and Love of Creation.

What else might you put in your new Sacred Bundle? What gifts have you gathered? Take a moment to listen deeply…

We ask for a blessing by and presence of: Eagle and Hawk Medicine that carry the message and powers of a new vision; Raven Medicine that helps transform the heavy hucha; the sight and wisdom of Owl that can see into the darkest recesses of the Shadow; Hummingbird Medicine of great joy and heart-fullness; Turtle Medicine for knowing your home and for the care of the Earth; Star Jaguar Medicine of the embodiment of the energies of the Star Beings of Light; Whale Medicine that can assist you in accessing the records past and future that are needed for humanity's evolvement at this time; Dolphin Medicine which assists you to contain even more Love and Light in harmony and great joy with your brothers and sisters. The Rainbow Serpent comes forth to bring in the colorful spectrum of the Wheels of Light and to unite together the spiritual medicine of all of these and so many more, too endless to name.

Are there any objects that may have come your way on the journey that speak to you with deep meaning and power? Have you gathered special stones, rocks, crystals, feathers, offerings, candles, medicines of power and spirit? If they have not come to you yet, ask and they will start appearing! Keep it simple and connected. Start with the container, the cloth or skin that is to hold these blessings. Instead of being flat like an Altar, you will wrap up your contents and tie them up in a bundle so that the energy is contained. This focuses the powers more strongly. I once witnessed a Light leaving my Mesa as I was getting ready to do a healing with it and opened it to show a client. It is important to keep the Bundle closed once you work it, and open it rarely so as to keep the powers concentrated.

Put your energy into the Bundle as you are creating it, with the many good intentions you carry. Make a stronger commitment to your destiny path that you have become more conscious of. Sit with yourself in holy meditation, gathering and focusing all that you have experienced, breathing it into realization and fulfillment. What kind of support do you require from the spiritual World to sustain you through these times? What energy do you want to create in the World so that you can be a lightworker for the transformation of humanity? What are the particular gifts you carry that are ready to be brought out into the World that you have downloaded from the highest realms of Love and Light? Let the answers gracefully come through to you as this Sacred Bundle is blessed with Divine Essence. It will be matched by the Holy Ones who look over you and your progress. You are important. You are here for a reason. It is important to know one's full spiritual medicine and to own it through the journey of the Thirteen Heavens. It is time for this in humbleness and appreciation for all you are. As we blossom in fullness we can then assist others to do so. We give thanks to every being, every Medicine that has crossed our paths including the Dance of the Shadows.

Have faith in yourself as a divine being connected to the Source of all life. Your divine authentic self is ready to help birth forth a new vision for humanity. Intend this with the full love force of your open Heart. Hold a vision that might contain wishes for:

1. Peace in the hearts and minds of all beings.
2. All children being fully loved and well taken care of.
3. The elements of Earth, Water, Fire and Air being purified and clean once again as the element Ether enters in.
4. Alternative forms of energy developed that do not pollute or use up the Earth's resources.
5. Species that have disappeared returning again, as well as better care being taken of those who are still here.
6. Abundance for all in a way that does not take from the Earth or from each other.
7. The Earth is totally honored and becomes a Garden of Eden once again.
8. Anger, lies, hatred, inequalities, control over others and abuse, as well as personal resentments are being transformed out of the darkness in a flash of Light and Love.
9. Weapons of war cease to exist.

10. Governments become Spiritual Centers that truly assist in the care of the people and their lands.
11. The human population is brought into balance to what the Earth can truly provide.
12. Diversity is honored and appreciated.
13. Each person is living a creative life, doing what they love best.
14. Ceremony, Spiritual Rites of Passage, and a strong connection to the Divine in all aspects of life, are the norm.
15. All people feel loved and are in loving relationships and communities.
16. The Holy Ones walk among us, reminding us of our divinity.
17. All of humanity is unified, as the five fingered race, joined by the One Heart and the Light and Love of Great Spirit.

As we believe, so it is. We begin here and now.

Let your bundle be a reminder to you to stay conscious and you will learn to work with it further in the chapter on daily rituals. Remember that this Medicine Bundle is a sacred object to keep you aligned with positive intent for your role in this time of great spiritual renewal and evolvement. You are the Light of the World and you are here to use your Light and Love to heal and transform the Dark, bringing back home the parts of you returned in Love. The Light returns to the Darkness; the Darkness opens to the Light. By being all the Light and Love you can, you assist the Shadow Beings to remember their original Source. The divine forces of Love and Light cannot be destroyed nor can they destroy. The World can be changed person by person, moment by moment, by what you have gathered. 'I am', as God created me in the Light, in the Love, in the Glory! The 'I am' presence is the part of us that is truly connected to the unified God Source.

We are in the change times and we are being brought to the wall of our fears and limitations. Your sacred Bundle will help you remember your connection to Divine Source. We must evolve or we will continue to suffer and cause suffering! It is our divine duty and divine right to bring Heaven to Earth. Thy will be done, on Earth as it is in Heaven. And it is very important that we remember in the process of 'healing and transformation' as we build our bodies of Light and Love, to give back to all in sacred reciprocity. The Sacred Hoop will be healed when we move onward in a beauteous spiral dance of inter-connectedness to 'all our relations.'

20

Giving Back to All ... 'Coming Full Circle'

We are the Circle, the Circle is healing us
Unite the people, We are One
You are One and I am One and We are One together
We can lift each other up; Higher and Higher

We have come a long way on our journey of healing and are thankful for all we have experienced. As we transform and 'come full circle' in our personal healing, it is important to expand our Sacred Hoop to reach out to others and to give from the fullness of our beings. The circle of 'healing and transformation' must not stop here. It is important to keep generating true Mana in order to be able to live in the Fifth World, the Land of the Flowers. The flow of energy must continue between and among us and the Three Worlds, as the Tree of Life is renewed and restored. We have become realized and renewed as a holy temple; we are the Light and Love.

Both Buffalo and Turkey are the spirit guides who present themselves to assist in bringing forth the great give-back of all we have experienced. They remind us how to keep the 'Sacred Circle' of Mana and life force circulating, returning fertility and abundance to the land and to our lives. Give thanks for their presence and invite them in to show you the way. Buffalo Medicine reminds us to give thanks for all that is so abundantly given in prayer and in giving back. As we feel the bounty of our own divine spirit and are filled up to overflow, we give thanks for our abundance and from this fullness we give back to the World and its inhabitants, without stress, without feelings of lack. But in full trust in Great Spirit, working through Mother Earth to provide us with all we need to live. The spirit medicine of Turkey reminds us that the more you give, the more you live, and to give thanks for all the gifts before they are even received; and that there will always be enough if respect is given to those that give of themselves.

There is a story from the Andean cosmology that speaks of the exchange of energies and Ayni between the Worlds. Ayni is the impulse towards sacred interchange and the spirit of reciprocity which is needed to sustain life, and is an integral part of the social and mystical traditions of Peru, as well as many other indigenous cultures. In their social system it is about giving back to others as a way of keeping society in harmony. In the mystical system, Ayni is the basis of all ceremony and ritual, for the shaman or Medicine person always makes sure there is an interchange of energies with the spirit realm.

There is an ancient story that speaks of how two rival Incan Rulers were in a power struggle for control of the Incan Empire, and that the civil war that resulted, weakened the empire and made it vulnerable to the conquest of the Spaniards. Because these brother-Kings forgot the sacred teachings of the process of Ayni, they were lost in competition instead of working together and were unable to collaborate and lost the Empire. When they died they descended into the Underworld, with all the heavy hucha they had gathered. Their task was to teach the Lowerworld beings how to perform Ayni, and when they had succeeded, the Lowerworld would rise into the Middleworld.

Our work as humans in the Middleworld, is to clean the heavy energy here and to cleanse our energetic and physical environment, so that the Upperworld of the most spiritually infused element Ether will descend to Middle Earth. Our work is also to not create more heavy energy, in the karmic exchange that may still be occurring in connecting to the Lowerworlds. If we keep aware of this great responsibility, maybe the Mother Earth will not have to purify herself in a manner that creates devastation and suffering for humanity. This may then create the paradisiacal World of which we have been dreaming.

We can also contribute to the realization of this Heaven on Earth by creating columns of Light that can help bring together and reconnect the Three Worlds. We can practice Ayni in the biggest sense of reciprocity, by establishing contact with the vibrantly alive divine energy of the Upperworld and pulling cords or columns of Light down to the Lowerworlds and the Inca Kings, in order to assist them in their job in the realms of darkness. As we bring back into the Light our own separated, unloved parts, we assist all the Kings, Queens, Priests and Priestesses, the Rulers, and those who once carried the higher energies and have fallen in their job of trying to practice true reciprocity, in coming back home cleansed and cleared of their heavy hucha and karma.

We are not separate in this great web of life and it is time to remember the sacred contracts that we have with each other and all of life. When we gather all this wonderful sacred Mana and evolve to our next levels of consciousness, it is important to work with this energy by using this holy power for a higher purpose. Know there truly is an endless source to this energy. This is not about giving in acts of codependency, based on feelings of un-love and need of approval. This is not about giving until you are empty and drained to the bottom of your being, but rather from the fullness of your Light and Love. This is where sacred reciprocity and grace come into play. This is how the renewal of energy truly works. Our consumer society trains us to accumulate material goods. Spiritual teachings tell us that the more we share our power and wisdom the more sacred and fulfilled you become. The more energy you give, the more you are open to receive an even more powerful influx of energy. This keeps the 'Circle of Life' force moving so that the spiral of evolution can continue to rise up to higher vibrational levels.

Let's take these teachings to the basic level of exchange between humans; that when you appreciate someone, you are giving them some of your living energy. When they receive good energy, they are better able to give to others and to pass it around. As you give you will be given to according to the spiritual laws of the Sacred Hoop. We have individuated to the extreme as a society, and need to come back to the basic truth, that we can generate collectively much greater power and good works than we can alone. We have gathered so much heavy energy in us in the journey of separation that we have created mirror distortions and relational issues almost everywhere we go. This changes as we come 'full circle in healing and transformation'. We have now gathered many of the gifts and sacred Mana of the higher frequencies and can enjoy sharing with others in grateful harmony. This truly heals the Sacred Hoop and releases us up to truly be able to take the journey of the Thirteen Heavens. Here we may begin anew.

As we learn true surrender and offer our free will to join with the Will of the Creator, we are able to hear more clearly what our true Spirit Path is here on Earth. There is much change to be made in the systems that we have created that do not serve the new paradigm being born in each and every one of us. Globally and locally, grassroots action is taking place that is giving a new role model for bigger change to pattern the New World from. Environmental issues, social change and equality for all people are being addressed bit by bit as new solutions are arising daily as the stark dichotomy of oppressive regimes and corporations are no longer being hidden or accepted. It is important to not go into overwhelm and to work step by step to find productive ways in which to make change. As we evolve our reactionary Ego parts and are directed in our actions by our Higher Self, it is more possible to give back to the World, our communities and each other, in a way where we focus more on positive change, than on attacking or further separating ourselves from the Heart of Creation. The Dalai Lama is one such representation who exemplifies divinity embodied in human form. We can aspire to forgive the most atrocious behavior of others, while striving to take positive action from

Love, to change what can be changed, and to keep giving positive prayers and intent towards the negativity that remains. If we truly have been able to see the bigger picture of our own Souls' journey, then maybe we can see the bigger picture of what is needed for productive change in the systems that have developed out of separation.

All life is connected and everything is sacred. The evolutionary journey of our inner beings will affect others positively, just by the vibration we exude; but we also must take action towards change in every aspect of our World, for that is what is being asked and called for as we learn to give from our Hearts. You are a unique being, possessing many gifts that you have rediscovered on your journey of healing; use them wisely, use them well, for every Soul is needed.

This is a give-away poem
You have come gathering
You have made a circle with me of the places where I
have wandered
I want to give you the first daffodil opening from the Earth
I have sown
To give you warm loaves of bread baked in soft mounds like breasts
In this circle I pass each of you a shell from our Mother Sea
Hold it to your spirit and hear the stories she will tell you
I have wrapped your faces around me, a warm robe
Let me give you ribbon-work leggings, dresses sewn with elk teeth,
Moccasins woven with red and sky blue porcupine quills
I give you blankets woven of flowers and roots
Come closer, I have more to give, this basket is very large
I have stitched it of your kind words
Here is a necklace of feathers and bones
A sacred meal of choke cherries
Take this mask of bark which keeps out the evil ones
This basket is only the beginning, there is something in my arms
for all of you
I offer you this memory of sunrise seen through ice crystals
Here, an afternoon of looking into the sea from high rocks
Here, a red-tailed hawk circling over your hair
May I give you this round stone which holds an Ancient Spirit
This stone will soothe you
Within this basket is something you have been looking for
all of your life
Come take it, take as much as you want
I give you seeds of a new way
I give the Moon shining on a fire of singing women

I give you the sound of our feet dancing
I give you the sound of our thoughts flying
I give you the sound of peace moving into our faces
Come, this is a give-away poem
I cannot go home until you have taken everything
And the basket which held it
When my hands are empty
I will be full

- By unknown Native Woman

21

Daily Rituals for Life: Everyday Is a Sacred Day!

I have been in the dreaming of the Moon time and now it is the Sun's turn. The Sun entices me to awaken and join it on its journey through the day. I feel it encouraging me to begin anew and listen to what it has to share with me as a messenger of the Creator. I am reminded to not take anything I do not need to carry from the day or night before, as I get a chance to be reborn again. I greet the day and I am hopeful that it will welcome me.

Each day we get to begin anew! We get to start the day off setting positive intentions for our day with the rising of the Sun. It has been a good and powerful journey of healing and it is important to know how to sustain the new energies on a daily basis. Even though we have gone through many gateways and have remembered the greatness of our Higher Self, it is still easy to move into forgetfulness because the collective of the Human Race is still evolving as a species. It is important to find a path, a spiritual practice, a ritual to do daily or as much as possible, to keep the higher frequencies embodied. If we start our day out in a field of positive energy, we are much less likely to get thrown off our center by challenging events, as well as be more able to create a higher vibration out in the World as we go about our daily lives. It is so simple but easy to forget. The Medicine Bundle is a place to build from and to begin with.

The changes you have made in your journey are not to be taken lightly and need care and intention to keep the higher frequencies generating. Daily devotions and practice have been a necessary part of almost all spiritual paths, such as meditation, chanting and prayer. Without it, we often fall back to sleep. Daily Rituals can provide a doorway to the Higher Self or Higher Power, to Mother Nature, as well as to the spiritual energies that surround us. Setting a little time aside each day to slow down and tune in to our higher guidance, and to listen to the whisperings of our guides, totems, angels and allies, is a must as the changes intensify. How are you going to maintain the connection to your center core Light, when the Earth is shaking and time is sped up so fast that you can no longer hear or feel your heartbeat? How will you remember the bigger picture, when the World is changing rapidly around you? How will you keep your Heart a clear and open channel of Divine Love? How will you maintain an enlightened perspective when the challenges of your personal life are overwhelming?

When you do not have much time in your day, even a simple prayer and candle lighting that takes ten to twenty minutes can focus a clear spiritual intent for the day. Even a few moments of tuning into the part of you that feels connected to Divine Source and the unified field of 'Oneness' will have a positive effect. Follow the traditions and spiritual path with which you are already in touch. Use the practices you are familiar with; but remember that you are in a different Medicine Field now and may need to change or add a few things. I am going to share some of the simple practices that I use or know that can assist one in keeping in alignment with the spirit in all life. I am not going to go into great detail on each one, for there are many spiritual paths and traditions to follow that have daily practices. This is a reminder that the Good Medicine journey continues and that it takes daily attention to keep the Tree of Life whole. This is a reminder so you pay attention to the importance of keeping your profound changes intact. I trust what follows will be useful.

It is important to establish a sacred, private place in your home where you can ground into your spiritual practice. This place needs to be where you can have both privacy and a sense of beauty and peace. Take time to attune to and locate this sacred space. You can sense it with your intuitive knowing or you can use dowsing rods or a pendulum. Once you have found its location it is important to cleanse the area, as well as to cleanse and feed the newly established Altar as you work with it. An Altar simply put, is a designated place of spiritual focus and connection. Smudge, herbs and sound, are a few examples of what can be used to clear the space, sacred objects and your personal Medicine Field. These tools also help create balance and harmony, and act as a way to communicate with the spirit realms. Smudging is the burning of certain herbs to create a cleansing smoke bath, and is a practice held sacred by many indigenous cultures, and is a powerful way to clear and renew spiritual connection. It is another way to clear the heavy hucha that is often generated on a daily basis. It is a very important aspect of Daily Ritual, as well as a helpful ally during difficult times.

Following is a list and brief description of the healing properties of these gifts from Mother Earth, as well as some of the other clearing tools.

Use them with great respect to clear yourself and your sacred space and objects.

The Sacred Four

Tobacco - is the forerunner of all other medicines and connects all living things; sooths the heart and eases the mind and creates spiritual unity and healing as a conduit to the higher vibrations, carrying your prayers and well wishes. It works in harmony with Cedar, to assist the prayers to be heard, and carries the more masculine energies.

Cedar - works both as a purifier and as a way to attract good energy and clear negative emotions such as fear and anger, while centering one's Soul, in order to make contact with Great Spirit.

Sage - clears and drives away negative thoughts, feelings and Dark Spirits, as well as keeping sacred objects protected and honored. Various types of Sage carry subtle differences in their effect. Sage works well with Sweetgrass, honoring both the Dark and the Light.

Sweetgrass - calls in the spirits, who can lift one up into the sweetness of life, and is a feminine plant medicine. It reduces anxiety and fear, and balances with gentle smoke.

The combination of the Sacred Four cleanses and centers from the Four Directions; bringing one's energy field into purity and balance, setting the Ritual Space.

Additional Medicines

Cornmeal (blue preferred) - is to set sacred space, calling in the assistance of the Corn Mothers, who not only balance and ground the energies but also offer a boundary, where only the highest good can enter in; feeding and welcoming Mother Nature's helpers.

Copal - is from the resin of special sacred tropical trees from parts of Mexico, Central and South America and is one of the strongest medicines available for clearing the negative energies that are created from this time of separation. It goes into the depths of the energy fields of a space or person, creating a doorway for the fragmented parts to come together and be raised into the Light. It is also used to feed the spirits.

Frankincense and Myrrh - cleanses and protects the Soul.

Lavender - brings in the grace of the breath of the Spirit World.

Basil, Rosemary, Rue etc. - aromatic herbs used in bundles like a broom, to cleanse the energy fields.

* Salt - to move very discordant and stuck energy or spirits; use with alcohol to burn, starting the fire in a heat proof container; works especially well to clear a space by focusing on the corners. Start with very little alcohol. Also to surround one in order to clear the energy field from outside negative influence.*

Bells or toning bowls - useful to dispel stuck energy and to get it moving while raising the vibration; assists in bringing in the Light. Different metals produce a variety of tones.

Selenite Crystal - carries the frequency of pure White Light, cleaning and amplifying energy of other stones. Functions as a doorway through which the vibration of the Higher Self can enter consciousness.

Now your space is ready for your new Altar. Let it speak to you and guide you on its placement. It may be time to build a new Altar or change the one you already have. If you do not have much room in your home, you can work with your Medicine Bundle. If you make changes to an existing Altar or start a new one, your Altar should exemplify that which you would like to bring to Earth from the heavenly realms you have journeyed to, symbolically honoring where you have been. Each sacred object you put here is to become a powerful conduit for your intentions and prayers, as we give our attention, our breath, our tobacco, as a way to utilize and draw in the presence of Spirit. We can assist inanimate objects to become spiritually alive and provide a physical space for guides to be more present in our lives. As we invoke various positive intentions and call in the Holy Ones while praying over these inanimate objects, they begin to come alive with the essence of Ether.

I was once told that many spirits are given offerings (like tobacco, chocolate, flowers and alcohol), because these are the things they miss from not being embodied, but it is also said that they need beauty to attract them back into the physical dimensions and to assist them in being more present here. We have been living in the dimension of free will and it is necessary to ask for assistance for these helpers to come forth.

Everything is alive and we were never truly separate from the web of life. The element of Ether, Spirit in Matter, is being made more readily available in our lives once again in every breath and every moment. We do not have to wait for the next ritual, or the next healing session to touch in. The time is now, every moment, everyday. We can help to see and bring the sacred back into daily life, not only by treating each other as sacred and by respecting all of Nature as holy, but also by bonding with and seeing power objects in this way. In this honoring it is important to do so from a place of detachment. These objects assist in bringing in the Beauty Way by how they carry such mystical allure, but at times we may be asked to bring in the gifts of Spirit just with our own presence. You may have a special crystal that you dearly love, but it is important to know that it really belongs to the Planet and that you may have to release it at any time, just as we must release our body to the Earth and our Souls to Great Spirit.

The new Altar you are creating can help focus your dreams of a New World, and be a reminder of your profound changes in consciousness. By bringing together in a beautiful way, visually and energetically that which one wants to now embody, we have a place of real spiritual power to access and return to, again and again. The Altar is like a control panel that can transmit energy and vibrations to the mind and Soul, being a reminder of the powerful journey you have just taken. They are important doorways into other realms and dimensions.

Carefully select the items you want here, understanding the meaning and purpose of each object. Follow your expanded intuition and trust your own knowing in what you create. Your Medicine Bundle is meant to be a portable Altar that you can transport to sacred sites and ceremonies, while the one that is now being created is stationary. But it is better to have a Sacred Bundle, to do Daily Ritual with (if you do not have the bigger space), than no Altar at all. You can surround it with candles and work with it still bundled together, since they are not meant to be opened very often. An Altar, with the objects laid out is a powerful visual reminder and is able to be accessed a bit differently. It is like the central control pad to the individual intentions of specific Medicine Bundles.

You may have some of the following on your Altar or not, it is up to your guidance. Try to keep it simple so as to be more powerful with each object being placed with pure intent, are the instructions that were given to me by a Bolivian Shaman who worked with me on realigning my Altar. Your Altar may contain:

1. *Candles to represent and be lit to call in the Four Directions, plus the Center or the Seven Directions, which include above and below (depending on your available space).*

2. *Use similar objects as put in the Bundle; such as crystals, stones, feathers, shells, animal parts, any objects from Nature, special gifts given along the way, pictures, statues, fetishes, etc. Some of these may represent your most important spirit guides and teachers.*

3. *Crystals and stones can be put in the directions as well, selected according to their particular attributes and gifts, representing the sacred energies of the Medicine Wheel; grounding the powers of each direction strongly to the Earth and to the Light. Crystals also assist in bringing in the Light.*

4. *Something very special to represent the feminine and masculine energies, as well as an object that joins the two.*

5. *Honor the Four Elements with whatever has meaning for you such as: a bowl of Earth from a special place, a container of blessed Water, a feather to represent Air, and candles in honor of the Fire. The element Ether is brought in by your prayers, songs, good intentions and offerings.*

6. *Have a beautiful bowl or shell for the particular offerings you may wish to give and remember to change them more often than not, keeping alive and present the vitality of the Sacred Powers.*

7. *A grid of the Sacred Three of the Triple Goddess that will provide an energetic womb space to birth the new creative energies that are now available into your World and as a way to keep these present. I use an amethyst crystal to embody the focused wisdom of the most ancient Goddess of Creation (known as the Crone), a rose quartz to radiate the Love of the Mother, and green adventurine to ground into the vibrantly earthy inspirational energies of the Maiden.*

Once again listen to what works for you. Arrange everything so that you create something beautiful. Consecrate this Sacred Space, drinking in the beauty and power of your little temple. It is such a grand feeling to be in a church, a temple, a mosque, a kiva, or any place where prayer and true connection to Spirit has been invoked over and over. But often we do not have the time to go to such wondrous places and if so, it is almost never a daily practice.

So we begin our day, 'a brand new day never been used'. The Sun rises and we share our dreams with each other or write them down, giving thanks to our Dream Keepers for holding the space for this doorway. Honoring the messages of the dream time is very important as a way to become connected to the unconscious, so that we may bring the dark recesses of our psyches into the Light, uniting night and day. We go outside to connect with the natural World and give an offering of tobacco to the Sun, which is a gateway to the Great Spirit's Light, beaming down on us, connecting us to the great Central Sun. We speak our intention for the day and our prayers for our beloveds and the World. Inviting the Sun into our Solar Plexus, we align our will with the Will of the Creator and start anew, as children calling in the wonders of the day. Bringing this Solar Light through the core of our bodies, we ground with the Earth through the bottom of our feet, offering her cornmeal in gratefulness that she allows us to walk another day upon her great beauty. We pull in her Light without a Shadow from the crystalline core Center of her great being back up through our feet, filling every cell with the template of loving 'Oneness'. Taking in any messages that we receive from the 'flying ones' who pass by while we drink in the beauty of the sunrise; breathing in the morning air and giving thanks that we are given yet another day to be all we can be.

Going to our Altar, we utilize a smudge of cedar, sage, or copal, to help clear the Shadows of the night. The directions are called in with the lighting of the candles and any invocations we wish to bring forth. We visualize ourselves in the middle of our sacred Medicine Field. From the center of this space we call in and reunite the three main aspects of our being, asking for them to be in communication and connection with each other. Bringing in the Higher Self from above one's head; align this spiritual vibration with the Conscious Self, the daily self you have come to love and respect, which is the part of you that you are most aware of, with the Basic Self or Inner Child, who now is able to embody more of the Magical Child. Now feel the awareness of Spirit throughout your body, making sure you are connected to the Earth Star beneath your feet, assisting you to ground and complete your 'Totem Pole' of wholeness. Take a moment to pay attention to the beating of your Heart and the feelings that are stirring, as the entirety of your being unifies here. Some form of breathing practice, healing chant or tone or song from your spiritual tradition; a moment of rattling or drumming, brings us home to ourselves, as well as informs the Spirits that we are available for connection. We call on our personal connection to Great Spirit and go deeper into the Heart and Soul of all of Creation; feeling filled up, by the outpouring of Light and Love that emanates from Source.

Asking for assistance or messages from our animal allies, as well as from teacher spirits and higher guides, we use a rattle, bell, or any other tool that we are attuned with, including our voice. The emanations of the royal blue Light of the element Ether assist us to tune into the higher energies. Using a pendulum, sacred stone, sound, animal totems or visualization; we go through our Chakra System with whatever method we have connected with, rebalancing and aligning with the energies of the day. Certain stones or crystals may stand out for us to work with as well as essential oils or flower essences.

Placing ourselves in the energetic grid of our personal Medicine Circle, aligning with all of our parts we invoke the activation of our Lightbody. Our core Light is contacted and brought forth and integrated into all of our bodies (physical, emotional, mental and spiritual), consciously attracting only that which we need for our highest good into our field. Remember to connect to this Light through the Earth Star of the Planet, where the Heart of the Mother beams forth the Light without a Shadow. Tune into her rhythm and her emanations, for she is going though her rebirth and wishes to take you along. If you work with this new Light the amount of suffering and disconnection that you experience from your essential self should be much less.

The Essence Self is the Soulful place that knows one's highest potential. From this place of pure connection, higher guidance may be given and it is a good time to ask meaningful questions that you may have. Stay connected with peace and grace and let go of the question for the moment, if the answers do not come forth easily. If it is an important and pressing question, take some time to rattle or drum in order to reach a further altered state of consciousness and to call in a trusted spirit guide or teacher. The guidance may come as a whisper in your psychic ear or in full visionary color. Open to the pure spiritual sight that may give you guidance and direction for the day. Listen to the messages and take them to Heart so as not to waste the insights and gifts that have been offered.

Focus your spiritual intent even more deeply than the morning's first prayers to the Sun for what you want to accomplish for the day, for the week, for the month, and provide offerings for the fulfillment of what you want to manifest. It is important to also pray for beloveds as well as the Earth and humanity at this time, seeing the Light and Love surrounding situations and people that need support. If we start losing our spiritual focus during our day, we can take a moment and breathe, asking assistance from our guides and allies to remind us. Take a moment to reconnect with the Higher Self so that all can be brought back into synergistic alignment.

Before you complete your morning ritual, either leave a candle or candles safely lit so as to continue invoking your prayers or put them out with respect. A great grounding practice that you can use throughout your day if you get overwhelmed is the personal Medicine Wheel visualization. See yourself in the Center of your Medicine Wheel, calling in the Thirteen Grandmothers and the guides of each direction to be with you, surrounding yourself in a Sacred Circle as a gentle reminder of the teachings of the Upperworld. The Central balanced Cross of the Medicine Wheel is running through your Heart Center, calibrating you with the Heart of the Heavens and the Heart of the Earth. You take a deep breath and experience the balancing of all parts of your being in wholeness; as below, so above, as within, so without.

It is also important to find a place in Nature that you can return to again and again, to tune into the Earth in a prayerful way. This place gets to be known by your guides and allies, especially by the ones connected to the land, and will aid you in keeping connected to Mother Earth and her rhythms while soothing you when you need comfort. Bring sacred herbs and offerings to this place to open the gateway of communication to the unseen World of Mother Nature. When you ask to enter in a respectful manner, all kinds of spiritual beings and realities may appear for you to learn from.

In this time of fast paced movement and technology, many have become disconnected from the relationship that we once shared with all life. Connect with Mother Earth as much as you can, because it is very important to not lose touch with that which will guide you and is part of you, in your survival on the Earth if you truly want to go through the Doorway to the Fifth World in consciousness. Our passage is not to be experienced by dishonoring and disconnecting from our Mother, but in harmony. We are made up of all her elements and need to remember this as the element Ether infuses us through our grounding in her. Visit your place in Nature because it gives you joy to do so, not only when you are in crisis. Trust in Mother Earth's guidance, from this most sacred part of Creation that acts as an intermediary and home for Great Spirit's aspirations for us to be carried forth.

If you have stones, crystals and feathers that you work with, notice which ones you may be attracted to, need to wear or to move to a different location. You are getting more and more sensitive to energy; and the more you respond and work with the subtle energies, the more magic and spiritual experiences you will have here on Earth. All stones embody Spirit, for they are the bones of the Earth Mother, as the trees and plants are her hair, the soil her flesh and the water her blood, the molten core her womb. Crystals are the record-keepers and the holders of much healing energy. Their presence in our lives can assist us to stay on track in a 'Walk of Beauty'.

As you go through the day you may have to remind yourself of the sacred covenants to which you aspire. We live in a World grown toxic by the misuse of energy in the physical, mental, and emotional realms. It is as important to keep ones energy field clean so as to not dump toxic materials onto the Earth. Come from the spiritual Center of your Heart as much as you can. Try to not create more karma by feelings of judgment of self and others. Watch the reactions of the emotional body when you feel threatened, misunderstood or not heard. Pay attention to what you think, feel and say. Use the Violet Flame to transform any places that get re-stimulated and hooked onto inside that have not been resolved. If issues show up to be resolved, take the time to do so, working with a trusted facilitator if necessary; for when we dive into the bigger energies left in the Unconscious a guide may be necessary to assist who is not emotionally blinded by the fears of the Shadow. Remember the middle place that resides within; the place where all roads, all nations, and all the multi-colors of the rainbow, meet in peace and harmony. Come back into balance and if you slip and fall back into the Shadow Dance, remember to release any emotional charge into the Earth (with respect and permission of course) or into the Light without a Shadow.

Have compassion for what you still need to bring back to Love within yourself and at what is being reflected back to you, from the great Smoky Obsidian Mirror that is becoming clearer all the time. Observe and be guided by what occurs in your environment, watching for synchronistic events, as well as animal messages. Remember to take the higher road when you can and remember why you have been brought to this heightened state of awareness at this time on the Planet. Be ready to let it go into the 'Watery Field of Grace' at all times. Watch your attachments to people, places and material objects, observing where you still need to let go another step further. Be at peace as much as you can, surrendering to the perfection of the moment.

As you come to the end of the day, be aware of the time of sunset as a powerful time to bring conscious awareness into the night. Light a red and white candle as suggested by the Mayan Elders, praying for peace in the World. Make friends with the dark of night. Reflect the setting Sun inside so that it will carry you into the dark, with a Light that never goes out. Before you go to bed at night, empty yourself of any heavy energy you have gathered once again; burning sacred herbs, collecting the negative energy at your navel, and once again releasing it to the Earth with permission and respect; bringing in the Light and Love from the top of your head, through your body and down to the Earth Star, then back up and through your Heart. Talk to the Higher Self of any person that you have had discord with, asking to clear the heavy energy between you and for resolution.

Give thanks for all you have experienced and to all who have crossed your path; to the Mother Earth for sharing her bounty with you and for allowing you to walk with her great beauty yet another day; to the Heart of the Heavens, for the Love you have been able to share, and to the Creator for the gift of the Spirit in all life. Have compassion for yourself, accepting whatever part of the journey you are on, forgiving yourself for any unconscious behavior you have exhibited on this day. When you remember, go outside and greet the stars, honor the reflections of the Sister Moon.

Ask the Dream Keeper who is the guardian of your dream World to assist in giving you guidance while you sleep, right before you put your head on your pillow. Put out an intention to take a journey through the dreamtime to dream yourself and humanity further awake. Remember the sacredness of all things and all beings, as we enter into the Fifth World.

22

The Fifth World

I *am Cosmic Consciousness, an awareness in the now of the many forces at work on every plane of existence in and beyond the World. In a sense, I am what has been referred to as 'the Fifth World,' when all is in balance and everyone lives in peace and harmony recognizing their oneness with each other. I am the end of an old Cycle and the beginning of a new one.*

I am a sign that all have learned to work with Nature, using the laws of Nature to benefit all. The streams and rivers flow, turning the water wheels; the wind gives its power to the windmills; the sun warms homes and gives light. Each element and being is recognized for its worth and utilized in beneficial ways, according to the Creator's plan.

You are now a conscious co-creator, taking part in the planetary transformation now taking place. Self and World are one being, breathing one life. You are the Dancer holding wands of male and female life force in perfect balance. The polarities within the self have been recognized and brought into a conscious creative working relationship. There is synthesis, crystallization, perfection, stability, all within the greater flow. You move consciously with the cosmos, understanding your place in time.

I dance freely and with power for I have faced the death of all that flows through me. In other words, I have transcended possession and desire for results. My actions are based on the fullness of the moment rather than on sacrifice for the future. I understand that now is all futures. I therefore live in death. It is death as a state of constant peace and surrender to what is. Thus, death is the ultimate balance during life. I have united the polarities of existence. As you approach the understanding of this within yourself, the World is yours. In Earth, I am through you."

From *Medicine Women Tarot,* by Carole Bridges

We have gone through another sleep cycle of the dream time and find ourselves awakening into a New Day. We feel renewed, inspired, and recommitted to the Beauty Way of Living.

I walk with beauty before me
I walk with beauty behind me

I walk with beauty above me
I walk with beauty below me
I walk with beauty around me
My words will be beautiful
                        From the Navajo Blessingway Chant

Much has been shared throughout this sacred journey, on what the Fifth World energies are opening us up to. I wish to revisit the vision once again so that you can hold it close to your Heart as you go about your 'brand new day never been used' and greet the morning Sun. As we approach this powerful dimensional shift, we can already sense the intricate streams of Light and the glowing presence of Love that are re-connecting us with all life and all beings, magnetizing us all towards the still point of Creation; offering us a chance to remember our 'Oneness.' It is said that it is truly necessary to move ahead in trust and surrender to the divine plan of Great Spirit, for the World we are moving into will be unlike anything we have ever experienced. Because you have gone through the journey of healing you are not the same as you were before. You have awakened to the possibility and, at times, to the experiencing of a greater reality by letting go of the untruth of separation from that from which you came. You are now connected fully to the profound emanations of Great Spirit and your sacred temple is infused with the wholeness of being of the renewed Tree of Life.

To name and get attached to what the Fifth World might be, look like, or feel like, is not what I am offering. We are in the creating, the dreaming, and the birthing of this New World, and it is in the total trust of our connection to the Heart of the Heavens and to the Heart of the Earth that we can open to the 'Flowering of our Soul.' We are very thankful for the many precious gifts that the many Wisdom Keepers have given so that during the 'Great Change Times' we may make some sense of the powerful journey that is being asked of us. As we become more spiritually informed, we will be more able to join our intent with the intent and Will of the Creator. Aligning ourselves to this can also give comfort and direction in a time of tumultuous and extreme change, in the dismantling of what we have believed makes up our reality. In this time of the purification of the old and preparation for the new, we are no longer held in fear of the unknown but move ahead in grace and trust in a higher connection.

I hope that this journey has not only stimulated you in your mind but more importantly in your Heart of Hearts, inspiring you to enlighten and navigate within the places of darkness, giving you a wake-up call for the importance of personal and global evolution. The change to a higher state of existence on the Planet can only come about one moment at a time, one breath at a time, one enlightened moment at a time. Remember to...

1. *Slow down and spend more time looking within.*
2. *Eat simple, healthy foods, and exercise your body often, especially using practices that work with energy not just muscles, such as Yoga, Chi Gong, and Tai Chi.*
3. *Live life as a Sacred Spiritual Journey.*
4. *Spend time enjoying and staying connected to Mother Earth.*
5. *Join with others in Sacred Ceremony and Prayer.*
6. *Consume less and give more.*
7. *Work on evolving yourself, for the purpose of life is growth.*
8. *Face and transform the fear based emotional reactionary states of past traumas.*
9. *Take time to be in good relationship with each other and your Sacred Self.*
10. *Send Love and Light to those people and places that need upliftment and spiritual renewal and contact.*
11. *Take greater responsibility as co-creators of this World, taking action from a much more enlightened part of your being.*
12. *Find joy in the moment whenever you can and deeply know that happiness is no longer conditional.*
13. *Be a caretaker of and live in balance with the Earth and all of her children.*
14. *Use your Creative Spirit to work together for the benefit of all of humanity as you believe in abundance and fulfillment for all.*
15. *Let the flow of healing Light touch and transform all aspects of you that need to be loved and nurtured back into spiritual wholeness.*
16. *Honor every being as Divine and remember we are all related.*
17. *Remain close to the Great Spirit and to the Heart of the Heavens and the Heart of the Earth.*
18. *Radiate to all, the Love and Light of the Creator.*

Remember that when we create from an expanded and united state of wholeness, only that which is for our highest good will flow. All else, we will feel resistance to. Look to manifest from higher feeling states, as the joy, abundance, and love you feel express in all parts of your World. Surrender to the knowing that you already exist within the Fifth World, where your roots have expanded to already be grounded in the New Earth, as you get to feel at home wherever you are. Your crystalline blueprint is now deeply reconnected to the crystalline core perfection of the Heart of Mother Earth, where you drink from her deep nourishment and perfection.

You are now able to be in contact with direct guidance from your Higher Self and the Higher Self of your Oversoul group, who are one with the true divine overseers of humanity's spiritual evolution. Your old Ego driven patterns will not fit here and will show up less and less; and if they still do, remember to Love all parts back into the wholeness of Unity Consciousness. Ask for assistance from the Christ and the Holy Mother, to transform whatever is still out of reach of the Love and the Light.

At Sunrise on December 21st, 2012, the Sun will rise to conjunct the intersection of the Milky Way and the plane of the ecliptic. This realignment of the true Cosmic Cross of stars and planets with the Heart of the Galaxy will recalibrate the sacred Tree of Life, showering all in direct relationship to it with the rarefied most spiritual essence of Ether that fills and permeates the Heavens and Celestial Space. We have been experiencing the effects of this on our way to this profound gateway. All time and space will come together and the veils of illusion will be lifted as we are given a chance to be 'born anew.' The separated Worlds of our earthly and heavenly dimensions will come together in reunion as we remember what we have learned from all the Worlds and Eras through which we have traveled, and take an evolutionary leap ahead with much greater consciousness than ever experienced before. The realms of the Thirteen Heavens will be as close to us as the kiss of the morning dew on the opening petals of a flower. We will once again feel and know the connection to the pure essence center of our beings, through the Center of the Mother Earth and the Milky Way.

As the powerful element Ether fully enters into our dimension, uniting with and spiritually transforming the elements of Earth, Water, Air, and Fire, we are being stimulated to return to the acknowledgement of the presence and honoring of Great Spirit in all life. Our Higher Self will be the overseer of our unified collective of personal wholeness. The rainbow spectrum of the blessings of the Universe are present for all to experience and know, giving us many more spiritual choices for our thriving, not only surviving. The Light of the Heavens without a Shadow, pulsing through the Mother Earth, will give us a new awareness of how to work with the spiritual Light and Love of a unified field on Earth, as the unseen forces become knowable. Contact with and embodiment of this great celestial essence will give us the conscious ability to tap into the Creation energies and powers that are for the highest good of the Earth and for all humanity. We will take a monumental leap of faith into creating from our Divine Source within and without. We will be drawn to create what gives us the most joy and learn through fulfillment and inter-connectedness, not through suffering. The most rarefied element Ether assists in the opening to the gifts of the Upperworlds and the Heavens, giving us access to the more conscious aspects of our Souls.

It has been said that we have needed the Dark to know and choose the Light. We have made the choice and brought the Light that is connected to the Love of the Mother, into the darkest recesses of our beings and into the World. This great spiritual awakening will continue to offer a path of transformation to all who choose to come back to grace and the presence of 'Oneness.' This will be a most glorious and unique experience, unlike anything we have ever known before in our embodiment as humans. The Tree of Life will hold up the Thirteen Heavens as its roots connect with Mother Earth. With the support of those who have been through 'healing and transformation' the Fifth World will light up, inviting those who have not yet been readied, to take a chance and open to the loving embrace of their brothers and sisters.

We will remember our 'Oneness' and sacred connection with all things, both earthly and celestial. We will remember how to merge with our environment and its elements so that we exist together in harmony. New governments and economies will rise out of the evolved spiritual consciousness. The inherent truths and unity of all spiritual paths will be honored. As the Heart of the Heavens is healed with the return of the Mother of all life to her rightful honored place in all of Creation, our Hearts will have been healed from all wounds created in this time of separation. The Heart and Spirit will reign together; Spirit and Matter will be rejoined. We will create realities that are in tune with our greatest good. The 'Waters of Grace' will assist us to be in a sea of our higher feeling states of Love, joy, and appreciation more often. We will no longer be afraid to Love and our Light will be in union with the Will of Great Spirit.

Negative influences will be transformed and the returned energy used for the positive evolutionary thrust of humanity. The life giving Divine Feminine energies will balance out this time of male dominance, evolving our hierarchical systems into a form which will honor the gifts of the many, as the Sacred Hoop is given space to heal, bringing in a time of intuitive guidance, harmony, mutual respect, gratitude, care of the Earth and all her inhabitants, and the fostering of cooperation and equality within our inner and outer communities. The new paradigm will flower forth with such radiance that the old ways will be outshined by its beauty and grace. We will awaken into a World where our greatest hopes will manifest instead of our greatest fears. We will awaken into a World where we are at peace with what is, instead of longing for what we do not have.

When the feminine is given its rightful place within and without, the masculine energies can be evolved to their higher states of being. Then the masculine and feminine dualities can come back into union with mutual Love and respect; creating a reality from true balance where the gifts of the Thirteen Heavens can be actualized. The polarities and dualistic ways of the Era we are leaving will be resolved as the unified Tree of Life holds up the New World. All races, nations, and colors of the Rainbow will come together and share their gifts, honoring the diversity yet keeping their individuality. All beings will be equally cared for and everything will come back into balance with the Earth, the Heavens, and each other. We will remember our connection in all ways to the 'Love of the Mother' and to the 'Light of the Father.' Let us believe that this is possible. So be it and so it is. Let's make it so!

To the 'Heart of the Earth' and to the 'Heart of the Heavens' and to All my Relations' for a blessed journey,

in Love and Light,
Michele Ama Wehali

Contact Information

email address: **earthstar3@earthlink.net**

Web site: **www. Journeytothefifthworld.com**

for current information on **workshops, groups,** and

individual healing sessions, as well as details on

sponsoring a talk or **workshop** in your area.

*The refining and evolution of human consciousness is as
important as the cleaning up of the Earth's environment.
As you gather, uncover, and align the energies of your
sacred self, you can experience a greater sense
of wholeness and peace, as well as be able to
take more conscious action in the World.
By healing psychological wounds as well as opening to the
higher frequency consciousness coming onto the Planet at this time,
we can manifest more gracefully the
life we have always dreamed of.*

To order more copies of this book contact www.llumina.com/store
Or call 954-726-0902 / toll free 866-229-9244

Printed in the United States
74546LV00003BA/1-93